# Lights Out
## Full Throttle

# Lights Out Full Throttle

### The Good, the Bad and the Bernie of Formula One

# JOHNNY HERBERT

## AND

# DAMON HILL

With James Hogg

MACMILLAN

First published 2020 by Macmillan
an imprint of Pan Macmillan
The Smithson, 6 Briset Street, London EC1M 5NR
Associated companies throughout the world
www.panmacmillan.com

ISBN 978-1-5290-3999-3

1 3 5 7 9 8 6 4 2

A CIP catalogue record for this book is available from the British Library.

Typeset by Palimpsest Book Production Ltd, Falkirk, Stirlingshire
Printed and bound by CPI Group (UK) Ltd, Croydon, CR0 4YY

Visit **www.panmacmillan.com** to read more about all our books
and to buy them. You will also find features, author interviews and
news of any author events, and you can sign up for e-newsletters
so that you're always first to hear about our new releases.

# Contents

# INTRODUCTION

Damon and Johnny here. F1's answer to Ant and Dec.

Between us we have about a hundred years' experience of driving motorcars quickly. We've competed in 261 Grands Prix, spawning twenty-five wins, forty-nine podiums, one World Championship and 458 championship points. We even have a win at Le Mans to our names, not to mention two crushed feet, a hair transplant and a pierced upper thigh. That said, when it comes to chatting about all things F1 we're still relatively intact, and can mix it with the best of them.

Despite its immense popularity, it's often been argued that F1 can be a bit too serious. Well, *nil desperandum*, ladies and gentlemen, because we, Damon Hill OBE and Johnny Herbert DNF, are here to prove the doubters wrong by swapping honest, forthright opinions and stories involving automotive derring-do. And derring-don't.

**Johnny:** For example, I took part in the very first FIA Formula One drivers' press conference at Silverstone many years ago, and had it been today I'd probably have been dragged from the room

1

by the scruff of my neck and fired from a cannon. To kick things off, the person running the press conference went around every driver and asked them what they'd be if they weren't in Formula One. For some reason the answers were pretty humdrum – astronaut or engineer, basically – so when he got to me I thought I'd try and be a bit creative and, after stroking my chin for a few seconds and trying to look reflective, I took the mic and said, 'I think I'd be a ball sniffer at Wimbledon.'

**Damon:** Hello Johnny, goodbye good taste. That didn't take long.

**Damon and Johnny:** Our double act started in 2013, when filming race-day show content for Sky F1 at Monza, prior to the Italian Grand Prix. As we'd both won a Grand Prix there, our employers thought it would be a good idea to have us reminisce about our experiences for the further edification of the viewers. After getting miked up, we went around Monza on a Vespa (with Damon driving, obviously) and chatted as we went. When watching the edit back in the Sky production office, some smartarse presenter who looks a lot like Simon Lazenby chips in with, 'Look! it's Dumb and Dumber!' and from that moment on an automotive entertainment behemoth was born. The audience seemed to like it, so we won in the end. Up yours, Lazers! We didn't mind a bit looking like a couple of chumps if that's what makes you happy. At last, we could drop the pretence of being responsible adults. Phew! What a relief!

Probably our biggest bugbear when it comes to broadcasting is that it's all a bit disposable, so whatever you say is usually forgotten about within a few seconds, which is why we decided to put pen to paper. We're not saying that every word that comes out of our sizeable apertures is revelatory, but chatting about F1 is something we obviously thrive on and the prospect of getting our opinions, experiences and stories down for posterity helps to redress the balance somewhat. It goes without saying that we're each going to ensure that the book is a true representation of our partnership – that is, we'll get everything out on the table, and then decide that Damon is right. That's the gag! You'll see.

Enjoy.

# CHAPTER ONE

## Monaco

**Johnny:** I'll start this one. Probably the most anticipated race of the year – globally – is also the most boring. Discuss.

**Damon:** No it's not? OK. I'll colour this one in for you, Herbert. Let's hype it up a bit at least. It's basically the most expensive film set on the planet. Monaco transcends motor racing. It's a carnival of excess. A celebration of massive amounts of wonga and bling. And one of the trickiest challenges a racing driver is ever going to have. I love it.

**Johnny:** OK. Good challenge. So if we're going to have a chapter about Monaco we really have to start with your old man, who used to be known as Mr Monaco, of course.

**Damon:** Indeed he did. Dad's reign in Monaco wasn't quite as long as Prince Rainier's, but during the 1960s, which is considered to be a halcyon era for so many things, he won it five times – half the years in that decade. So he was 'The Man'. Somehow he managed to fit in winning the Indianapolis 500 in 1966 as well, which was a week after Monaco. He must have had to qualify the car in the USA for the Indy, then fly back to do the Monaco GP, finishing a modest third, then fly back out to Indy to win that. Busy man.

Fascinating fact is that when Dad first went to Monaco, while doing his National Service in charge of the engine room of HMS *Swiftsure*, he'd never even heard of the Monaco Grand Prix and knew nothing at all about motor racing. He even went to the Casino and won a few quid. Maybe a portent of things to come? Just five years later, in 1958, he was in his first ever Grand Prix, the Monte Carlo, racing for Lotus. He tells a very funny story in his book where, about forty laps in, he's sitting there in third place thinking, *This motor racing lark's a piece of cake!* when his left rear wheel promptly fell off.

One question that gets asked a lot is why my old man was so successful at Monaco. One of my theories is that the track appealed to his mind in a way that other circuits did not. There's no time to think at Monaco and no time to relax. You cannot take your eye off the ball for a split second. I think Dad's biggest talent was his power of concentration, and his stamina from years of rowing, and a modicum of skill, of course – all things in high demand at Monaco. That's my theory anyway. The motor racing historian Doug Nye put it well: 'When it comes to Monaco,' he said, 'Graham Hill strode that stage like a Colossus!' Quite a good quote, but he didn't just mean his racing performances. He meant Monaco was a stage in every respect and that Dad somehow bagged the leading role. An amalgam of David Niven, Errol Flynn and Terry Thomas, Dad had that thing that made everyone feel he was doing it for them as much as for himself. He had the famous Kipling 'common touch', could hang with the Rainiers, yet mix on the level with everyone else. He was as comfortable standing in the terraces watching Arsenal (wearing a Savile Row suit, mind!) as he was golfing with Sean Connery or shooting with the Queen.

He was a guy who'd come from humble beginnings and risen to the top without becoming a snob about it. The previous Prince Rainier said something nice about him. He described him as 'Mediterranean', meaning British but without the chilliness. That's class, that is. Know what I mean, Herbert?

**Johnny:** Class. It's my middle name. Did you ever go to watch him race there?

**Damon:** No, I never went, which is a bit of a shame. But I remember seeing him win in 1969. The Monaco Grand Prix was hardly ever on television in those days but it happened to be that year. We were at a friend's house somewhere in Kent and I was playing in the garden with Major Matt Mason, which was a kind of bendy rubber toy astronaut, not a friend of the family!

**Johnny:** I thought it was the family dog.

**Damon:** Funny name for a dog? No, Herbert, it was a kind of Buzz Lightyear toy and it was bloody lethal. Inside each of the rubber arms and legs was a wire and if you bent them round too much the wire would poke out. Anyway, as I was busy impaling myself on Major Matt Mason my mother came out and said, 'Come inside, Damon! Now! Quick! Dad's winning the Monaco Grand Prix!' I'm not sure what kind of reaction she was expecting but I sort of lazily got up, reluctantly dropped Major Matt Mason and dragged my grumpy little arse indoors. The TV reception in remote Kentish villages was almost non-existent in those days so all I remember seeing was a foggy black and white picture of my dad waving to the crowd as he drove through the gasworks hairpin on his last lap. I wasn't too impressed with the picture, but I do remember getting a shot of something like pride to see the old man at work. Maybe that planted a bit of a seed? I wonder. I was too stupid to know what I thought about anything back then. But I knew if you bent Major Matt Mason's leg too many times you'd get stabbed in the finger. Ah, happy days!

So what was your first experience of the Principality, Johnny?

**Johnny:** The first time I went was in 1987 for a Formula Three race. It was a support race for the Grand Prix and I remember being absolutely wowed by the place. You were there too, I think, weren't you?

**Damon:** In '87? I was, but I didn't qualify, damn it!

**Johnny:** I'd never been anywhere like it before in my life. It was just so different to everywhere else. Can you recall the first time you ever walked the track? I do. Or at least I remember the first time I attempted to walk the track. You couldn't really do a full track walk in those days, but thanks to the people at Benetton, whom I already had a connection with, I managed to do about half of it. My first thought was, this isn't a bloody racetrack, it's just a concrete den of iniquity. How fabulous! There were empty bottles of beer absolutely everywhere and even the odd body. Not dead bodies, of course. Bodies that had been soaked in rather too much alcohol and for rather too long. It was absolute carnage from start to finish. What I remember most, though, were those turbo V6 engines knocking out 1,200 bhp at 12,000 rpm – experiencing that was genuinely life changing for me. The hemmed-in track also made everything – the sounds, the speed, the smells, the mistakes and the danger – very, very real. There was no get-out clause at Monaco. Or at least that's how it felt when I walked part of the track. You were either on it or in the wall. Until I first raced at Monaco the most dangerous track I'd ever raced at was probably Oulton Park. This place, though, was just ridiculous.

**Damon:** The only track you could compare it to back then was Pau. Did you ever race there?

**Johnny:** Nope. I should have when I was racing F3000, but I crashed the race before in Vallelunga in Italy and had concussion so was not allowed to drive. I do remember driving F3 at Monaco, though, for a one-off race. The F1 paddock was where it always is but we were based by the tennis courts, which is about a mile away. That meant we had to drive our cars to the track, so basically on the open road. We did so at about six o'clock in the morning prior to qualifying, so while all the residents were trying to get some sleep, a parade of F3 cars would take to the roads – which were not closed like the ones that made up the track, by the way – and basically cause mayhem.

That 1987 F3 race was genuinely the highlight of my life up until that point. The only run-off was at Sainte Devote, and I remember experiencing this mixture of intense terror and intense pleasure. I'd obviously experienced that before many times but not to such an extent. Death or a serious accident wasn't just close going around Monaco, it was sitting on your bloody shoulder, going, *Won't be long now, Johnny. One tiny little mistake and I've got you!*

**Damon:** What about the first time you raced there in F1?

**Johnny:** That would have been in 1989. At the time, Monaco was the third race of the season. Despite finishing fourth at the first race in Brazil, I'd struggled with braking, and at race two in San Marino I qualified twenty-third (one behind Martin Brundle!) and finished eleventh. My feet, one of which had been almost severed in an accident at Brands the previous year, were in absolute agony and I'd had to be lowered into the car in Brazil. In hindsight, it was

9

too soon for me to be racing. After finishing fourth in Brazil (behind Nigel Mansell, Alain Prost and Maurício Gugelmin) I naturally gained a bit of confidence but ultimately it was a false dawn. There are nineteen corners at Monaco and you spend 21 per cent of the lap braking. If ever a track was going to highlight my problem, this was it.

I don't want to turn this into some kind of moan-fest, but because of everything I'd been through I was seen as being damaged goods and the only person apart from myself who had any faith in me was Peter Collins. Not only was I desperate to repay Peter's belief in me but I also wanted to prove all the naysayers wrong. What was I supposed to do, though? Ask Peter to wait until my feet didn't hurt anymore? They still give me jip today so I'd still be waiting. I had to give it a go. At Monaco, as with San Marino before that, I had to brake with my heel and unfortunately it only really worked once every seven or eight laps. Then, at the Circuit Gilles Villeneuve in Montreal, which is somewhere you have to brake hard and often, I was well and truly found out – and that was the end of my first stint with Benetton.

**Damon:** Binned off by Briatore?

**Johnny:** Yes. Which was fair enough. A driver who can't brake isn't much use really.

**Damon:** My feet have been neither crushed nor amputated but the first time I raced in Canada I couldn't walk when I got out. My right foot was burning from having to be hard on either the throttle or the brakes all the time. Seriously, you have my sympathy, Johnny. Like, ouch!

**Johnny:** Thank you, Champ. Anyway, sod Canada. Let's get back to Monaco.

**Damon:** Agreed. Leaving the pits at Monaco and driving up the hill is certainly one of the most exhilarating things I've ever experienced. It's even better when you have to pass another car. Every race has its fair share of squeaky-bum moments, but going up that hill always used to evoke a round of profanities from me, which was rare. You remember in *Star Wars* when the Millennium Falcon goes into hyperdrive and all the stars start whizzing past? Well, that's what it's like when you drive an F1 car out of the paddock and up the hill at Monaco. It's like doing the Kessel Run in twelve parsecs (one for the geeks there). Once again, it's because everything's in such close proximity to the car. On a motorway, you often don't notice how fast you're going until you hit a slip road. Why? Because everything narrows down and your speed becomes more relatable. At Monaco, you can tell how close you are to the barriers by the noise. The louder it becomes, the closer you are. There are times when you can hear, better than see, how close you are to the barrier. It's a good sphincter test that one. All rather wee-inducing.

**Johnny:** All rather wee-inducing? You're like something from another century!

**Damon:** I'll take that as a compliment, Johnny, but I'm not quite Jacob Rees-Mogg.

**Johnny:** Qualifying at Monaco was, in my mind, the biggest single challenge there was in F1. That's how I used to regard it. These days the track's quite flat but that wasn't always the case. I think it's the madness of being able to drive a car with that amount of power around such narrow streets that makes it so enthralling. It's difficult to conjure up an everyday equivalent, but I suppose it would be like the government removing the speed limits on every road, street and motorway and then handing out Ferraris to everyone and saying, 'Here you are boys and girls. Go and fill your boots!' The people of Great Britain would be like, *Really? Can I? That's fantastic!* Which is basically what we were like when we first began to grasp what Monaco was all about.

**Damon:** You've hit the nail on the head there, Johnny. One of my biggest fears when I first went around Monaco was whether my car was going to fit on the track. That's completely absurd, of course, as the cars clearly do fit on the track. Just. To drive an F1 car around Monaco is to enter the Twilight Zone. Take your lap times, for instance. The first lap out always seems to take about thirty seconds, but it's really closer to two minutes! But as the weekend goes on a lap seems to take longer and longer. The track is actually expanding your mind and time is slowing down in an Einsteinian time-warp paradigm. Are you writing this down, Johnny?

**Johnny:** Making mental notes. Yes. (*Aside:* He's blooming mad!) I love that bit when you drive up over Avenue d'Ostende and then down towards Massenet. I always used to think to myself, whatever you do, do not understeer going into this corner! The relief I used to feel when the car turned was immense.

**Damon:** Going back to that F3 race in 1987 for a moment, do you remember where you finished?

**Johnny:** Yes, I finished third behind a French driver called Didier Artzet, who didn't progress, and my fellow short-arse and former teammate, Jean Alesi. I was behind Nicola Larini for most of the race but managed to overtake him right at the last minute. By the time we actually got to Monaco, I'd won four of the first seven races of the 1987 British Formula Three Championship, so I was on a roll. Subsequently, I was keen to impress the bigwigs from F1, and they were all there – Enzo Ferrari, Frank Williams, Ken Tyrell, Ron Dennis. The only man in F1 who makes me look like a giant was there too – Bernie Ecclestone. Before the race an idiot from our team (I was driving for Eddie Jordan at the time, who became my mentor) went and put a spool differential on my car and it turned out to be a complete disaster.

**Damon:** Don't tell me. That idiot was you?

**Johnny:** How did you guess? The reason I put it on (I'd used it in previous races, by the way, and to great effect) was because I hadn't experienced any understeer with it and I was convinced that it would work around Monaco. My engineer, Dave Bambo, thought I was bonkers but as opposed to pooh-poohing my suggestion he allowed it for first qualifying. The moment I went out I thought, *Shit, what the hell have I done?!* I could hardly manoeuvre the bloody car. Dave was obviously teaching me a lesson and the spool came straight off. I still go red thinking about it. By the way, my podium finish at the 1987 Monaco Grand Prix Formula Three was the best result by a Brit since 1984, so all in all my first experiences of Monaco were good. Apart from that bloody differential.

**Damon:** I wish I could say the same. I was driving for a team called Intersport in 1987, alongside Martin Donnelly, but the Toyota engine we had was just too heavy up top for that particular race. Neither of us qualified, so it wasn't exactly a success. I did still win a couple of races in the 1987 British Formula Three Championship, though – at Zandvoort and Spa – and I believe I finished a meritorious fifth in the standings.

**Johnny:** Fifth, eh? What an amazing effort. Just out of interest, who won the Championship?

**Damon:** Now you've got me. Some forgettable cove. Diminutive in stature and bereft of character and personality. Johnny . . . something or another. Anyway, back to F1, which is fortunately where the two of us ended up.

While I agree with you when you say that qualifying at Monaco is probably the biggest single task a Formula One driver faces in a season, I'd probably expand on that slightly and say that, front to back, it's the hardest race of all. It demands an entirely different approach at every juncture, so getting yourself into the 'zone', as it were, with everything that's going on, is nigh on impossible. It even starts a day earlier than the other races, so instead of arriving on the Thursday you have to arrive on the Wednesday. You do get a break on the Friday, but that's kind of detrimental in a way, as you just want to get on with it. The trick is to keep busy and fortunately that's not difficult over there. That said, even the simplest of pursuits, such as going out for a meal, have to be planned like a military campaign. First of all you have to try and get a table, which isn't always easy on race weekend, regardless of who you are. Should you manage to book one, you then have to try and get yourself and your guest or guests to the restaurant itself. As we've already said, things can get a little bit hectic in the Principality during the fifth month of the year. Even a short walk can be fraught with danger and every route seems to be barriered off.

Should you succeed in reaching your eatery of choice, you then have to try and make sure that you don't get bombarded by autograph hunters for the duration of your meal. Some people, such as Johnny, absolutely love being set upon by hordes of adoring people (who are usually quite refreshed in Monaco), whereas I prefer them to take a ticket and form an orderly queue. Even getting from the hotel to the paddock is a nightmare. Or at least, it used to be. The track closes at 6 a.m., so regardless of where you were staying you'd have to work out how to get to the paddock via an alternative route. It was like something out of the *Krypton Factor*. In the late 1980s and early '90s, which is when you, me and Brundle burst onto the scene, some of the smaller teams such as Ligier, Lola and Minardi would be based way up in the multi-storey car park, which is almost in France. To be fair, the amount of cars we had in those days was almost double the amount we have now, but you didn't want to be in an 'overspill team'. You end up walking miles and climbing mountains. In 1989, for instance, which is when laddo here arrived, thirty-nine cars were entered for the Monaco Grand Prix and twelve of them failed to qualify or pre-qualify. That must have been complete and utter madness. The above certainly isn't a complaint, by the way. It's obviously an honour, a pleasure and a privilege racing at Monaco. I'm merely trying to describe the myriad differences a driver faces at Monaco, and how we go about dealing with them. The issues we face are obviously what you'd call first-world problems, but unless you're properly prepared you can be exhausted before you even do a lap.

**Johnny:** A lot of it is obviously down to the individual. It's non-stop from the moment you arrive until the moment you leave, so if you're gregarious it's manna from heaven and if you're shy it's manna from hell. I could never sleep because of all the bloody fireworks.

**Damon:** One year I was there lying in my hotel room trying desperately to get to sleep and there was a couple having sex in the next room. And then the bloody fireworks started going off at the same time! I don't think the two were meant to be synchronized. Bloody impressive if they were! It seemed to go on almost as long as the flipping race, too. I remember thinking to myself, *One day I'm going to come back here as a spectator and see what I've been missing. Experience it as a fan.* Not necessarily like the couple next door did! But it is one of the frustrations about Monaco that, for the entire weekend, you're surrounded by tens of thousands of people who are, for want of a better phrase, on the lash. So if you are lucky enough to go to Monaco one day, spare a thought for all the poor racing drivers trying to get some sleep, would you? 'Turn that bloody racket down!' Can't see that happening somehow. Some drivers claimed they could party all night and still be on top form the next day, though. People like Eddie Irvine and a few others. Maybe they could?

**Johnny:** The same as James Hunt, I suppose. They just threw caution to the wind and joined the throng! So what's the worst experiences you've had at Monaco? As a driver, that is.

**Damon:** Well, the worst experience I've had was in 1994. Monaco was the first race after the funerals of Ayrton Senna and Roland Ratzenberger and F1 was in a very dark place. We all felt very down, and the atmosphere in the grandstands and on the streets was similar. The sky may have been blue but there was a dark cloud hanging over all of us. I remember I went into the changing room on the Thursday and opened a cupboard and there was Ayrton's T-shirt still hanging up. That really took my breath away. For the first time ever, I think, nobody really wanted to race or even be in Monaco. Do you remember it, Johnny?

**Johnny:** Yes, of course I do. We almost lost Rubens Barrichello at Imola too. I wasn't as close to Ayrton as you were, Champ, but we'd always had a laugh together and he'd been an inspiration to me. Do you know, he used to pinch my bum as we were leaving the drivers' meetings? I was probably closer to Roland really. Thanks to Gerhard Berger giving me a lift in his plane, I was able to attend both funerals. As Ayrton's teammate, though, it must have been incredibly difficult for you.

**Damon:** I guess it was. I had to try and keep the team's hopes up and I'd be lying if I said I was up to the challenge. I watched a report on the race some years later and the presenter made the very valid point that during the minute's silence that was held shortly before the race the countenances of some of the younger drivers displayed fear and confusion. F1 was being accused of being a barbaric sport at the time and, in hindsight, remembering two deceased drivers like that before such a challenging race probably wasn't a good idea. Then there was Karl Wendlinger's accident, of course. He was driving for Sauber and during first practice he exited the tunnel and lost control of the car under braking for the Nouvelle Chicane. After hitting the wall sideways his head struck a barrier. He was in a coma for several weeks and didn't drive again for the rest of the year.

If anything good came out of Imola, maybe it was the reformation of the Grand Prix Drivers' Association (GPDA). I forget how long the association had been disbanded for but after a meeting at the Automobile Club de Monaco on the Friday, between the current drivers and some former drivers such as Niki Lauda, a request was made for the FIA to recognize the existence of the newly formed association and to work with us to improve safety in F1. We elected Martin Brundle as chairman and Gerhard Berger and Michael Schumacher as directors. Almost to honour the reformation, it was those three who ended up on the podium! It worked for them, then!

Come on then, Johnny. Let's hear your worst Monaco experience before moving onto more uplifting stuff.

**Johnny:** Well, my worst personal experience as a driver – apart from aquaplaning off in 1998 after qualifying in seventh, which was a bugger – would have to be my last Monaco, which was in 2000. Twenty years ago! Bloody hell. Throughout my entire career Monaco had always been the highlight of my season and I knew I was going to miss it. For a working-class boy from Essex with two dodgy feet to even get in sniffing distance of the world's most glamorous sporting event was incredible, but to race there ten times and bag a podium was the stuff dreams are made of. Or at least my dreams. Knowing that I'd never get that buzz again was an incredible wrench and afterwards is probably the closest I've ever come to having withdrawal symptoms.

My name is Johnny Herbert and I am a Monaco-holic.

**Damon:** A Monaco-holic? You're not on your own, Johnny. Certainly not in terms of that feeling when you have to stop racing. My dad should probably have retired several years before he did but the fact was he just couldn't give it up. It's like breaking up a marriage. Not many drivers have spoken publicly about it but I think it's a very real problem. Rubens Barrichello's solution was to keep racing! Since retiring from F1 in 2011 he's spent eight consecutive seasons racing stock cars in Brazil. I'm assuming he doesn't need the money so he must still be hooked. But there's nothing worse than having to retire out of necessity rather than choice. My least favourite experience at Monaco in terms of racing was when my engine blew up in the tunnel in 1996.

**Johnny:** That was my best, because on that occasion I finished third!

**Damon:** That's another fine podium you owe me, Stanley. But in all honesty, you finishing third did obviously alleviate some of my massive disappointment. Very considerate of you. After I retired from the race I stood by the barrier with my engine smoking, thinking, *I do hope Johnny comes through and ends up on the podium* – not! On a more positive note, I think my best Monaco experience was taking the pole lap in 1995. I beat Michael Schumacher by almost eight tenths of a second, and looking back it was probably the closest I ever came to producing a perfect lap. Timed to absolute perfection, even if I do say so myself. And as everyone knows, if you have pole at Monaco, you have to be a complete idiot not to convert that into a win. But I managed it. Michael Schumacher got ahead during my first pit stop and led for most of the race. You finished fourth, didn't you, Johnny?

**Johnny:** I did, which, despite being lapped by you and Michael, was a big thrill for me. Not as thrilling as the podium, of course, which is my all-time favourite Monaco moment, but a thrill nonetheless. The podium at Monaco is totally different to anywhere else. Prince Rainier was still around when I made it up there, and that I found impressive. Working-class Essex boy, you see. It doesn't take much.

**Damon:** You and Prince Albert are mates, though, aren't you? You two used to go down the pub.

**Johnny:** Absolutely! I lived in Monaco for about fifteen years and Albert and I, or Bert, as he's known to his mates on the dominos team, used to frequent the Monaco boozers quite often. 'Get me a brown ale and some pork scratchings, would you, Johnny?' he used to call out. 'Yes, Your Royal Highness,' I'd reply. 'Have you got a euro for the jukebox, and a stool so I can reach?' He's actually a really nice chap and he loves his racing.

One of the most shocking off-track stories I've ever heard about Monaco involves the late, great Roy Salvadori, who was around in the 1950s and early '60s. After a fabulous career racing for Ferrari, BRM, Lola and many others, Roy ended up living in Monaco and one day in the 1990s, who should move in underneath him but Jason Plato.

**Damon:** Really? Plato? Oh my God, that's horrific! What happened?

**Johnny:** I read this in Jason's autobiography – apparently after Roy came down to complain about Jason's music one day they became friends. It's still shocking, though. Fancy having to live above Plato. And in the 1990s!

**Damon:** In some ways it's actually more difficult being a pundit at Monaco than it is being a driver. When I say difficult, I don't mean in terms of hardship. When all's said and done we're treated like kings really, or at least dukes, but when you're there as a pundit you'll be up at seven every morning and you won't finish until at least 9 p.m.

Johnny, I think I can hear violins?

**Johnny:** That'll be the readers, Damon.

**Damon:** Bless them all. While we're here, I want to add two favourite moments as a spectator at Monaco. We were talking earlier about the turbos, well in 1987 I watched Nigel's pole lap at Monaco, which was incredible. At the time I used to be able to get a pass from Bernie and could just walk around the edge of the track. There was no catch fencing at all, so in hindsight it was ridiculously dangerous. I was quite lucky, really, because as I was standing by Massenet, Philippe Streiff in the Tyrell crashed right in front of me and I got covered in brake fluid and carbon fibre shards. That was interesting.

Best of all, though, was watching Nigel on qualifiers in that turbo Honda. He came up the hill and I had real trouble moving my head fast enough to keep up with him. His unfeasibly large testicles, which you mentioned earlier Johnny and to great effect, were obviously larger still that day. I remember thinking to myself as he flew past me, *Shit, he's not going to stop!* I genuinely thought Nigel Mansell was going to die that day. He obviously didn't, thank God, and made it round in one piece. You'd never know by talking to Nigel, who can sound a bit like a retired bank manager, that he must be one of the bravest human beings on the planet. Earlier in the weekend I'd been standing on the bank on the exit of Casino behind Eddie Jordan. You remember the pop-off valves that used to crack open when you changed gear? Well, they were sort of mini explosions. When one of the Ferraris went past the valve popped and I swear Eddie's wig jumped off his head. I used to think that perhaps the Jordan syrup story was a bit of blarney, but it wasn't. Eddie's wig did a jig! I saw it wid me own eyes. That's my generic cultural appropriation accent.

**Johnny:** I'm actually crying listening to that. You do know that he glues it on these days?

**Damon:** Really? I had no idea. How do you know?

**Johnny:** We were once on a plane to Jerez and me and my mechanic, Bruce Stewart, had a bet to see if we could find out how

Eddie made his wig stay on. Fortunately Eddie fell asleep during the flight, so I took my chance and investigated. These days, whenever I'm alone with Eddie I always start looking quizzically at his hair, just to make sure it's not moving. Whenever I do he immediately starts talking to me in a very schoolmasterly way. 'Johnnyyyyyyyyyy,' he says. 'Steady on, Johnnyyyyyyy.' What an absolutely fabulous man, though. We only tease him because we love him.

**Damon:** Oh! I wouldn't go that far! Just kidding, EJ! He's our link, really. You drove for him at the very start of your career, Johnny, and I drove for him at the very end. I won him his first Grand Prix and you won him the Formula Three Championship and his first win in F3000. He's a bit special, is our Eddie. Life would be a lot less colourful without him. And balder.

**Johnny:** I'll second that. Speaking of links, before we leave the Principality we should give a mention to the film we made with Sky F1 in 2014. It was just a short film, but it was a heck of a lot of fun and is one of the most popular things we've ever done as pundits. Apart from putting down our microphones and going home.

A few weeks before the 2014 Monaco Grand Prix somebody suggested that I make a comeback as a driver. Although it was obviously a joke (although not that obviously), Sky thought there was mileage in the scenario and asked Champ and me if we'd like to go over there a bit earlier and make a film about me making a comeback.

**Damon:** Some would say you were never there in the first place.

**Johnny:** Be that as it may, I played myself, the excitable yet perhaps slightly over the hill racing driver, and you played my manager. For one shot in the hotel, the director wanted us to get in bed together, à la Morecambe and Wise. Damon was supposed to be wearing his dressing gown and reading *Le Monde* while I was supposed to be wearing my race suit and reading the *Beano*. It would have been fabulous, but one of us said no.

**Damon:** I know you were disappointed, Johnny, but I have my reputation to think of. What I found slightly unnerving was how naturally the whole thing fell into place; the excitable racing driver who has to be calmed down by his slightly po-faced but much more mature manager. It all felt oddly familiar. One of my favourite scenes, apart from us both impersonating Sir Jackie Stewart, is when the team went and asked the likes of Lewis Hamilton, Alain Prost, Daniel Ricciardo and the aforementioned Sir Jackie what they thought of the mighty atom making a comeback. Can you remember the verdict, Johnny?

**Johnny:** That I might just have been carrying a little bit too much weight.

**Damon:** I think we'll leave it there, shall we?

# CHAPTER TWO

## Team orders: good or bad?

**Johnny:** In my opinion, they're shit, and that's all I have to say on the matter.

**Damon:** Well, that was an interesting discussion. Very insightful! I had a feeling this was going to be a potentially contentious chapter, for the simple reason that it is, and always has been, a contentious issue. I'll tell you what, shall we start again? Maybe be a bit more objective this time?

**Johnny:** Oh, all right then. As far as I'm concerned team orders are in complete contrast with what we're there to do. And what the fans are there to see. They put the whole thing in reverse. Think back to when Mika Salo was ordered to give way to Eddie Irvine at Hockenheim in 1999. Michael Schumacher had broken his leg at Silverstone and Mika, who'd driven a few races for BAR earlier in the season, was brought in as a replacement. Eddie was going for the Championship and because Mika was in front of him he was told to give way. Mika did as he was told, Eddie won the race, and a few weeks later Mika was on his way again. I've spoken to Mika about this and, to this day, he regrets doing as he was told.

**Damon:** Why?

**Johnny:** Because he never got another opportunity to win a race, and probably knew that at the time. Also, in his mind, if he had gone against Ferrari's wishes and won the race they might have respected him more.

**Damon:** No they wouldn't! They'd have said, hang on a minute, this guy seems to think he's more important than Ferrari! But I wish he'd done it.

**Johnny:** I suppose I'm looking at it from the underdog's point of view, or, in mine and Mika's case, the number-two driver's. Had I been like your good self – a World Champion with oodles of power and film-star good looks – then I'd have experienced the other side of the coin.

**Damon:** You mean you'd have known what it was like to benefit from team orders and film-star good looks?

**Johnny:** Yes, which means I wouldn't have wanted to throw things at people afterwards. That's what I mean! I'm sorry, but in my opinion team orders should not be part of F1. Perhaps I'm being naive, but that's the way I feel about it.

**Damon:** Unfortunately they're a necessary evil. There's this thing called a racing team and as a driver you are part of that team. Sometimes you simply have to toe the line. I'm certainly not saying that I'm a fan of team orders, but ever since the sport created two championships within the same championship back in 1958 there has been a conflict of ambitions and objectives. As a driver you have an objective, which is making the most of your career, and sometimes that fits with what the team wants. But sometimes the team asks you to sacrifice that objective for what they would probably call the greater good. It's always that way around because the revenue is tied to the Constructors' Championship instead of the Drivers' Championship and the teams regard you as an employee. I'm not saying I agree with that, but it's the way they look at it.

**Johnny:** My argument with that would be Michael's era, when he used to have the Championship wrapped up by July. Most of the team orders issued by Ferrari in that period were for the betterment of Michael Schumacher, not the team, and certainly not any of his teammates. Take the Eddie Irvine and Mika Salo incident. Barring an accident or a breakdown, Ferrari were going to finish with a one-two that day no matter what, so the theory that it's all about the Constructors' Championship doesn't rub. Nine times out of ten the Constructors' Championship will be won by the fastest car. Sometimes it might happen a little bit later if you don't issue team orders and occasionally it might not happen at all, but that's just life. I suppose the drivers are in a unique position really. The Constructors' Championship is all about the team, whereas the Drivers' Championship is all about the driver. The thing is, if a driver was asked by his team to sacrifice a race win so his teammate could win the Drivers' Championship, what should happen?

**Damon:** It would be his call, ultimately, but in my opinion he should sacrifice the win. And that should be what the team would want him to do.

**Johnny:** Why should he sacrifice the win?

**Damon:** Because without the team, which by definition is more than one individual, he wouldn't have been in that position in the first place and, assuming he can't win the Drivers' and his teammate can, he'll be helping the team's morale and reputation and

27

the team are likely to love him for that. Although there is no extra prize money to the team if their driver wins the Drivers' Championship, to the best of my knowledge, which sucks a bit if you ask me.

However, you will get situations where drivers' career trajectories flatten because they obey a team order and are asked to do something against their will. I do think it was a bit rough on David Coulthard to be asked to move over for Mika Häkkinen in Jerez in 1997. But if he'd said no, maybe the relationship with the team could have been a bit tetchy. But, that's my point. He's got a responsibility to himself, too.

By way of contrast, in 1965 my dad was racing with another Scot, Jackie Stewart, in the Italian GP in Monza. Both were BRM teammates. BRM knew they had the race in the bag, so partway through Jackie and Dad were told by the team not to go beyond a certain rev limit. They were heading for a one-two and wanted to protect the result. Dad was numero uno in the team, so everyone expected JYS to move over eventually and let him take the lead. Jackie claims he never disobeyed the order but he kept on mysteriously overtaking Dad, which is normal at Monza, what with the slipstreaming etc. Actually it can be difficult not to catch up the guy in front! But, sure enough, he crosses the line first without giving the lead back to Dad. Meanwhile, the team are going apoplectic and were furious with them both after the race, as they had a comfortable sixteen-second lead over Dan Gurney in third place. But you can't keep JYS from his victory! It was his first ever. He had arrived!

Twenty-eight years later at the same Grand Prix and same racetrack I was playing Jackie's role. It was my first year at Williams, and I was number-two driver to the great Alain Prost. On the first lap I sort of clipped Senna's rear wheel, catapulting him into the air. Quite spectacular! Really annoyingly, that damaged my front wing and I had to pit for a new one. But just like that Droopy cartoon character, that just made me mad! It's probably quite hard to imagine me being pumped up, but give it a go, if you would.

So there I was, charging through the field like a lunatic, when all of a sudden the team came on the radio. 'Damon,' they said. 'Would you mind slowing down a bit please. Alain's worried you're going to catch him.' Because I was so pumped I wasn't in the mood for being charitable so instead of acquiescing to my masters' wishes I basically told them to get stuffed. 'Tell Alain I will race! I WILL race!'

After a moment the team came back on the radio and said, 'OK. Thank you, Damon,' and that was it. It was as if I'd made them all a cup of tea or something. Had my new-found butchness scared the team into submission, I wondered.

**Johnny:** I was lying fifth until I spun off and hit the tyres at Parabolica. Who won the race, then? Was it the diminutive Frenchman? The one with the big nose and even bigger brain? Or was it the awkward Brit? The one who's butchness and masculinity turned his team to jelly?

**Damon:** 'Twas I! But it wasn't because I'd intimidated the team into submission. Actually, we never got to find out what I'd do, because Alain's engine blew to smithereens just as I was about to catch him going into Curva Grande. Huge cloud of smoke and I was home and dry! Lovely. Poor Alain, though. I did feel for him. A bit.

Recently I was having an email conversation about this with my engineer at Williams, John Russell. I said to him, 'You do realize, John, that in Monza I said that I *would* race Alain, not that I *wouldn't* race him?' He just said, 'Yeah, Damon, I know.' Ha! Funny.

Anyway, back to your earlier point about team orders being catered to specific drivers. Does everybody cross the start line at the London Marathon at the same time? Parity in F1 is impossible. It's very fair on paper but, unfortunately, due to a number of practicalities, it just isn't in reality. For instance, if a team is trying to sign a new driver and he demands to be given number-one status in the team, what are they going to say? I'm sorry, Mr Herbert, but we reject your outrageous demands and all we're going to offer you is parity with the eighteen-year-old novice we signed last week. Real F1 life isn't like that. If a team wants the best driver they will make accommodations. And if that means the snotty new boy has to learn from the master, they will impose team instructions to that effect.

Your Michael Schumacher example is a good one. He basically negotiated to have an entire team all to himself, which at the end of the day is the ideal scenario for any driver who is serious about winning the World Championship. Who wouldn't want to go into battle with an entire team fighting your corner? When I raced against Michael and had DC as a teammate I had an intra-team battle against him on my hands and an inter-team battle against Michael. Michael, on the other hand, only had to worry about the inter-team battle, as his teammates were there to support him. Because DC couldn't win the Drivers' Championship and I could, I didn't think it unreasonable for me to ask Williams if DC could support me for the remainder of the season, but Williams weren't interested in the Drivers' Championship. The only thing they were interested in was the Constructors' Championship, so my request for DC's assistance was refused. In a sense, they were doing the right thing for the sport as they were allowing their two drivers to race, but the cost to me was that I had to fight two opponents whereas Michael only had to focus on one. Me! My argument was also that the big story is the Drivers' Championship. Fans and the press don't give a stuff about the Constructors'. I admit I wasn't thinking about the fans when I asked, but it should be as important for the team to win the Drivers' as the Constructors'. But it isn't.

Speaking of the public . . .

Maybe we should mention the fans? The ones whose money we happily take? They're the ones who get cheated because of team orders, and on occasion it's rendered the sport guilty of selling something under false pretences. When fans sit down to watch a race they do so in the belief that the drivers are going to race. Understandable, I think. Then, something like the 2002 Rubens and Michael fiasco in Austria happens, when Rubens was forced to yield to his teammate on the final lap, which to this day makes me want to run behind the sofa and hide. The crowd, quite rightly, booed throughout the entire presentation ceremony and the press conference afterwards was excruciating. The entire episode was an utter disgrace because they had effectively been deceived into thinking they were watching a real race. Actually it was a pretend race. Then there's Monaco 2007, when Lewis had to literally follow Fernando Alonso for most of the race, faking it. Yet again, the public believed they were watching a race, when in fact they weren't. It was a McLaren parade. To me that is trading under false pretences. The public are sold a ticket to a race. These people have paid good money to watch a no-holds-barred battle between drivers. That, regardless of all the other permutations regarding team orders, is where F1 loses respectability.

**Johnny:** I just want to touch on what you said about the Drivers' Championship, as it made me think about the Prost–Senna era.

Even though the Constructors' Championship was around in those days, nobody apart from the teams gave a stuff about it. Not because it wasn't important, but because you had two of the best drivers ever battling it out on the track week after week. Neither were being controlled in any way, shape or form. It was, in every respect, a golden era.

**Damon:** When you've got a dominant team you can allow your drivers to do that.

**Johnny:** It doesn't always happen, though. Look at Abu Dhabi in 2016. Mercedes had already won the Constructors' Championship by then and the winner of the Drivers' Championship was going to be either Lewis or Nico. Nico only had to finish third to win it, even if Lewis won the race, so as a climax to the season it had real potential. While leading the race, with Nico in second, Lewis slowed up a bit in the hope of bringing Sebastian Vettel and Max Verstappen into play. Had they both caught Nico and overtaken him, Lewis would have won the Championship, so in my opinion it was worth a try. The moment Lewis started slowing down the team were on the radio telling him to speed up, but Lewis, to his eternal credit, told them to get stuffed. 'I'm in the lead so I control the pace,' he said, and he was absolutely right. In the end Paddy Lowe got on the radio and ordered Lewis to do as he was told. Could you imagine telling Prost or Senna to do the same? That'd be interesting. It was even suggested that Lewis might face disciplinary action after the race, but it never came to pass.

What would you have done in those circumstances, Champ?

**Damon:** Knowing what I know now, I would have lured Nico into trying to overtake me and then accidentally not seen him! No, I think I'd have done the same. I certainly wouldn't have just sat there for forty laps wondering how I was going to congratulate Nico. But trying to be objective for a moment, I think there were reasons why the team got involved, and although we may not like or agree with them, they're part and parcel of today's sport. I'm referring, of course, to the commercial side of our sport, which is a necessary thing. Everything the teams do has to reflect their sponsors' or owners' ethos. Having their cars bashing into one another and bitter feuds between drivers is not the PR message of their dreams. Nor is using unsporting methods to win. I'm not saying that will have been the only reason for the team getting involved but it's bound to have been a consideration. My, how times have changed. I think we need a discussion about it myself. I love a bit of argy-bargy!

**Johnny:** Do you know, I think I'd go as far as to ban radio in F1.

**Damon:** Have you lost your mind, man? Is it too hot in here or something? Seriously, I do think there are times we need a radio.

**Johnny:** Such as?

**Damon:** Erm, how about, 'Johnny, your car's on fire!' What about mirrors, though? I think we should ban them. I don't think people have given this enough thought, I really don't. You see, if a driver doesn't have mirrors they're going to stick to the same line and just drive as fast as they can. The drivers behind will know the guy or gal in front won't have seen them. Also, they won't be able to turn into you on purpose. I'm super sensitive about things like that.

**Johnny:** What, so now teams are going to have spotters then, like in IndyCar?

**Damon:** Well, if they have spotters we'll have to junk the radio then! No mirrors and no radio. Let's put that to the teams, shall we?

**Johnny:** I would seriously ban radio, though. For anything that isn't an emergency. It's the one aspect I genuinely don't like about racing. Every five minutes it's, *Ooh, your left front's a bit cool. Do this, change that.* It's constant interference. Bugger off! You do all that stuff on the Friday and the Saturday, then on the Sunday, you race.

**Damon:** I take it we've expanded this chapter, then, from 'team orders' to 'team orders and team interference'? I'm with you 100 per cent on this. It wasn't *that* long ago that we were racing and there was neither an ability nor a necessity for teams to keep telling us every five minutes what we needed to be doing. They expected you to be able to work out if your tyres were being overused – that was part of your skill. You'd obviously talk tactics beforehand but generally speaking you'd tell them if and when you wanted to come in. That rarely happens now. It all comes from the garage.

I'm going to use Lewis again as an example, this time at the Brazilian Grand Prix in 2019. What a great race that was. The serious bit was over and the drivers and teams had started playing with their strategies and making – heaven forfend – alternative decisions! This obviously flew in the face of normality, as everything is normally set in stone. This time they tore up the script. Hooray! There was a beautiful moment when Mercedes told Lewis he had an option on strategy. I forget what exactly. But Lewis had clearly become so used to them telling him what to do that when the option was eventually put to him he said, 'Well, I don't know! What do you want me to do?' The team appeared to be equally nonplussed, as they must have thought he wanted to choose, and there was a lovely bit of toing and froing between Lewis and the garage. I think it ended with him saying, 'It doesn't matter, I'll come in anyway,' or words to that effect. I remember thinking to myself when I heard it, that's racing! It's the adrenalin factor – the drama. There's a driver and he's in a dilemma. He's got to make a decision – and quickly! What's he going to do? Granted, the exchange between Lewis and the garage did lack that slick decisive clear thinking we've become so familiar with, but it was entertaining and exciting instead!

Sometimes the radio is really entertaining, like Monaco in 2019 with Lewis's tyres. He was on the radio saying 'She cannae take it, Cap'n! She's gonna blow!', or panic to that effect. Meanwhile, Peter Bonnington is as cool as a man in a swimming pool with a piña colada. He's whispering sweet platitudes into Lewis's helmet. It was nail-biting stuff. Whether or not it was done for entertainment value I'm not sure, but it was damned exciting. The tyres did last to the end of the race, so perhaps it was? Who cares, though. We loved it.

For drivers from our generation and older that was very much part of what we did, reacting to what the tyres were doing. These days the drivers are informed when their tyres are at the optimum temperature, whereas we had to try and gauge that for ourselves. Sometimes we missed it and sometimes we got it right. That particular skill, like so many others, is no longer required. Some drivers have it, like Lewis, Kimi Räikkönen, Sebastian Vettel and Sergio Pérez, but mostly they have to drive to the engineers' data, which is a shame, I think.

**Johnny:** Well said that man! Lewis and Sergio are excellent when it comes to gauging the condition and temperature of their tyres. I can't remember exactly when this has happened, but in recent times I've definitely heard them telling their engineers that their tyres are actually OK when they've been told to pit. Is that rare these days? Yes it is. Is it necessary for the job? That's debatable. Damon and I would obviously say it was in our day, but then we were driving very different cars, weren't we old boy?

**Damon:** We were indeed. Us and those before us had what you might call a more sensory experience, rather than data-driven. The reason we had to be so in tune with our cars was because we were our own engineers, so to speak. That seems to be a thing of the past.

One of my favourite films is *The Right Stuff*, which is the story of how the first US astronauts insisted on having controls in their rocket and a window, otherwise they were just going to be specimens sent up into space, 'Spam in a can!' they called it. If we're not careful, that's what's going to happen in F1. The GPDA have become more outspoken recently about the amount of control being relinquished by the drivers and I believe Lewis and the older guard have been helping them clarify what they're after, which is basically more self-determination within a race situation. They don't want to design the cars but they do want to have some say on safety. It's their lives, after all. I doubt they'll have much luck, but at least there's some fight in the GPDA and a desire for things to change.

When I stopped racing in 1999, the engineers were just getting to the point where they did all the set-up work and I thought to myself, so what am I supposed to do? Just drive around. Is that it? One of the things I liked about driving a racing car was playing with all the kit and getting the right balance. These days, and from the very beginning of a driver's career in single seaters, that's all done for them, and you're told how to drive the car. Whether you like it or not, you have to learn to drive the way the engineers want you to and to me that's the wrong way around.

It's like telling Roger Federer how to serve or hit a backhand to make the most of the racquet design. Some people have a certain style of driving and they need to be able to employ that style in order to achieve their potential. The car is obviously their tool and it's the engineer's job to help them get a feel for it. Look at Sebastian Vettel. He's been up and down like a fiddler's elbow over the past couple of seasons because he can't get the feeling he wants. When he gets what he wants he's blindingly quick again.

**Johnny:** The value of drivers such as Niki Lauda and Alain Prost, who could basically sit in a car and within minutes tell you exactly what was right or wrong with it, was never lost on the public. In fact, it was one of the attractions of F1. Intuitive geniuses – or genii, as Julius Caesar might have said.

**Damon:** Don't try talking Latin, Johnny. It hurts my brain. Rubens Barrichello was another one. He was highly regarded as a test driver and had better sensitivity to what the tyres were doing than Michael did. The tyre technicians actually requested him over Michael. I loved doing testing but I don't think I had freaky sensitivity like Rubens did. I think you were more in Rubens's camp, Johnny?

**Johnny:** You were better than you think.

**Damon:** That's very kind. OK, I was better than I think! I think what I was good at was getting the car to work for me. If I didn't have your natural talent, Johnny, I'd have to make my car better than yours! Some drivers' set-ups were mad. There's this thing we used to use for balancing the car called an 'anti-roll bar'. Jacques Villeneuve would come in and say, 'I wanna stiffer bar! What's the stiffest bar you can make me?' in his best cheeky brat way. That's literally what he would say. The team would then go, 'Er, we can make one infinitely stiff Jacques, if that's what you want?' So that's what he ended up with, the infinitely stiff rear bar! I should say now that it is absurd to have an infinitely stiff rear bar, because it can't move, which means it's not doing anything. It's solid. He wanted one, though, because he thought that would prove to everyone how intense and extreme he was. It was basically like going into a curry house and asking for a vindaloo with extra chili just to show how hard you are. To be fair to Jacques, he actually made it work, but it was still daft.

**Johnny:** Do you remember Niki Lauda's fuel trick? He always used to save a bit for the end of the race. Everyone else would charge off using their turbos and when they started running out of fuel Niki would pop up and say, 'I've got loads left mate. See ya!' The same with Alain Prost, of course. They really were masters of their craft.

Shortly before my first season at Benneton in 1989 I had to have my seat made. I turned up to Benneton HQ at about ten o'clock one night and there was just me, Rory Byrne, who was the chief designer, and his daughter. He said to me, 'Johnny, I can design the best chassis and we can have the best tyres and the best engine. There's just one weakness, though, and that's you.' To engineers that's exactly what we are, a weakness, because we're the ones who make the mistakes. I don't mean this in an arrogant way but we are the sport, and the reason we're the sport is because we're fallible. Today F1 is all about seeking perfection and, as I just said, the only thing that realistically prevents them from realizing it is the likes of us. The drivers. We're the ones who create the entertainment, and again I don't mean that in an arrogant way. It could be by winning a race or a championship, but it could also be by telling your engineer to naff off when he asks you to speed up, and causing a shunt. It's all part and parcel.

**Damon:** I'm not sure that's quite right, Johnny. After all, the members of the team are also fallible. Mercedes, for one, got in a right old two and eight in Germany last year, when Lewis came in for a new front wing and they weren't ready for him, resulting in a fifty-second pit stop. The rest of it is science and engineering really, but there's plenty of sport to be had both in and out of the cockpit if you know where to look.

**Johnny:** Could you imagine Nigel Mansell working with a team these days? That man could have driven a brontosaurus on wheels around Suzuka and he would still have made it purr. Gonads like planets, I tell you. Planets! He was probably the mightiest driver I ever drove against, but he also had skill. Lots of skill. It wasn't all brute force. Nigel's fan base was also massive (probably bigger than any other driver's, apart from Ayrton) and the attraction, in addition to his delightful facial hair, was obviously the way he drove.

**Damon:** There was always a bit of a buzz when Mr Mansell turned up. Back to why you mentioned him though. If you said to Nigel, 'Look, Nige, we want you to go around ten seconds off the pace because we need to save fuel', he'd just look at you and say (I can't see how I can possibly do my Nigel Mansell impression justice in print, so you'll just have to access your inner Brummie), 'Urrrrr, that's no blooddy foon, uz it?' No. Can't see it happening. It'd be a complete non-starter. I'll tell you what, Johnny, thank God we don't have to reach any conclusions about this. Too many variables.

At the end of the day you want the whole team around you, which begs the question, why do we have to have teammates?

Imagine you're in a nursery and you're surrounded by lots of fabulous toys. There you are having the time of your life when one day some other kid turns up and starts nicking them. It doesn't stop there, though. Later they start making friends with all your friends and before you know it they're being bought better toys than you are and you're no longer popular. There's always a honeymoon period when a new driver arrives. Every-body hangs on their every word and is extra nice to them. You could feel a bit jilted, if you were thin-skinned. Which I'm not, Johnny, am I? Am I? Don't answer that.

**Johnny:** Sticking with that comparison for a moment, I've been the new kid before, but with the understanding that I was about to enter somebody else's nursery, and I always ended up with second-hand toys! That was the case with both my stints at Benetton. The first time it was Alessandro Nannini's nursery and the second time it was Michael's. Even after finishing fourth in my first Grand Prix, the bigwigs at the team, like Flavio Briatore and Luciano Benetton, didn't even hang around to congratulate me. In fact, they never said a word. Blatant favouritism can make people do some very strange things, and it harks back to your point about teams treating their drivers unequally.

**Damon:** In hindsight, you could have crumbled when that hap-pened, as many drivers might have, but you didn't. You kept on going. And it was a bit of a sensational story, you finishing fourth in your first Grand Prix. Didn't Jean-Marie Balestre, the President of the FIA, ask the other drivers to give you a round of applause at the next race?

**Johnny:** That's right. It was at the drivers' meeting. Before the start, he said, 'What Johnny Herbert did in Rio was absolutely amazing and I think he deserves a round of applause,' or words to that effect. It was very nice of him.

**Damon:** I don't get it, then. So why didn't Flavio and Luciano hang around to congratulate you?

**Johnny:** Because their man, who was obviously Italian, had been beaten by a disabled Brit.

**Damon:** I totally get the feelings of paranoia. Once you give a driver a reason to suspect that there's something going on, they're all over the place. You could see it with Senna, even. They start to see subterfuge everywhere. It can easily spiral out of control. Drivers are often seen by teams as being temperamental or unpredictable, so they try to humour them. The problem is they don't really understand how to motivate a driver. Most engineers and designers don't get drivers. If a car goes wrong they know exactly what to do but if it's a driver having problems they just look baffled and embarrassed. Maybe they're more comfortable relating to inanimate objects! Sometimes a team will realize that in order to keep their prized asset happy they'll have to give them everything they want – within reason. Some more insightful team members understand that a happy driver is a quick driver. People like Adrian Newey appreciate the fact that his car isn't going to work without the driver and the more he gets to know the driver the better chance he has of seeing his lovely car running at its full potential. Whether Adrian has to put on a facade every so often is neither here nor there; he knows what makes a racing driver tick. But generally here is such a divide between the drivers and a team. I always thought they were thinking, *Oh God. Not another one!* And they say you're part of the team, but you're not. Not really. A driver is not a permanent part of a team. They can build a team around a driver, but because of the time a driver usually spends with a team – not to mention how much money they get paid – they're not really part of it. It's a temporary residency, a political relationship, and some people are very good at it, very adept, and some aren't. The ones who are good at it know how to work the system, and ultimately the success they have can often be far greater than their talent. You're not going to get what you deserve just because you're a good guy or because you have talent. Also, nothing we go through beforehand, whether it be karting, motorcycles, Formula Renault or even Formula Two, can prepare you for the monster that is Formula One. There's a moment of realization when you reach F1 that everybody around you knows more about you than you do. A lot of it might be hearsay or rubbish, but everybody has an opinion or some information on who you are, where you came from, what you do best, what you do worst, and how you're going to fare. It's very unsettling and you spend half your time thinking, *Where the hell did that come from?* You have to accept this as soon as you're able, because regardless of where you are on the grid, it's never going to change.

What we see on the outside are two guys in overalls in front of a team of people with their thumbs up, looking happy, but inside there's all kinds of craziness going on. It's you or him, kid! There can only be one winner in this relationship. It used to be more overt. In fact, Frank Williams used to like having two drivers who didn't get on, as he thought he would get the best out of them if they hated each other's guts! Maybe he was right, but more often than not you end up with a very destructive atmosphere, just like you had with Prost and Senna at McLaren. There are also times – and I'm going to include you in this, Master Herbert – when you get somebody who is very talented but unfortunately isn't a political animal. I think I'm the same, in that I was never very political, although I would always fight my corner if I had to. Not always comfortably, it has to be said. Like you, Johnny, I'm not a fan of confrontation.

Before we move on, can we have the closing statements, please, for Johnny Herbert versus Team Orders and Team Interference? I'll speak on behalf of the accused and I think we should try and include a personal experience or two, if we can. You first, Johnny.

**Johnny:** I'll give you two examples, M'lud, one off the track, and one on it, and while we're here, I'd like to ban Flavio Briatore.

**Damon:** From what?

**Johnny:** Everything! Flavio was the one who ignited my hatred of team orders and team interference and he made my life a misery at Benneton. When he signed me up for the 1995 season (I'd also driven the final two races of the 1994 season for Benneton), he told me that I would have the same equipment and the same amount of support as Michael, and like a fool I believed him. As well as being the reigning World Champion, Michael had also been at the team since 1991, so it was actually quite naive of me. What I think Flavio thought he was getting by signing John Paul Herbert was a talented but ultimately subservient number-two driver, and had I known that I would never have signed. It was written into my contract that I had to score a certain amount of points by Silverstone or the team could replace me, and I believed that my reward for achieving that goal would be a crack at the World Championship.

It took about two days for the cracks to start appearing. I was doing an interview and the man with the notepad asked me what my ambitions were for the season. 'To win races and become

World Champion,' I said. It was a bit of an innocuous statement really, as every driver at every one of the top four teams would have been saying exactly the same thing. Mr Schumacher, though, was not impressed, and the following day he made reference to my comment in an interview. I forget what Michael's exact words were but he claimed I was being political and said that if I thought I would be challenging for the Championship I had another thing coming. Until then I'd got on really well with Michael and although we were never at each other's throats thereafter, he obviously went from seeing me as an obedient little helper to a potential threat.

After that, life became a bit of a nightmare for me and the part that's relevant to this chapter is when I was suddenly prevented from seeing Michael's data. He was allowed to see my data, but I wasn't allowed to see his. Flavio's orders, apparently. I'm not one for conspiracy theories but at my first race for Benetton (this was my second stint), I qualified less than half a second behind Michael, whereas my two predecessors at the team, Jos Verstappen and JJ Lehto, had qualified, on average, 1.9 and 2.2 seconds behind him. At the following race I qualified 1.5 seconds behind Michael and that was pretty much the pattern thereafter. The car just didn't feel right from then on. Anyway, that's neither here nor there. My evidence for the court, M'lud, is not being able to see Michael Schumacher's data because of an order from on high. I could ask for several other incidents to be taken into consideration, but suffice to say that Ferrari wasn't the first team he had wrapped around his little finger, and the whole issue of what happened at Benneton in that era has even been the subject of a book.

**Damon:** Outrageous behaviour. We should have him flogged!

**Johnny:** Who, Flavio? Definitely. Anyway, silence in court, or I'll have you removed. My second piece of evidence is an episode that happened in 1998, which was my third and final year at Sauber. Until then most of my teammates there had been Italian drivers, but for 1998 Peter Sauber decided to ditch them in favour of a fiery little French one called Jean Alesi. Jean and I had known each other for donkey's years and we always got on well. He was also one of the most competitive drivers I'd ever raced against, so I knew it was going to be interesting. I certainly wasn't expecting any favouritism, though. Jean, who had replaced me at Benetton, had finished fourth in the Drivers' in both his seasons there, which is where I finished in 1995. As far as I was concerned, we were going to be racing equally and nobody at the team had said anything to the contrary.

Funnily enough, the opening race of the 1998 season is famous because of an issue involving – would you believe it – team orders! It was when DC had to make way for Mika. That was very contentious. There were also accusations of radio tapping after Mika pitted without being asked to do so. Do you remember?

**Damon:** I do indeed. What a fiasco that was. Poor old DC. That can't be right, can it? Same thing as Jerez? I was driving for Jordan alongside Ralph Schumacher and finished about tenth. My evidence *for* team orders also comes from this season.

**Johnny:** Don't tell me, Spa?

**Damon:** How did you guess? Anyway, carry on. The jury are getting restless and so am I!

**Johnny:** By the time we got to the A1 Ring in Austria it was about even-Stevens between Jean and me, both in terms of qualifying and racing. Then, during qualifying, everything started to change.

It had been raining shortly before the session started but by the time it got underway the track was starting to dry out. After my first run I was lying eighth and ahead of Jean, and it was the same after my second. Before my final run I came in to change to slicks and shortly after going out again Peter came on the radio. 'Let pass Jean,' he snapped, as if I was holding him up. I assumed Jean was right behind me but it took him two laps to pass me. By this time I only had about a minute left to start my flying lap and although I managed to do so my tyres were freezing cold. As a result, I ended up qualifying in eighteenth position whereas Jean qualified third. I found out soon afterwards that by the time I was asked to let him through he'd already completed his fast lap so why the hell Peter had asked me – sorry, ordered me – I had no idea. I was bloody furious! Poor old Jean went off, by the way, after colliding with Giancarlo Fisichella, and I finished in eighth.

**Damon:** Poor old Jean my foot. I bet you were delighted.

**Johnny:** *Moi?* Anyhow, at the next race in Hockenheim, Jean and I qualified eleventh and twelfth respectively, so apart from us wishing we were higher up the grid it was all tickety-boo. I was on a one-stop strategy, Jean was on a two, let's go racing! Five or six laps before Jean was due to make his first pit stop, Peter came on the radio again and whispered seductively, 'Let pass Jean.' *Not again*, I thought. *He can't even say it right. It's 'Let Jean pass', you Swiss cheese!*

'I'm sorry Peter,' I said defiantly. 'But I won't. He's on a two-stop, I'm on a one, I'm in the lead so no, I will not let pass Jean.'

The Swiss cheese wasn't happy.

'Let pass Jean,' he repeated angrily. 'Let pass Jean!'

'No, no, no!'

This went on for about two laps and in the end I got so worked up that, as I was trying to do as I was told and let Jean pass, I spun off into the bloody gravel! Fortunately the marshals managed to push me out (they were allowed to do it then) but I was so angry that instead of carrying on racing I went straight to the garage with one thing on my mind. I was going to kill Peter Sauber.

**Damon:** So you're now admitting attempted murder, Johnny? Would you like me to get you a lawyer?

**Johnny:** Almost! Fortunately Peter wasn't around when I came in (he was probably hiding in the loos), and by the time I eventually found him after the race Jean was bending his ear about something so I left them to it. It was probably for the best. I did speak to Peter the following day and he tried to convince me – badly, it has to be said – that he was doing it for the good of the team. Had Jean been fighting for the Championship at the time then I'd have understood, but we were both in a similar position.

**Damon:** So what was his reason?

**Johnny:** I reckon it was because Jean had driven for Ferrari. Peter was always a huge fan of the team (they were also Sauber's engine supplier at the time) and I think he had a soft spot for Jean, just as Peter Collins at Benetton had had a soft spot for me. What Peter Sauber failed to appreciate, however, when dishing out team orders, was the effect this would have on me personally. I'd been at the team three years and we'd had not an inconsiderable amount of success together. I think that's what annoyed me the most.

**Damon:** I've said it before and I'll say it again, F1 teams often have a very unequal way of treating their drivers. My evidence for team orders happened in exceptional circumstances, and although I too am generally against them, I do believe that they have their time and place in the sport. That said, it's such a grey area and because of all the different interpretations as to what might constitute a team order I doubt the practice of issuing them could ever be totally eradicated. It'd be impossible. The problem is one of semantics. What is a team order? How many angels can dance on the head of a pin? Is blue more green than red? You get the idea.

The 1998 Belgian Grand Prix is one of the most talked about races of the 1990s and a lot of people I've spoken to say that they remember where they were when it took place. It was full of incident.

**Johnny:** I remember where I was. Halfway down the grid at the start of the race and then right in the middle of one of the biggest pile-ups in F1 history.

**Damon:** You and about thirteen or fourteen other drivers. It'd been raining most of the weekend but instead of starting late and with a safety car, like it had done the year previously, the race started on time and without one. As we accelerated like maniacs out of La Source at the start of the first lap, DC hit a long metal drainage grid that caused little or no concern in the dry but in the wet required caution and respect. As DC hit the grid he had his right foot planted firmly on the throttle and as the rear wheels spun on the metal he went sideways towards the wall. I was right behind him and realized that after hitting the wall he was going to rebound back onto the track. I wasn't sure at the time whether to stay where I was or try and get in front of DC before he rebounded and in the end I decided to stay where I was and sit it out. As soon as he'd done so I went merrily on my way but the carnage that was then unleashed behind me has been etched into the annals of F1 history. It was all a bit hairy really.

**Johnny:** All a bit hairy? Is that honestly the best you can do?

**Damon:** Am I failing to evoke a sense of drama, Johnny? Apologies. Unsurprisingly, the race was stopped, but I decided to stay in the car. I was absolutely busting for a pee but I didn't want to break my concentration. Because of where we'd qualified – me third and Ralph eighth – there'd been a real buzz in the team prior to the race and we'd been cautiously optimistic. I'd even turned down a request from the marketing director at Jordan to visit some sponsors, which had angered Eddie, but I hadn't wanted anything to get in the way of our preparations.

After taking our original positions on the grid, the race was restarted and I got off to an absolute flyer, he said modestly. After the race restarted, Mika Häkkinen ran Michael Schumacher wide and then spun backwards into the path of one of the Saubers. But which one? Was it the Sauber being driven by the diminutive French driver or the Sauber being driven by the diminutive English driver? That's right, it was the one being driven by the diminutive English driver. The pride of Essex, no less. As my old F3 team manager used to say at moments like that, 'You can't beat bad luck!' Nice, eh?

On lap seven my old foe, Mr M Schumacher, passed me to take the lead and despite the conditions, which were still appalling, only a fool would have bet against him clinching the win. Shortly after the halfway point, DC, who was towards the back of the diminished field, started running into trouble and he began to slow down. Sticking to the racing line in order to minimize the effects of the spray, he was on his way into the pits when Michael, whose sight was obviously impaired and who probably thought he was running into the slipstream of a fast car, ran straight into the back of him. Because Spa is so fast and protected by trees the spray is worse than any other track. You simply have no idea how close you are to another car, or at what speed they're travelling. In addition to losing his right front wheel Michael also lost his head, and after alighting from his three-wheeled Ferrari in the pits he made his way rather briskly to the McLaren garage where, after locating DC, he was almost certainly intending to shake him warmly by the throat. Luckily for everyone concerned, but especially for Michael, I think, a rather burly McLaren engineer intervened and sent him on his way. While Michael no doubt sat remonstrating with Jean Todt about what bad luck he'd had and how big a cannon the FIA should fire DC from, DC went back out and ended up finishing seventh, just one place off the points.

As Murray and Brundle were having fits about the handbags in the pits, the remaining nine or ten drivers continued aquaplaning merrily around Spa. I was in first, my teammate Ralph Schumacher was lying second and Johnny's teammate, the diminutive Frenchman who shall not be named, was lying third. Sorry, Johnny. You missed all the fun in that one. The next driver to go off was Eddie Irvine, and then Giancarlo Fisichella, in an incident reminiscent of the DC–Schumacher shunt, ran straight into the back of Shinya Nakano's Minardi. This brought out the safety car, which in turn, after I dived in for a set of wet tyres, brought Ralph Schumacher within touching distance of the gallant race leader. My evidence is obviously being written with the benefit of hindsight but at the time the only thing on my mind was the fact that Jordan, which had never won a Grand Prix in their history, were on course for a possible one-two. In reality we'd been hoping for a podium, so this was potentially pretty damn special.

As we crawled along behind the safety car it dawned on me that the biggest threat to our potential one-two was the restart. Ralph was on a different set-up to me and had been faster as he tried to make up lost ground. I was concerned that if we had to race each other it could all go very wrong. He was obviously pumped up for the win, like I had been in Monza in 1993. Normally there would be a discussion about what we needed to do next, and I waited for some instruction to this effect, but there was silence. Having spent several years dutifully coming second to the team leader at Williams, I thought, *OK, now it's my turn to say what I think should happen.* I said, and these were my exact words: 'I'm going to put something to you here, and I think you'd better listen to this. If we race, if we two race, we could end up with nothing, so it's up to you Eddie. If we don't race each other, we've got an opportunity to get a first and second, it's your choice.'

Some people have construed this move as gamesmanship, but to me it made perfect sense. As the senior driver I was merely taking responsibility for the entire team's race weekend result. We were sitting on an almost guaranteed one-two, but if Ralph was going to race me, I would have to race him and we could both end up in the gravel. As renowned and significant as this race undoubtedly is, it would be even more so had Ralph and I flung it away at such a late stage. Brundle, who must have been suffering from dehydration and eye strain by this time, concurred with my assessment of the situation but astutely added a key considera-tion that might have been playing on Eddie's overloaded brain by that point: Ralph was leaving the team at the end of the season and therefore had little incentive to obey team orders. Eddie also had to consider the fact that I was a main player in his key spon-sor's plans. The horns of this particular dilemma maybe had him thinking a bit longer than usual. So much to think about and so little time!

In the end, Eddie ordered Ralph to stay where he was. I believe it was done reluctantly, as nobody wants to kill a race (well, almost nobody), but it was obviously for the greater good. Just to be on the safe side, I drove the remainder of the race flat out. I wasn't convinced that Schumacher Jnr wouldn't suddenly be overcome by a wave of insubordination, and anyway, he had to press on because he had Alesi chasing him down. The relief I felt when I finally crossed the line was massive. It had been a helluva long afternoon.

The alternative ending to this scenario was played out at the 2013 Malaysian Grand Prix between Mark Webber and Sebastian Vettel. I won't repeat the back story, as it would take forever, but worried by a potential collision towards the end of the race, Christian Horner gave Vettel, who was running second behind Webber, an order in code. Because team orders had been outlawed, the phrase Christian had to use was 'Multi-21', which meant keep your positions. Maybe Mark thought he could trust his teammate at that point, but Seb decided to race, and overtook Mark to win. Like me, Mark had obviously been informed that Seb had been given his orders, but he was probably more trusting than I was, and when Seb made his move it seemed to take Mark by surprise. Afterwards, Seb was absolutely defiant about his actions and summed it up succinctly with the following words: 'I was racing, I was faster, I passed him, I won.' A lot of people sympathized with that racer's attitude. But there was an uncomfortable feeling about Seb after that, I have to say, as it suggested a pretty selfish and perhaps even deceitful side to him. I think Mark lost respect for him after that episode. It also sowed the seeds of suspicion that the team would protect Seb at his expense.

**Johnny:** Do you remember the following year, on the eve of the Malaysian Grand Prix, Sky asked us to recreate that whole controversial incident, complete with drivers, vehicles, and even the pit wall crew? You played Webber and one member of the Red Bull pit wall team, and I played Seb and the other, who was Christian Horner. The vehicles we were given were golf carts that would only go about 5 mph, so when it came to filming the actual overtaking incident it took bloody ages! Great fun, though.

By the way, did you manage to have your wee?

**Damon:** I did, thanks for asking, and then I immediately managed to jar my back.

**Johnny:** While having a wee?

**Damon:** No, this was on the podium. The jarring, that is. Not the wee. After the race Ralph and I were put into a car and taken to the podium. Ralph had a face like a bulldog chewing a wasp and I understand from Eddie that afterwards Michael stormed into his motorhome demanding to know why he hadn't let his brother win. I think Eddie was expecting Michael to congratulate him, as Schumacher the elder had obviously been with Jordan at the beginning of his career, but after his shenanigans with DC he obviously had his blood up. Eddie gave Michael short shrift, apparently, so he failed to get satisfaction. Anyway, back to my back. When I got onto the podium I thought, *Right then, I'm going to give it the full Michael Schumacher jump in the air!* Unfortunately, I was so cold and wet that when I jumped I only went about six inches from the podium and when I landed I jarred my back.

**Johnny:** You twit. Look, I get the fact that it's ultimately up to the teams whether or not they issue team orders, but unless it's for safety reasons or to prevent a disastrous cock-up, which I think covers what happened at Spa (dear Ralph might disagree, but who cares), then I think it's detrimental not only to the sport's reputation, but, as you rightly said, to the fans. But that's just my opinion.

**Damon:** Agreed. Can we move on now please?

**Johnny:** Yes, and that's an order!

**Damon:** A team order? I will defy it, Herbert!

# CHAPTER THREE

## Can F1 be green, and should it even aspire to be?

**Damon:** Think back to the oil crisis of 1973 – global oil supplies were restricted due to Middle East politics and made everyone realize how dependent we were on oil. When people saw F1 cars happily burning it up for their own amusement when there was a country-wide 50 mph speed limit in the US to save fuel, it made F1 look like it didn't give a hoot. Which was obviously bad. I'm pretty sure that was the first time – or at least one of the first times – that F1 came in for criticism for using fuel frivolously. The analogy they used then to deflect criticism was that all the cars for a whole season used less fuel than a single jumbo jet flying from London to New York. But people rightly argue now that the problem is fuelled (sorry!) by the logistics involved as opposed to the racing. While that's a valid criticism, there are certainly other forms of entertainment that are as bad, if not worse, than F1. Take the music industry, for example, of which I have a rudimentary knowledge.

**Johnny:** You mean you play the guitar a bit?

**Damon:** A bit badly, yes. So I never got to do a world tour like the Rolling Stones. When they go on tour they'll have two or three stages on the road that will leapfrog each other from venue to venue. The logistics involved in moving these stages – not to mention the lights and PA etc. – will be on a biblical scale, but do they come in for the same amount of criticism? I think not.

**Johnny:** A lot of it has to do with profile, I think. If F1 didn't get any attention, it wouldn't get any attention, if you see what I mean. It's one of its main objectives. When the first ever Formula One World Championship race took place at Silverstone in 1950, hundreds of thousands of people turned up and clogged the roads. Why? Because they wanted to be entertained. Even if the world is warming up that isn't going to change in a hurry, and despite the fact that F1 has come in for more than its fair share of criticism over the years it's done more than most to try to clean up its act. The advent of Formula E hasn't helped. In fact, it reminds me of my time at school.

**Damon:** You went to school, Johnny? I want proof!

**Johnny:** Well, briefly. Before I went out picking pockets. The point is, I had to try really hard at school as I wasn't academically gifted and just when I thought I was getting somewhere a swot would pipe up with all the answers and make me look useless. F1 is me, and Formula E is the swot. The darling of the motorsport world!

**Damon:** Mmmmm. We'll get to Formula E later. But let's not forget about all the technology F1 has created over the years. Or should I say the teams have. In 2017, Mercedes-AMG, in their quest to further the development of the apparently redundant internal combustion engine, achieved a 50 per cent thermal efficiency rating for its Formula One engine, which essentially meant it had a better power-to-waste ratio. Power to waste, I hear you cry? That's right, power to waste. The thermal efficiency of an engine is determined by the amount of energy it can extract from the fuel it runs off. Before Mercedes-AMG made their breakthrough with the 1.6 turbocharged V6, the average thermal efficiency for an internal combustion engine was between 20 and 30 per cent, so basically they've doubled it. It's hard to overestimate the significance of an achievement like that. Imagine every road car in the world running with that kind of efficiency.

**Johnny:** So why hasn't the technology filtered through to the road car industry yet? After all, road cars are Mercedes' bread and butter.

**Damon:** Good question. Don't really know. Mercedes-AMG have actually managed to transfer the technology to a road car (it's called the ONE and will be released sometime in 2021), but each unit will cost upwards of £2 million. Peanuts to Bernie, perhaps, but if I wanted one we'd have to start doing panto or something, Johnny. F1 doesn't communicate these advances to the wider world, which is where I think they're missing a trick. You can't just leave it up to the manufacturers. The fact is, if it wasn't for F1 the technology wouldn't exist, and that's a pretty powerful statement. This isn't a recent thing. F1 has always hidden its light under a bushel, yet it's responsible for producing a plethora of bona fide geniuses. Or genii, as the Romans would have said. Every sport has them – geniuses, that is – and in this particular case I'm not talking about the chief protagonists. How many sports were built, and have advanced upon, foundations created by technical pioneers? I can't think of another. The upshot has been a marriage of entertainment and innovation that has lasted, so far, for over seventy years. What makes F1 different to, for instance, a huge engineering company is the sport element. The modus operandi of a Formula One team is to get one over on their competitors, and that brings out a different kind of creativity and ingenuity.

**Johnny:** You mean they tend to take the piss a bit more?

**Damon:** I mean they tend to take liberties. Watch your language, Johnny – think of my reputation. People in F1 will always try and push the boundaries – not just of what is possible, but of what is allowed, and in an ultra-competitive environment. That, in a nutshell, is the difference between an engineer who works in F1 and an engineer who works for, BAE Systems, for instance. A famous example would be the measurement of ride heights back in the ground effect days. Ride height is the amount of clearance between the bottom of a car and the track, Johnny. OK. I know you knew that. Back in the late 1960s, when Peter Wright and Tony Rudd from British Racing Motors came up with the idea of using the underside of the car to create 'suck', or downforce, they realized that the ride height would be critical. Their idea was put on the shelf for a number of years because of lack of money but in early 1976, Peter and Tony showed their idea to Colin Chapman of Lotus and together with Martin Ogilvie they created the amazing Lotus 78, or the 'wing car', as it became known. As you know, Johnny, the panels that were fitted to the side of the Lotus 78 created a seal which produced an unprecedented amount of downforce, which gave the car more grip and thus higher cornering speeds.

**Johnny:** Which is where the term ground effect comes from.

**Damon:** Go to the top of the class.

**Johnny:** Lanky streak of . . . Anyway, I know the rest of this story; eventually the FIA put rules in place to prevent these wings from being too close to the ground, didn't they? The increase in performance was considered to be dangerous, so to all intents and purposes the fun was over. Or was it? Instead of doing as they were told, the designers at Lotus simply fitted hydraulic rams to the wings which would enable their drivers to either lower or elevate them as and when. Out on the track they would obviously lower them and get the increased performance but as soon as they were in the garage they'd flick a switch and become legal again. It was blatant but they got away with it. I think they'd found a loophole in the wording of the rules. Something about the cars having to be in a legal condition when presented for scrutineering, which they obviously were. As soon as they were out on the track, however, it was wings down and away we go! Nowadays the cars have to be open for scrutineering any time over the weekend, but that original loophole enabled Colin, Peter, Martin and Tony to create a moment in time that has become engraved in F1 history.

**Damon:** My God, it's like listening to Wordsworth! Poetry, Johnny. But the reason I mentioned the above is because I think it exemplifies the motivation to win, which is obviously what drives not just F1, but every sport on the planet. The motivation to do it ethically, however, is now the big challenge, and it's finding that balance between doing the right thing, providing entertainment and safeguarding the future of your sport or team. Incidentally, I've just realized that Johnny and I are sitting in front of a huge log fire at the moment, which obviously isn't helping the environmental cause!

**Johnny:** I think F1 has always been seen as being a little unethical, or even a bit questionable. Look at tobacco sponsorship.

Tobacco sponsorship was absolutely everywhere in the 1960s, '70s and '80s, yet despite it being a thing of the past in other sports it still has an association with F1. While that's probably down to the amount of money that was invested in F1, it merely strengthens the argument. Then there's James Hunt, of course. I think James went to bed with an unlit cigarette in his mouth ready for the new dawn.

**Damon:** Did you ever smoke, Johnny?

**Johnny:** I did, when I was in my teens. It was at a karting event and after swallowing the smoke instead of inhaling it I was sick on my friend's trainers. That was it for me. I'd also heard from someone that it could stunt your growth and that terrified me! But it's not just fags and fuel that are to blame. F1 has always been quite wasteful in terms of resources, and while the tobacco firms have largely gone and a reduction in $CO_2$ emissions has become a genuine work in progress, there are other issues that are still outstanding. Tyres being one of the main ones. At the Abu Dhabi Grand Prix in 2019 Pirelli advertised the fact that they'd be bringing 4,500 tyres for the weekend. Not a wise thing to shout about, in my opinion.

The contradiction here (Professor Hill would probably call it a paradox) is the amount of time and effort teams and drivers spend trying to make efficiencies in order to win races, which means driving an F1 racing car is actually an ecologically friendly endeavour. Don't get me wrong, the drivers and engineers aren't thinking about saving the planet while making these efficiencies. It's just the way it works. In 1989 I raced at the Circuit Gilles Villeneuve in Montreal for the first time, which we mentioned earlier demands a lot of braking. I was told by my engineer that the brakes wouldn't last the race if I didn't take really good care of them and for the first few laps that was all I could think about. After lap seven or eight I got bored with this and the concern about my brakes went out of the window! That's just me, though. Saving fuel is obviously a more relevant example, as is saving tyres. The more I think about this subject, though, the more hilarious it sounds. A sport that runs on mastering efficiencies is famously inefficient. Brilliant!

**Damon:** If we're going to talk inefficiency, surely we have to mention the Mazda 787B, which a certain Johnny Herbert drove to victory at Le Mans back in 1991. Aesthetically, it's one of the most magnificent cars ever created, although not so ecologically. Am I wrong in thinking that as well as guzzling rather a lot of fuel it used to spit flames out of the side?

**Johnny:** Nail on the head. The rotary-powered 787B was an absolute beast of a car and when I first drove it in 1990 the flames, which would spit out after coming off the throttle, were at least two metres long. By the time I won the race the following year the FISA – the old governing body – had intervened and, in an attempt to prevent us from roasting spectators, they ordered Mazdaspeed to reduce the flames to about a metre. Killjoys! All it was doing was burning off fuel and oil, but the effect was amazing. Add that to the scream of the R26B engine – not to mention the colours of the car, which were bright orange and British racing green – and you had before you one of the most popular cars ever driven at Le Mans.

While we're here I think I'll share one of my favourite Le Mans stories. It involves a broken car, a big lie and a VERY angry Frenchman who was born in Luxembourg but once identified as being Belgian.

**Damon:** Bertrand Gachot?

**Johnny:** The very same. He and I had raced against each other in Formula Three and he had a reputation of being a bit of a hot-head. In 1990, when Mazdaspeed started building the 787B with a view to competing at Le Mans, they went against convention by hiring three drivers who had next to no endurance experience. The three were Bertrand, Volker Weidler and my small but beautifully marked self. The reason they decided to hire the three of us and not some endurance drivers is because the car was a bit slower than the main contenders and so basically we were going to have to get a wiggle on. In that first year we managed to complete 148 laps before the electrics failed. The car was generating too much heat (it happened inside and outside!) and unfortunately this played havoc with them.

When we retired the car, which was in the early hours of Sunday morning, I was the one driving and after getting out and shaking everyone's hand I sat down to take stock. We knew there was a problem with the car so it was no great surprise. Anyway, as I was sitting there I suddenly remembered that Bertrand had been due to take over from me and would probably still be asleep in the team caravan. Sure enough, our French-Belgian Luxembourger was still fast asleep and so to cheer myself up a bit I decided to have some fun – at his expense. He obviously had absolutely no idea that we'd retired the car so after barging through the caravan door I grabbed Bertrand by the overalls and shouted, 'BERTRAM, YOU'RE LATE! YOU'RE SUPPOSED TO BE IN THE BLOODY CAR. GET UP YOU TIT. THE TEAM ARE GOING CRACKERS!'

Have you ever seen a French-Belgian Luxembourger poo his pants? It's quite something. To be fair, Bertrand was up and at 'em like a Jack Russell in a room full of rats, and when he finally got his bearings he started shouting like an excited child. 'Oh my God, Johnny!' he screamed. 'Why didn't anybody call me sooner? Quick, throw me my boots!' he shouted in a very heavy French accent.

**Damon:** You're digressing, Johnny.

**Johnny:** I never did throw Bertrand his boots. Why? Because I was on the caravan floor wetting myself.

'Why are you laughing, Johnny?' he cried suspiciously. 'What is uuuurp wiz yoo?' Then Bertrand realized what was uuuurp and went absolutely, get-the-elephant-tranquillizer-gun mental!

'You English sink you 'av zis amazing sense of 'umour, but really, Johnny, you are a dick!'

And then he went for me.

'You can't hit me,' I protested. 'I'm disabled!'

He did see the funny side, eventually, and by the time we won Le Mans the following year he was almost back to normal. He's quite a character, is our Bertrand. Off his box, of course. Just like most French-Belgian Luxembourger racing drivers.

Incidentally, I was that exhausted after winning Le Mans (I was the last man in and ended up driving an extra session) that I failed to make it to the presentation ceremony. Story of my bloody life!

**Damon:** Stop whining man! However, it's yet another example of trying to balance entertainment value with ecological responsibility. I don't miss what the 787B was potentially doing to the planet, but what I do miss is not seeing and hearing it, and its like, on a racetrack anymore. That's the price of having a greener footprint, I'm afraid. One of the main complaints from F1 fans at the moment is the reduction in noise, but the reason there's no noise is because the cars are more efficient. The FIA did relent slightly in order to try and appease the fans but the engineers argued that the energy used to create that extra noise could be better used elsewhere. You see what an enormous quandary this is?

Talking of noise, or lack thereof, I was invited to a Formula E race in Paris in 2018 and the shortage of noise got me into rather a lot of bother. I was making my way to my seat, which was in a grandstand by the first corner, trying not to step on everyone's feet and thinking I had timed it to perfection when suddenly the bloody cars flew past!

*Neeeeeeeeeeeeeeeeeeeeeeeeeeeeeeeeeeeeeeeeeeeeeee!* (That's roughly the noise they make.)

All you can hear is tyres squealing. You can't hear them coming and there is nothing to tell you the race has started. So the poor people who had got there in ample time and had been waiting patiently for the most exciting moment were not amused to have a big bloke blocking their view, even if he was a World Champion. A bit embarrassing.

What is the collective noun for Formula E cars? It must be a 'neee'. The first thing I heard was a neee of Formula E cars whizzing around the first corner at what must have been, ooh, at least 60 mph. Maybe more! I have to say it's one of the more surprising forms of motorsport I've witnessed. Silent racing! Oh, for Mr Herbert in his flame-throwing Mazda!

In all seriousness, I do believe Formula E works as a form of entertainment and has a place in the future of motorsport. There's a little bit of argy-bargy here and there and even the odd shunt, so if you can stomach the noise, which almost doesn't exist in the first place, you have the makings of a decent afternoon. And the youth seem to have taken to it. My son, who still qualifies as a youth, will often say to me, 'Dad, did you see the Formula E race earlier?' 'Afraid not Josh,' I usually reply. 'I was washing my beard.'

The organizers of Formula E are obviously conversant of the fact that, as time goes on, *neeeeeeeee* will become the norm. It certainly won't be everyone's cup of tea, but as concern about the environment grows its offering will undoubtedly become more and more attractive. In twenty years' time young motorsport fans will sit patiently at the feet of the likes of Johnny and me, and as we wax poetic about the joys of hearing a V8 engine for the first time they'll say to themselves, 'Isn't it time for their medication?'

Do you miss the sound of a V8, Johnny?

**Johnny:** Yes, of course I do. Apparently, if they ever sort out the hydrogen issue, the sound will come back. It'll be different, but it'll be big.

**Damon:** That's because hydrogen burns with a loud bang. And how do I know hydrogen burns with a loud bang? Because I once blew up my chemistry lab at school. We were taught that the test for hydrogen is that it burns with a pop. But after testing it I can confirm conclusively that it is definitely a loud bang. Either way, if the engines in F1 start popping or banging there'll be a lot of happy people in the grandstands.

**Johnny:** And in the cars, I think. To me that's all part of the buzz. One of the biggest buzzes I get during the F1 season is when an F18 jet fighter flies over the track during the third day of the Australian Grand Prix. It happens every single year and every single year Mr Hill, for want of a better term, craps himself! It invariably happens just as Simon Lazenby turns to Damon and asks him for an opinion about something. You can hear the thing coming about ten minutes beforehand but because we've got earpieces in and are trying to concentrate we only get the main event. Every year it gets the old boy. He's fragile and a bit nervous, you see. Like an old dog.

The fact is, though, apart from F18 fighter jets, a lot of humans just love noise. Take fireworks, for instance. Sure, they look nice, but can you imagine silent fireworks, or fireworks that go *neeeeeeeeeeee*? No, of course you can't. It's unthinkable. Fireworks are only enjoyable when they make a noise.

I've been to a MotoGP race and the noise the bikes made at the start of the race was just incredible. It really surprised me. It created a kind of sonic wow factor which is now missing in F1. I know we take the Mickey out of Formula E but the only reason we do that is because we've experienced the sound of twenty V8 engines roaring on a starting grid. That's where the wow originates from. It's now a thing of the past, more's the pity, and the sound of F1 no longer moves its public like it used to.

It makes me think of the first ever British Grand Prix I attended, at Brands Hatch in 1976. Although I'd had some success in karting I was hoping to become a metalworker when I left school. Well, not hoping, exactly. Metalwork was the only thing I was really interested in at school and I hadn't even considered racing as an option. The details of the race itself are long forgotten, save for the fact that the winner, James Hunt, was later disqualified after an appeal by Ferrari. I can still picture him signing autographs with a fag in his mouth, a pen in one hand and a glass of champagne in the other. He was also flanked by a couple of stunners, of course! I'm surprised witnessing that didn't make me want to become a racing driver. I think I was just a bit too young to appreciate it. Anyway, the part of the day I remember most is the ten seconds prior to the start of the race. That will stay with me for the rest of my life. I couldn't see a great deal as I was about three foot five, but the noise the cars made seemed to engulf the entire track and everyone around it. It was terrifying. Genuinely terrifying! It was that noise that made me decide to become a racing driver. I was just twelve years old at the time but from that moment on it was all I thought about. At the British Grand Prix at Silverstone in 2019, Jenson Button took his 2009 Brawn out for a spin and the noise it made took me right back to that day at Brands. It was a real déjà vu moment.

**Damon:** It can go too far, though. Those very high revving V8s made more noise than power. At Silverstone for the 2009 British Grand Prix, I'd just become President of the British Racing Drivers' Club (BRDC), and we were standing to attention on the hospitality suite balcony next to the FIA and the RAC's suits, all of us Presidents dutifully paying attention, and you could hear this terrifying noise before the cars came into view during the warm-up lap. *WAAAAW WAAAAAAAW WAAAAAAAAAAAAAW*, it went. Not *Neeeee, Neeee, Neeee. WAAAAW WAAAAAAAW WAAAAAAAAAAAAAW.* It literally sent a shiver down your spine. But when the cars eventually appeared they were pootling along like Fiat 500s. It was quite a disappointment really. Not so much a wow factor. More a, Oh, really?

So what's the most amazing noise you've ever heard from one car, Johnny? I think I have two. The first came from Ayrton's legendary MP4/4 which he won the World Championship with in 1988. At Interlagos in 2019 Bruno Senna took it out for a very emotional spin and the moment I heard that deep rasping growl I was in raptures. It also carries a great deal of emotion for me, as does choice number two. This one's a little bit more obvious.

**Johnny:** Was it made by Williams-Renault, by any chance? Circa 1996?

**Damon:** It was indeed. My FW18. The last time I drove it was in 2019 at Silverstone and I couldn't wait to hear that Renault V10 engine again. You obviously get a very different perspective in the cockpit than you do from a grandstand. It's like being sung to. I could listen to it all day long.

**Johnny:** If you're going to have two, so am I! The first one is my one abiding memory from the 1983 Formula Ford Festival at Brands Hatch, and believe it or not it brought a tear or two to my eyes. It was my competitive debut in single seaters and during one of the support races I heard a Ferrari V12 going down the back straight into Westfield. It brought me to a standstill and I genuinely did start to well up. A bit.

I'd like to follow this up by telling you that I triumphed at the 1983 Formula Ford Festival, but sadly I can't. I even made a bit of an arse of myself during the quarter final. I became . . . petulant.

**Damon:** Well, we have to think of our readers, Johnny. Pray tell.

**Johnny:** I have a feeling you're going to enjoy this.

Unfortunately I'd been a bit of an also ran at the festival and by the quarter final stage my best result had been fourth in one of the heats. Because I'd been used to winning in karts I didn't like this and at the start of the quarter final I could feel myself starting to become angry. You could count the amount of times I lost it as a racing driver on the fingers of one hand and the result of this particular 'wobbler' was fortunately a one-off. I got so worked up that when I got to Clearways about halfway through the race I deliberately drove off. 'Sod this,' I remember saying. 'I'm out!' What makes it even more ludicrous – if that were possible – is that I was actually running tenth at the time and could easily have made the semis and even the bloody final!

Throwing your toys out of the pram is one thing, but trying to break them is quite another.

**Damon:** You're nothing more than an automotive masochist. A compact kamikaze.

**Johnny:** I've been called worse. My second choice would have to be the Wankel rotary engine inside the Mazda 787B. There are obviously emotions attached to this one too but the scream that engine makes is ear-piercing. Get a couple of flames running alongside and you have the ultimate racing car.

**Damon:** I don't want to speak on your behalf Johnny (although I'm going to) but I think we agree that the sport we fell in love with all those years ago was made up of three elements – speed, noise and obviously a bit of racing. The idea of F1 being expected to fix things for society is going a step too far and the idea of its green credentials going hand in hand with the aforementioned three elements is just wishful thinking. We should obviously do our bit – and we do. But it's not just F1's problem. It's everyone's problem. If F1 contributes anything to society, it's that it shows what is possible. Like the way Lewis has galvanized other drivers to support the fight against racism so effectively. This would have been inconceivable only a few years back.

**Johnny:** And look at crash structures. Engineers within F1 have worked a lot on how to absorb the energy from a crash, and that research can be repurposed.

**Damon:** Very true, Johnny. In 2014, the heart surgeon Professor Martin Elliott delivered a fifty-minute lecture at Gresham College London on Formula One and its contributions to healthcare, all while wearing flame-retardant racing overalls. He said in his introduction, 'At first sight, there is little relationship between the high tech, high cost, high speed and highly competitive world of F1 and heart surgery for children. Yet Formula One, with its extraordinary teamwork, rates of innovation, commitment to excellence and relentless pursuit of safety has taught us a great deal.' If you ever get a spare fifty minutes and are interested in this subject then please have a watch. It's absolutely fascinating. I obviously won't go into detail here but in a nutshell the professor made a link between a present-day F1 pit stop and transferring an ill newborn baby from a maternity unit to a hospital such as Great Ormond Street. At first glance that sounds quite ridiculous, but the process is essentially similar. In human terms they each require quick-thinking, skill, leadership and synchronicity.

Professor Elliott and his team had spotted this link, and approached F1 teams about it; the likes of Ross Brawn, Dave Ryan at McLaren and Alistair Watkins, who is the son of Sid Watkins – Professor Sid was F1's medical chief for years. F1 basically wanted to help if it could. And it could! Over a period of months, they and their teams assisted Professor Elliott and his team in identifying where lessons might be learnt from F1. The late Nigel Stepney, who was then at Ferrari, went to Great Ormond Street Hospital to observe such a procedure and when reporting back to Professor Elliott he was pretty caustic in his assessment. 'I was amazed at how clumsy and informal the handover was,' he said. 'I couldn't work out who was in charge.' Professor Elliott described Nigel's assessment as damning, but it acted as a catalyst for some pretty strident improvements.

When we read about the lecture and its backstory we both felt incredibly proud, and the attitude of everyone involved in F1 was, in our experience, typical of the sport. F1 should always do what-ever it can to support society and it should definitely make more noise about its achievements. If that happens, perhaps more opportunities will be identified, like has happened with this nasty virus. All the F1 teams rolled up their sleeves to see where they could help, with their ability to rapidly prototype and produce parts for ventilators, for example.

With regards to the whole environmental issue, we like the fact that F1 is becoming greener and while we continue to mourn the passing of the V10s and V8s we appreciate the importance of it happening and the magnitude of what might happen if it doesn't. Then there are the wider issues, of course, such as the transport of equipment and what happens when a hundred thousand people turn up to a race weekend. In November 2019, Formula One set out its plans to have a net-zero carbon footprint by 2030, and in January 2020 they signed the United Nations' Sport for Climate Action Framework. That's obviously admirable, but at the end of the day F1 fans want one thing – entertainment. Formula E may well be the bee's *neeeeeeeeeeeeeeeeeeees* to some folk, but we F1 fans like our *WAAAAAAAAAAAWS*, however quiet they may be.

# CHAPTER FOUR

## Lewis

**Johnny:** How could we possibly write a light-hearted book about F1 and not include a chapter on the laughter machine that is Lewis Hamilton.

**Damon:** I was about to say that being facetious doesn't suit you, Johnny, but it does! It's a part you were born to play.

**Johnny:** I'm only joking. As you know I'm a huge fan of Lewis's. In fact, in November 2019 I wrote a piece for the *Guardian* in which I, Johnny Herbert, proclaimed him, Lewis Hamilton, as the best there's ever been.

**Damon:** What I think is most impressive about that statement is that you wrote a piece for the *Guardian*. A wonder which will never cease to amaze me.

**Johnny:** I had help. Anyway, the reason Lewis Hamilton is the greatest F1 driver I've ever seen is that whatever situation he's in, he's always able to impress me.

**Damon:** So the definition of greatness is whether or not you can impress Johnny Herbert? The Johnny Herbert Test.

**Johnny:** In Johnny Herbert's head, yes! It used to be Ayrton, but I've been watching Lewis for such a long time now and he seems to get better and better. 'Who's the best F1 driver ever' is one of those conversations that could go on forever, and I think you can only do it by era. For instance, I know that Juan Manuel Fangio and Jimmy Clark are considered to be two of the best F1 drivers there's ever been, but because I never saw them drive in the flesh and have only seen clips of them on YouTube and on DVDs I can't really comment. Not in any detail. I'm relying on reputation. If I ever had to provide an argument as to why I think Lewis is the best there's ever been, however futile that may be, it would be down to the amount of pressure he's under compared to drivers of yesteryear. For example, in 1955 the Formula One season, which was won by Fangio, consisted of seven Grands Prix and in 1966, which was Jimmy Clark's second and final championship win, it consisted of ten. In the 2019 season, which was won by Lewis, there were twenty-one Grands Prix, so more than those two historical seasons put together. The first took place on 17 March in Australia and the last on 1 December in Abu Dhabi, and Lewis won eleven out of the twenty-one. To be able to perform to that standard, not just week after week but year after year, is just mind-boggling.

**Damon:** I have to ask. What about Michael?

**Johnny:** He may have won more championships but Michael's win to race ratio is found wanting compared to Lewis's. Out of 308 starts Michael Schumacher won ninety-one Grands Prix whereas at the end of 2019 Lewis had made 250 starts and had won eighty-four Grands Prix. I'm no statistician, but even I know which figures are more impressive. My next comment is probably quite predictable, but something else Lewis has over Michael is that he's always been happy racing alongside a competitive teammate.

**Damon:** I'm going to agree with you. One definition you can use for a great driver is whether or not they define an era and he most certainly does. This is the Hamilton era and he's been dominant. Ever since his first Grand Prix back in March 2007 he's been a contender and in my opinion he should have won the 2007 season. Going back to what you said about pressure, Johnny, with the advent of the internet and social media, Lewis has had to contend with an almost forensic interest in his life. Yes, he obviously courts the attention to a certain extent, as do most of them, but the amount of words that have been written about Lewis over the years would probably fill a thousand books. Apart from the odd faux pas, which we're all entitled to, I think he's handled himself splendidly since coming to prominence. Most importantly, though, that attention, which I freely admit would have bothered me big time had it been there when we were driving, has never really affected his ability to drive and win races. Or should I say, he's never allowed it to. That's impressive stuff.

**Johnny:** Now it's my turn to agree with you. If you go back to the 1960s, '70s, '80s and even the 1990s, you very rarely heard anybody criticizing you and if you wanted attention you had to go out looking for it. These days, partly because of social media, you get criticized all the time.

**Damon:** There's an expression about blowing smoke up skirts, which I think means constantly praising someone, but it's tricky not to with Hamilton! But we get paid to be at least a bit critical. Herbert and Hill, a couple of trolls. Who'd have guessed?

I don't quite agree with you, though, with regards to being criticized, Johnny, as in the 1990s I suffered quite badly from it. I'll come to that in a minute. I do know what you mean, though. It's all a matter of degree, and being criticized in the 1990s was a very different experience to being criticized today. It's like comparing a conker fight to a nuclear war!

You're certainly right about the 1960s. In Dad's era he'd have had to do something pretty outrageous to get a fraction of the attention Lewis gets. And believe me, he tried! He'd have had to dance on a table with his trousers around his ankles or something. Oh, he did! Anyway, the exception proves the rule. Front-page story but in a fun way. Supportive even. 'What a jolly good bloke!' kind of thing. Imagine that today. Today it's different. Smartphones give everyone the opportunity to record events and give their own spin. Whereas the editors of the past might have gone, 'Oh, I've met Graham Hill. He's a good chap. Go easy, boys,' today papers have to compete against almost infinite competition that has no mediation or moderation. If my dad came out of a restaurant a bit worse for wear and was accosted by a reporter and a photographer, the following day's headline would be something like, 'Hero Hill enjoys night out with wife and chums'. If Kimi Räikkönen did the same it'd be, 'Rampant Räikkönen worse for wear – AGAIN!' Or words to that effect. I think we're slowly starting to realize that whatever you say or do, whether it be winning a World Championship, falling out of a nightclub at 2 a.m. with a girl on each arm or talking to people about clearing up plastic bottles on a beach, which is something Lewis did a couple of years back and got slated for it, there's always going to be somebody who is determined to try and call you out or criticize you. It's inevitable. If you can learn to just ignore that stuff and treat it as white noise then you'll be fine. You've got the opportunity with social media to say what you want to say and then leave it. You don't have to get involved with tit-for-tat arguments that ultimately serve no purpose.

**Johnny:** I'm afraid I got put off social media by people like that. Not because I used to engage in silly arguments, but because I got fed up with posting information and opinions and then receiving abuse for it. It's a shame for the people who are interested, but the people who shout loudest tend to be the ones with the sharpest tongues. In the end I gave up. Anyway, that's just me. I think Lewis has definitely become more engaging over the past few years. Not just with the public but with diminutive TV pundits. He's more relaxed these days. I'll tell you who I'd use as a comparison – Andy Murray. When he first came to prominence everybody thought he was a miserable git. He wasn't of course – he just sounded a bit dour – but the press and public had made their decision and that was that. Then he goes and wins Wimbledon and cries in public a few times and wadaya know, Andy Murray's not a grumpy sod after all, he's a sensitive soul who's been misunderstood. I think Lewis's change has been more organic, in that there hasn't been one single event that made the public like him.

**Damon:** Perhaps he's just matured a bit? He's still only thirty-five years old, remember, and it feels like he's been around forever. I think Lewis is basically just a nice guy who wants people to like him. Not because he's an egomaniac, but because if you are public property it's nicer than being hated. I could be wrong, but I think social media has helped Lewis in that respect. Together with his burgeoning maturity, of course. As you say, he's definitely relaxed a bit and people have warmed to him. But he's also shown he's not afraid to put all that on the line by supporting the Black Lives Matter protest. I think this is the even more mature Lewis who is happy to trade being universally liked for principles he is passionate about if needs be.

The criticism I mentioned earlier was a consequence of me

being humiliated by the brilliance of Michael Schumacher. You see, I can say it now. But only after years and years of therapy! At the end of the 1995 season he was celebrating his second Drivers' Championship whereas I was licking my wounds having yet again received the wooden spoon. The infuriating but mercurial German had got one over on me for the second year in a row and subsequently I'd been slaughtered by the press. This I found baffling and quite frightening, and by the end of 1995 I was in a pretty bad way. Also, my relationship with Frank Williams and Patrick Head was on the wane and I was at my wits' end.

The catalyst for me seeking help was, rather ironically, a piece the BBC had made – about Michael Schumacher. In that piece was an American lady called Mary Spillane, who apparently advised politicians and sportspeople on how to conduct themselves in interviews and how best to behave in the public domain. When she was asked what Michael had that Damon Hill did not, she began to list my faults. This, as you can imagine, was quite a sobering watch for me. According to Mary these faults included looking haunted and holding my head down and looking at the ground instead of looking at the world. Funnily enough, my mum used to say exactly the same thing. More to the point, her comments sounded very similar to the ones Patrick had been making at the time. In short, I was far too withdrawn and did not exude the confidence Michael did.

**Johnny:** You could have powered an entire continent with the confidence of Michael Schumacher. Everybody used to look quite downbeat in those days. Even the likes of Ayrton. Not Michael, though. Confidence was part of his arsenal, not just on the track, but off it.

**Damon:** And don't I know it. Mentally I was in no position to go into battle with anybody in that respect, least of all an uber-confident German who already had the upper hand on me. I was taking the world onto my shoulders and I suffered as a consequence. The only good thing about Mary's inventory of inadequacies was that there was plenty of room for improvement, and after watching the piece I decided to give her a call. My family and I were living in Ireland at the time and she came out to see me. On her first day I was pouring my heart out to her, when she suddenly put her hand up and said, 'Stop! Save it for the book.' With that one comment she sorted me out. It was amazing. It was as if somebody had just hit me over the head and brought me to my senses. After that she gave me some golden rules, which were roughly: focus on your job; always look for the positives in whatever happens; don't get distracted by what the press are writing but, if there are any inaccuracies, correct them immediately; always come across upbeat whenever appropriate; don't invite the world to pile in on top of you and don't say more than you need to.

**Johnny:** What went wrong?

**Damon:** Typical! I come clean with you and all you can do is slap me in the face. Call yourself a friend? Don't answer that. Actually, Johnny, that was the best piece of advice I have ever been given. Seriously, it changed my life. I was able to approach the 1996 season in a completely different manner, and as opposed to fixating on any rivalry between me and Michael, or between me and my new teammate Jacques Villeneuve, I was able to allow myself the space in which to maximize my opportunities.

**Johnny:** It sounds like an epiphany. Why didn't you pass all that on to me, by the way, instead of just letting me go to pot? I could have done with some words of wisdom.

**Damon:** Something else Mary advised was to not take responsibility for other people, so I'm afraid that would have been out of the question. Anyway, what about the future of Lewis Hamilton. Where do you think he'll be in five years' time?

**Johnny:** We've been through this, haven't we? A lot of people reckon that Lewis doesn't care about stats. My foot he doesn't! He'll want to beat Michael's championship record *and* Michael's race win record. What's more, he'll know exactly where he is at the moment and exactly what he has to do in order to beat it. I could be wrong, of course, but I think that's his main motivation these days. To be the best ever. It probably always has been, the same as it has been for every other driver. The difference being that at the beginning of Lewis's career, and all the way through most drivers', it was just a pipe dream. Now, for him, it's close. Desperately close. The engineers aren't the only ones striving for perfection.

**Damon:** Of course, at time of writing this COVID thing has put a bit of a spanner in his assault on the summit. He'll have to keep his powder dry for a few more months. Maybe a year? What if he loses that motivation? Stranger things have happened.

**Johnny:** If that happens, the world will be his oyster. He's got squillions of pounds in the bank, squillions of followers on social media and a loving family. He's already got a clothes label, and I'm pretty sure he's into music. I've never heard him sing, though. If all else fails he should open up a butchers and call it Ham's Hams.

**Damon:** That'll help him stick to a plant-based diet, won't it, Johnny? In fact, I think you should suggest it to him the next time you do a piece together for Sky Sports F1. You mentioned the clothes label. How many sports people, apart from Fred Perry, have started a clothes label either before or after they've retired that has stood the test of time?

**Johnny:** What you've just said is actually an allegory for the difference between F1 stars these days and F1 stars when we were around and before. When you say that Fred Perry is the only sportsperson who has started a successful clothes label, you're probably right – in the UK. If you cared to venture overseas – he says, frantically googling sportspeople who have started successful clothes labels – you'd find that Michael Jordan, Cristiano Ronaldo, LeBron James and Serena Williams, to name but a few, all have successful clothing labels that have been established for a number of years. They're the people I think Lewis wants to align himself with, which obviously makes perfect sense. By the way, Jack Nicklaus also does a nice line in apparel, so there's hope for us yet. Anyway, the point I was trying to make is that Lewis Hamilton is an international sports star – he's a global brand. F1 has never had that before.

One thing I don't see Lewis doing is staying in F1 after he stops driving. I could be wrong, of course, but I'd be very surprised. If he did, I personally think that would be great for the sport as his popularity transcends F1. How many of his 14 million Instagram followers or his 4 million Facebook followers are F1 fans? Quite a few will be, I should imagine, but a lot won't be. As long as he's associated with the sport he'll obviously be flying the flag.

**Damon:** I don't think Lewis enjoys the paddock enough to want to stay in F1 beyond his driving years. But returning to the present day for a moment, let's talk about Lewis trying to beat Michael's record. I certainly think it's possible, but it's going to get harder and harder as time goes on. Not just because he's getting older, but because Ferrari and Red Bull are getting stronger. Before

COVID I would have said he *had* to win the 2020 Championship to stand any chance of securing eight championships. But now it's all up in the air. Maybe the deferring of the 2021 regulations to 2022 has increased his chances, though? If the new regulations make Mercedes less competitive, then his run will probably be at an end. Not forgetting that, at time of writing, he has yet to sort out his contract. And he won't go to Ferrari. Not in my opinion. He'll bow out as a six-time World Champion and then open a chain of vegan sausage roll shops.

The great Murray Walker once said, 'I don't make mistakes. I make prophecies which immediately turn out to be wrong.' Well, I do actually have form when it comes to failing to appreciate the motivation of F1 drivers, so don't take any notice of anything I say. The most relevant example is when I said that there was no way Michael Schumacher would ever *try* and win seven World Championships, let alone achieve it. I was basing everything on my own feelings and experiences, and I just couldn't see how anybody would want to do that.

**Johnny:** Lewis is definitely that way inclined. He'll want to leave a legacy and if his legacy is one World Championship behind Michael Schumacher he won't be happy.

**Damon:** I think you might be right there, especially as he's so close to achieving his goal. Who was the second person to run a mile in under four minutes? Mr Herbert is now looking at me blankly, ladies and gentlemen. Exactly, Johnny, nobody remembers. What's more, nobody cares. That was Gary Player's famous quote; 'The only people who remember when you come second are your wife and your dog!' I'm obviously not saying Lewis is that person, because he's not in so many ways, but if he retired now he would be forever known as the driver who was *almost* as dominant and successful as Michael Schumacher. That won't satisfy Lewis. He wants to be the GOAT. He did the old 'I don't care about stats' thing at the 2019 Sports Personality of the Year Awards. The host asked him via video link if he could beat Michael's record and he said he wasn't interested. Yeah, right!

Do you know what I think? I think Lewis has got a colour-coordinated chart in his bedroom and every time he gets home from a Grand Prix he updates it. I can see him now. After alighting from the bus he'll run to his house, burst through the front door, make himself some beans on toast, race up to his room, lock the door and then get out his box of chart stickers.

'Pole position? Yes. That's a green sticker.'

'First to the first corner? Yes. That's a blue one.'

'Nice quick pit stop? Yes. That's a yellow one.'

'Race win? Yes. Ooh, that's a gold sticker. A gold sticker with a number one in the middle!'

There's a row at the very bottom of the chart that Lewis only updates once a year, and only if he's won the World Championship. These stickers are kept in a matchbox under his pillow and have a cup in the middle of them. These are special stickers. You know what I'm referring to, don't you, Johnny? That's right. There are currently six stickers on the chart, and two empty spaces.

The chart is framed, by the way, and it takes pride of place above Lewis's bed. Once he's filled in the chart Lewis finishes his beans on toast, gets into his Power Rangers pyjamas, jumps into bed and then pulls his Johnny Herbert duvet over his head before dreaming about beating Michael's record.

**Johnny:** There you go, readers. An insight into the rather strange private world of Lewis Hamilton.

# CHAPTER FIVE

## Is it harder for people from poorer backgrounds to make it in F1?

**Johnny:** Another contentious one. Neither of us had a pot to piddle in when we stepped onto the first rung of the F1 ladder. A lot of people assume that because of who Champ's dad was he must have glided into the sport on a silver spoon, but nothing could be further from the truth. Don't get me wrong, we were lucky in that we had some support and I'm sure that Champ had some good connections, but even taking into account things like inflation the difference between motorsport then and motorsport now with regards to cost is astronomical. That's not to say that people who don't have rich parents or bene-factors don't break into the sport. They do. It's becoming ever harder, though, and as the technology progresses – not just in F1 but in karting and every other formula – financial consider-ations become more and more prevalent. When I started kart-ing, my dad used to take tyres out of the bins at race meetings and turn them 180 degrees so the inside was facing out. It used to stave off having to buy some new ones.

**Damon:** *reaches for his violin* You had to suck on a damp cloth too, didn't you, Johnny, and eat a handful of hot coal? Charles Dickens would be reaching for his pen listening to this. I love it. I understand that it's much harder for people without money to get into motorsport – today more than ever, and I take my hat off to you and your dad, Johnny, for persisting against impossible odds. It's very like the Hamilton family story, but what it shows to me is that if you're motivated enough and you really want to do it you'll find a way. It's certainly a problem when you get to the door of F1 and there's a seat going. Then, if you haven't got money, you'll almost certainly be passed over in favour of somebody who has. Don't forget that Ayrton Senna brought money with him, as did Niki Lauda. Alain Prost had Renault to give him a leg up, but had they not been there things could have been very different. But if you're rich dad doesn't want to help, all hope is not lost! Richard Williams, former chief sportswriter for the *Guardian*, has recently published a book about the racing driver Richard Seaman. Seaman's credited as being one of the greatest pre-war racing drivers and despite having very wealthy parents his dad wouldn't have anything to do with him racing. So he got his mum to pay for it in secret! Sad ending, though. He crashed at Spa during the 1939 Belgian Grand Prix and died from his injuries. He was only twenty-six. But you see what I mean about being motivated enough? Richard Seaman may have been financially privileged, but he still had obstacles. He absolutely would not give up on his dream, even if it meant conniving with his mother to deceive his dad. It's an incredible story. You can't trust racing drivers!

**Johnny:** But your family had money, didn't they? You went to a posh school and all that?

**Damon:** I did. Until Dad died. Then the money ran out, and I had to make it on my own just like he did. *He* didn't have a pot to piss in. Grafted his way up as a mechanic for Colin Chapman in return for drives. He was famous for making a pint of beer last all night at the Steering Wheel Club in Mayfair, which was low rent in the '50s! So I was not loaded, JH. The only money I had was what I earned as a despatch rider and a labourer.

**Johnny:** Another difference between our day (and before) and the present day – you've already touched on this with the Richard Seaman story – is that for generations of racers the parents generally didn't want their children to go into motorsport, so they'd often end up defying their parents' wishes and going behind their backs. Today it's completely different. In fact, there are parents queuing up these days to take their kids karting. You never had that in the '60s, '70s or '80s. My parents were the exception as opposed to the rule – they engaged with my ambition to become a professional racing driver. Things were definitely starting to change by then – as in more and more parents were getting involved – but it was still frowned upon by the majority. And why wouldn't it be? After all, drivers were still being injured or killed on a regular basis in F1. What self-respecting parent was going to bankrupt themselves in order to put their child in a position where they could easily get killed? Put like that, you wonder how F1 survived in those days, but there was never any shortage of drivers. Those who weren't supported by the parents just took a different route. Look at Nelson Piquet, who I suppose comes from the generation before you and me. He had to race under his mother's maiden name so his father wouldn't find out he was racing. It's all about motivation. As you rightly said, if you want to do it, you'll find a way.

**Damon:** You remember my mother, Johnny? She could be a bit intimidating if she thought her boy was not getting the right treatment. Maybe she should have spoken to Flavio for you? She didn't have any money so couldn't just write out the cheque. But after a conversation one day with a guy called Mike Knight, who ran the Winfield Elf School in France, whose alumni included, among others, Alain Prost, Jacques Laffite, René Arnoux, Patrick Tambay (you get the picture), she managed to get me in there for nothing.

**Johnny:** Hang on. You weren't even interested in cars.

**Damon:** I know! Mum just said to me one day, 'Damon, I've managed to get you a place at the Winfield Elf School in France.' To which I replied, 'I'm afraid I'm not interested in cars.' I was racing bikes at the time and was paying for it all myself. It was great fun. I wasn't about to swap two wheels for four. No way.

'It's free,' said Mum.

'OK,' I said. 'I'll do it.'

**Johnny:** I bet one of the reasons she got you in there was to get you off the bikes.

**Damon:** I think there were definitely conversations going on to that effect. Which, as a parent myself, I now understand. You can almost hear the conversation. 'What's Damon up to now, Bette? He's not still on that bike is he? You need to get him off that.' They probably didn't mean, 'and straight into a Formula One car', but that was what happened. The next thing I know I'm racing you in F3. What a way to make a living!

This might sound quite naive of me, but I remember hearing Bernie talk about how much F1 was worth one day – this was years and years ago – and he mentioned a billion pounds. *A billion pounds!* I remember saying to myself. *How much is that?* I genuinely had no idea there was even a thing called a billion pounds back then. These days there are at least three billionaire dads in F1 who have managed to get their kids into a car. I'm not saying that's a bad thing, necessarily, and I'm not saying they're not good drivers, but have they ever had that moment when they didn't know if they were going to go racing next year? Of course not. We used to experience that all the time, didn't we? It was always there. There were always people going, 'Come on, you've got kids and a mortgage. Shouldn't you be thinking about looking for a proper job?' Half your brain would go, *Good God, you're right,* and the other half would go, *Piss off and mind your own business. I am not giving this up!*

**Johnny:** Do you know how much it costs to go karting these days? This is on the European circuit. About half a million pounds a year. And that's for one kart. A bloke in China paid £800,000 a couple of years ago. Eight hundred grand! You're right, though. If you have the motivation to succeed you'll do it. Or at least give it a good go. If you just paid attention to the stats about how much it costs to go karting or to race in F2 and F3, or how many billionaire dads there are in F1, you'd be straight down the job centre. Obviously you've got to have talent. Which, together with some good connections, a bit of luck and an awful lot of tenacity, is what got you and me into F1. You also have to have desire, of course, and that's ultimately what carries you through. Everything else comes and goes throughout the journey. The only thing that's there from start to finish is a desire to race in F1. I was very lucky. The races I won at the start of my career seemed to attract the people I needed who helped me get to the next steps. People like Eddie and Peter Collins. Had it not been for them I would never have made it.

Charles Leclerc and Esteban Ocon have had similar journeys, I think. Because he's a Monégasque people assume Leclerc is wealthy but his parents didn't move there as tax exiles. That's where he was born. And then there's Lewis, of course. His dad, Anthony, worked every hour God sent to keep Lewis in a kart, and one might say it has paid dividends! The point being they were all from working-class families, and are some of the best drivers in F1 – and Hamilton is one of the best there has ever been. The fact they didn't need a silver spoon is a good thing.

**Damon:** But surely that's what gives you the edge? If you've had to fight tooth and nail to keep racing year after year and you finally make it to the top, you're not going to let the other blokes get past, are you? One thing I'm conscious of not doing is starting a rich versus poor argument. How futile would that be? On one side you'd have Ayrton, Niki and James Hunt, and on the other you'd have Lewis, Fernando, Nigel and even Michael. His dad was a bricklayer, for heaven's sake. Of course there are going to be more rich kids in F1 than poor kids. It's unavoidable. What levels the playing field a bit is that determination and competitiveness that the richer kids might not have. Emphasis on the word *might*. Here's a question for you, Johnny. If you could start again and you had a choice, would you take the potentially easier route into F1 via billionaire parents or would you take the potentially more difficult route without the billionaire parents and with a shedload of sacrifice and worry. Don't just say the difficult route for the sake of it. Think about it for a second. You and I have already taken the latter route. What might it be like not to have to worry about anything other than winning the next race?

**Johnny:** Hand on heart, I would still take exactly the same route, and that's even discounting those idyllic years karting. In the early days, before it all became serious, me and my mum and dad (and my sister, if we could persuade her) would spend every weekend travelling up and down the country attending kart meetings. We all slept in the back of the van, which was also the workshop, and we had just the best times. 90 per cent of our social life was based around those meetings. It was what we lived for. I mean no disrespect whatsoever to those who haven't had to worry about whether they'll be able to afford to race, but in my opinion it's an advantage and I'd far sooner take my chances with bugger all. Seriously. That's my final answer. Same question to you.

**Damon:** I'd take the billionaire parents. Then, after one season in karting, I'd drop out, buy an island in the South Pacific and surf, with just my trust fund for company. No, in all seriousness I'd probably get bored without having to fight for something. Definitely. Secretly, I believe there are some drivers in F1 who don't even want to be there. We can't mention any names, of course, but you can just tell. Sometimes – this is more so at karting level – you'll have drivers who are basically just playing out the dreams of their fathers. It sounds like some cod Freudian psycho-analysis, but I believe it to be true in a lot of cases.

**Johnny:** The same thing happens at kids' football matches, I think. The difference with karting is that the parents will often be shelling out ridiculous amounts of money. As well as making the pressure on the child even greater, this heightens the emotions of the parents. I don't want to go into detail, but I've heard some absolute horror stories about what happens at karting tracks.

**Damon:** What, you mean fisticuffs?

**Johnny:** I'm afraid so. And we're not talking Queensbury Rules here. There's also a prestige element these days, which doesn't help. People are a lot more aspirational than they used to be and that can certainly cloud your judgement. Is social media to blame for that? Partly, I think. Everybody wants what everyone else has got and more. At the end of the day, these kids should be left to make up their own minds about whether or not they want to race. The thing is, when do you know? I think not being too aspirational was one of the biggest things I had going for me in my early karting years, for the simple reason I was able to enjoy it. I was always competitive, but not to the point where I wanted to take on the world. That came later. Had that pressure and aspiration been there at the very beginning I'm not sure I'd have enjoyed it nearly as much and I may well have been turned off by it. My parents, too, were never pushy in that way, so the only expectation they had was that I enjoy myself. When I eventually decided that I did want to take things seriously, my parents knew that I was doing it for the right reasons, which gave everybody one less thing to worry about. I also knew that if I changed my mind I could say to Mum and Dad, 'I don't want to do this anymore.' Not every kid has that luxury I'm afraid.

Getting back to the original discussion, is there anything the sport could do to make it more accessible to people from poorer backgrounds?

**Damon:** I believe there is a way. When I didn't have a drive and things were really desperate, I was invited to take part in a charity karting event which was being held in a bus depo in Clapham. Salubrious, eh? I didn't have a budget to go racing so I had to treat this race like a real competition. All the top drivers were taking part so it might as well have been. Do you know what, Johnny, I learnt more about getting the best out of something while driving that cheap little kart that didn't handle well around a makeshift kart track made out of old tyres in a bus depo than I did during any of my seasons in F3. Seriously. It was absolutely invaluable. There was one race. One opportunity. I could have turned around and said, 'Hang on a second. I was driving in F3 a few weeks ago. I'm not driving this!' But I had to grab it. It was all I had left! When Josh, my son, said he wanted to be a racing driver (it was a bit later really, as he was sixteen) I looked at karting and I thought, 'We don't know anything about this sport. We'll get murdered.' If you read Jenson Button's book you get a glimpse of how technical and involved it is. There's a whole lot of black art going on in that sport, which of course you know only too well, Johnny. Anyway, instead of buying a kart, spending a fortune and making a mess of it, we decided to join a karting club instead, called Club 100. With a karting club, the deal is that they supply the karts – you could be driving anything, by the way, and some karts are better than others – and everybody mucks in and helps to look after them. It's like a cooperative, I suppose, and puts everybody on a level playing field. If you're any good, you'll get to the front, and if you're not, hopefully you'll still enjoy yourself. The ones who aren't very good will go backwards, even in one of the good karts, so there's no ambiguity. The model enables people to try motorsport without any significant outlay and despite it being centred around people having fun, first and foremost, it can obviously help to identify talent.

If the FIA wants to distance itself from the accusation that F1 is an elitist sport then it has to do more to enable people who can't afford to dive headfirst into karting to at least dip their toes in the water. If you use football as an example, which is certainly not regarded as an elitist sport, their model of identifying talent at grassroots level is something that's taken very, very seriously, and as far as I can tell, it pays dividends. You can't legislate against the presence of multi-millionaires and billionaires in the sport, but what you can do is make it possible for people without that kind of money to reach a level that's respectable without having to mortgage their houses or, worse still, just give up and walk away. The reason Johnny and I feel so strongly about this isn't because we're a couple of socialists (our politics is between ourselves and the ballot box, thank you very much. Vote Monster Raving Loony!), it's because the prospect of widening the talent pool, even marginally, could revolutionize Formula One.

**Johnny:** Hear, hear!

# CHAPTER SIX

## Silverstone

**Johnny:** What's your first memory then, Champ? Early 1960s?

**Damon:** Silverstone memory? I was definitely taken there in the early part of that decade but because I was only just born in September 1960 I don't really remember a great deal. My first Silverstone memories, which I should think would be from 1965 or '66, are of old buildings and wind! Those relentless sou'westers that used to batter the area for what seemed like days on end. I suppose I grew up there, in a way, despite not remembering the very early days. You remember odd things, like buildings. There used to be a very old timing hut there which was the headquarters of something called the Doghouse Club, which my mum was involved in. Sort of a cross between the Women's Institute and the Salvation Army. They raised a lot of money for charities besides organizing a safe place to leave your kids and provide a refuge for exhausted and infuriated WAGs of racing drivers. Let's face it, we can be a touch tense when we're racing, can't we, JH? I talk about it in my autobiography, because between the ages of about two and thirteen, I spent quite a lot of time there. Nice cakes!

The name of the club came from Jack Brabham's wife, Betty, in response to him not paying her enough attention at a party. She told the other wives he was in the 'doghouse'. So they formed the 'Doghouse Owners' Club'! Over the years the club, which was also known as the WMRAC, became very famous for its charity fund-raising cabaret balls, held in the Grosvenor Hotel in London. It was quite something seeing all the wives doing the cancan, I can tell you! Whatever, it was kind of a safe haven for family and friends, so it became the base for me and my sisters and was a place where Mum could leave us while she went off and did the timing for my dad. She was something of a dab hand at it. Actually, a lot of the WAGs would have a job with the team doing the timing. But my mum, armed with only a pencil, a rubber, and about four stopwatches, was able to time virtually the whole F1 field, to the extent that her times would often be used as a fallback if the official times were ever called in to question. It was part calculated distraction, as it kept her occupied rather than just waiting and worrying, but also a properly important job for the team. I mean, BRM and Lotus used her timing! In addition to wives and children, the Doghouse Club also used to be frequented by the 'dolly birds', as my mum used to call them: glamorous girlfriends of drivers who were still bachelors. Quite nice when I got a bit older! Not appreciated so much by the wives, though.

**Johnny:** The Doghouse Club's quite famous, although I never went myself. Wasn't there a control tower nearby?

**Damon:** That was on the other side of Woodcote. Fantastic commentary box on stilts where they could see almost everything. Looked like the one in Scalextric. But that was the one problem with the Doghouse at Silverstone. It was on the inside of the corner so all you saw was cars flashing past. If you went to Brands you could see about a third of the track but because Silverstone runs around an airfield it was always difficult. It's obviously a great venue, though, and the history of our sport in the UK is centred very much around Silverstone.

What was your first time at Silverstone, Johnny?

**Johnny:** I'm afraid I can't remember the first time I went there as a spectator. It would have been sometime in the seventies, I'd imagine, so about ten years after you. The first big moment that I had there was at the Formula Ford Festival in 1983. You remember, when I heard that V12 and then cried my eyes out before losing the race? My first win there happened a year later, in a round of the Formula Ford Championship. I beat Bertrand Gachot, the world's premier French-Belgian Luxembourger, on the line and by a hair's breadth. It's a very special place for me. Not just because of those early days, of course, which were incredible, but everything that's happened since then. My win in 1995, which I'll come to, to going arse over tit on a hoverboard in front of tens of thousands of people and being helped to my feet by Simon Lazenby and Daniil Kvyat. I notice you didn't try and help me. You just stood there silently looking wise. I actually thought you were levitating at one point.

**Damon:** And I thought you were, when in fact you were falling off a hoverboard. What did I say afterwards?

**Johnny:** You said, 'I was going to tell you to take a bow but you just did.' Comedy gold, Champ. I'll tell you what makes Silverstone special – for me, at least, and I'd wager you're the same – is the aforementioned crowd. For me the British fans are the best in the world and as much as I love the venue, they're the thing that makes Silverstone really special. I'm certainly not denigrating the

97

venue, but just like any other track it only really comes to life when it's full of people, and the people who fill up Silverstone are a breed apart. Regardless of what I've been doing there, whether it be racing, spectating, punditing (I know that's not a real word) or making a tit of myself on a hoverboard, I've only ever received love and support from the fans.

**Damon:** You are such a lovie, Herbert. Can I add a bit of blood and guts?

**Johnny:** Be my guest.

**Damon:** Silverstone always reminded me of a medieval battle-field.

**Johnny:** He's lost the plot, folks!

**Damon:** Silence, you miserable peasant! I am your king! OK. Maybe not. But I always think, when you turn up and see all these tents and flags, it looks like an army amassing for battle. Think *Lord of the Rings*! Then, if you're a driver like we were, you go out to do battle and the masses all cheer and support you. It's all very visceral. Fortunately, this is something we've both experienced, Johnny. It's what connects us. We're old victorious warriors. You can relate to that rare experience of leading the British Grand Prix and being steered by that incredible wave of support that ani-mates every inch of every stand. It's quite spine-tingling, isn't it? Nigel used to say that the crowd were worth a second a lap and he's probably not far off. Maybe six tenths?

Normally I don't like receiving too much attention because I'm naturally modest, aren't I, Herbert? But at Silverstone it's different. The atmosphere pulls you in and it brings out the exhibitionist in all of us. Herbert here is the real fans' favourite, which is just as well as Johnny craves attention like Brundle craves Werther's Originals. I can't think of any other driver or pundit who engages with the fans like Johnny does and it's a pleasure to watch. Take the aforementioned hoverboard incident. There was only one person the crowd wanted to see take that thing for a spin and that was him. If it had been me it might have been vaguely amusing, in a dad-dancing kind of way. Johnny's a man of the people, though, and can laugh at himself. Which is just as well.

When you were racing did you always drive to the track, Johnny?

**Johnny:** What, you mean as opposed to catching a helicopter? Yes, of course I did. Where you drove in from depended on where your team was based but the furthest I ever came in from was Milton Keynes, which is about fifteen miles away. Many years ago I got stopped by the police on my way in and almost missed the race.

**Damon:** Which is why you should have got a helicopter!

**Johnny:** Shhhh! I was running a bit late and, with the traffic all queued to one side, I decided to use the empty lane, which would get me to the drivers' entrance. As I drove along this police helicopter started flying alongside me. It had a camera on the side and I didn't know whether to wave, stop or speed up. In the end I tried to ignore it and when I arrived at the front of the queue I was stopped by the police.

'Get into that queue,' one of them said, pointing at the line of cars.

'But I'm driving in—'

'Do as you're told, sir,' interrupted the policeman. 'We'll be with you as soon as we can.'

When they eventually got to me, another policeman said, 'Oh, it's you. 'Ere, you're cutting it a bit fine, aren't you?'

'Yes, I know!'

I then decided to go on a charm offensive.

'I don't suppose I could have a police escort, could I?'

'Sorry sir,' he said. 'You're a racing driver, not a royal. Now move along please.' I have to say it's a hell of a lot better now than it used to be. The traffic, that is.

**Damon:** A few years ago they had some massive problems because everybody seemed to turn up on the Friday night, including about a thousand caravans. The year after they put in a rule that said anyone bringing a caravan has to be here on the Thursday, and that's definitely helped. At the end of the day, though, I think the venue and the police cope tremendously with the onslaught.

The issues we still have at Silverstone, with regards to infrastructure, are almost a metaphor for the problem we have with motorsport itself in this country, which is that it's still seen as being something niche. It's not football, it's not cricket, it's not rugby. It's an alternative world – a world that's perceived as being exceedingly wealthy and more than capable of looking after itself, and maybe that's true. But you could see Silverstone as a national asset worthy of public investment, because preserving it for the British Grand Prix is valuable for the country as a whole. We have had some small dispensations from the public purse over the years, but we've had to work very hard to get anything.

**Johnny:** We're back to what you said earlier about F1 hiding its light under a bushel. I don't think it's the country's fault, as such. I do agree, though, that Silverstone should be treated more like a Wembley or a Twickenham. The thing is, how long have Wembley and Twickenham been the homes of English football and rugby union? A hundred years? As well as it not being as old as Wembley or Twickenham, Silverstone's had to share the big event with Brands Hatch and, earlier, Brooklands, so it doesn't yet have that brand exclusivity. It's certainly getting there, though, and even has a hotel now!

**Damon:** The history of Silverstone's quite interesting. I can see Johnny's eyes glazing over as I speak. Don't worry, we'll get to the racing soon, I promise. It was built on the site of a Second World War Royal Air Force bomber station, RAF Silverstone, which was the base for No. 17 Operational Training Unit. I don't know how many airfields were built in the 1940s – tens of dozens, probably – but they popped up in only a few years. And there appeared to be no planning, as such. Silverstone, in particular, is a little bit all over the place. It's three runways, which were built in the classic Second World War triangle format, and still lie within the outline of the present track. The first time it was used for motorsport was in 1947, when a group of locals held an impromptu race there. One of the friends, called Maurice Geoghegan, ended up running over a sheep that had wandered onto the airfield. The sheep was killed, the car written off, and ever since then the race has been known as the Mutton Grand Prix. The following year, the Royal Automobile Club took out a lease on the airfield and began transforming it into a racetrack. The rest, as they say, is history. OK, Johnny, you can wake up now.

**Johnny:** Don't worry, I'm all ears. In fact, I have an interesting fact for you. In 1948, another training base, called RAF Snitterfield, was one of two disused airfields being considered to host the 1948 British Grand Prix. The other one being, RAF Silverstone!

**Damon:** Mmmmm. Doesn't have the same ring to it really, does it? The Snitterfield Grand Prix.

**Johnny:** I've got another story about getting to Silverstone. In 1992 I was driving for Lotus alongside Mika Häkkinen and we were staying somewhere near Milton Keynes. On the Sunday, Mika got up late and while going through Silverstone village he did the same thing as me – got on the other side of the road, floored it, and hoped for the best. He hadn't got far before he was stopped by the police, but instead of being asked to join a queue he was arrested and taken to the police station. I've seen Mika when he's really flustered and believe me, it's a joy to behold.

**Damon:** Like when?

**Johnny:** Well, there was that time when I was sharing a room with him in a hotel. He went for a bath and after a few minutes he shouted to me and asked if I could fetch him a towel. 'Of course I will, Mika,' I yelled. I then took off all my clothes, put a flannel over my privates, walked into the bathroom and said, 'Here you are, Mika. Would you like me to get in with you?'

**Damon:** I honestly wish I hadn't asked.

**Johnny:** When Mika's really flustered he starts spluttering, which is what he did in the bath, and I had visions of him sitting in the police station doing just that. It's cruel, but it did make me titter a bit. I ended up having to do the warm-up in both cars and went four tenths quicker in his!

**Damon:** The things you have to do to nick your teammate's car. You could have done with a chopper, not a copper! Ha! Sorry. Actually, the Grand Prix weekend used to be responsible for the world's biggest gathering of helicopters – if you looked at the sky it was like *Apocalypse Now*. I'm not sure if that's the case these days, but in our day it looked like a gigantic beehive.

**Johnny:** Like Monaco, my first experience of the British Grand Prix as a driver was racing F3 in a support race. That again was your big chance to impress the bigwigs. Or at least, that's what we thought. When you get into F1 you realize that nobody with any clout gives a stuff about the support races. To be fair, I think it's a bit different these days and I know the drivers will often watch the F2 races. At the end of the day, though, as an F3 or an F2 driver, Silverstone will be the biggest crowd you race in front of all year so that itself is a huge buzz.

I can't believe your old man never won the British Grand Prix.

**Damon:** It's strange, isn't it? He had two seconds and a third but never made it onto the top step. Funnily enough, the British Grand Prix could actually have been Dad's first win in F1, as in 1961 he was leading the race but spun off. He did win the International Trophy at Silverstone in 1971, which was driven under F1 rules but was classed as a non-championship F1 race. He drove a Brabham BT34 lobster claw, and that was his last win in an F1 car. Jim Clark won the British Grand Prix five times, as did Alain Prost. Lewis has now won it six times, but if you said that to him he'd probably just say, 'Really? Have I?' He's very good at being humble.

One of the most memorable British Grands Prix I remember as a driver was 1992, when Nigel won. Yes, him again! It was actually my first ever Grand Prix – we'd entered the previous five races but hadn't managed to qualify. I was in a Brabham and qualified 7.4 seconds behind Nigel. My only responsibility that day – apart from finishing the race, which I did, in last place – was not to get in Nigel's way and the reason that became an issue was because he kept on bloody passing me! God knows how many times he lapped me. I think it was five in the end. He'd just lapped me for the last time when we crossed the line and this idiot ran out onto the track right in front of me! But I enjoyed knowing what it might be like to win the British GP, as I followed 'Our Nige' on the slow-down lap. We got as far as Club before a full-on track invasion started and while Nigel was being held aloft by his adoring public I was trying to avoid being trampled to death. There were people literally jumping up and down on my car. It was incredible. You finished about seventh, didn't you?

**Johnny:** No, I retired. I should have finished in the points but had a gearbox problem late on. That track invasion was one of the most amazing things I've ever seen in my life. I watched it back recently and the amount of flags being waved as Nigel comes over the line is just astonishing. There are literally thousands upon thousands of Union Jacks. Then, when he emerges for the presentation, the noise is almost deafening. A hundred and fifty thousand people going absolutely bonkers. It was his seventh win out of nine races so there was a lot to celebrate. Speaking of which, my favourite part of the post-race coverage is watching Nigel celebrate. It just doesn't work for some reason, but it's great to watch.

**Damon:** At least he didn't bang his head on a gantry that time! Amazing to think, though, that the following year I was driving for Williams and in with a real chance to do a Mansell. All I had to do was beat three-time World Champion Alain Prost, and there was no way in the world a British team were going to order a British driver to wave through a French driver at the British Grand Prix. Can you imagine? Anyway, although he outqualified me by about a tenth of a second, Alain started poorly, so I was able to snatch the lead. There could be no stopping me. Except . . . It was all going swimmingly until, shortly after a restart following a safety car, my engine erupted with a plume of white smoke, accompanied by a collective groan from the crowd. Just moments before I'd been out there loving it, Mansell style, giving the fans something to cheer about and the next minute I'm rolling to a halt in the infield. I got out and decided to show the crowd how cheesed off I was, so I kicked the car and looked angry. Later Patrick Head had a quiet word in my shell. In his best headmaster's voice, he said something like, 'Look, Damon, I don't think it's a good idea for you to be seen kicking the car, if you don't mind.'

'Yes, sorry Patrick,' I said. 'Won't happen again.'

**Johnny:** I had no idea about that. If I ever tried kicking a car I'd end up losing a foot! Things worked out a bit better the following year, though, eh Champ?

**Damon:** Absolutely! Pathetic attempts at histrionics notwithstanding, I was gutted not to have won the British Grand Prix. By the following year, however, I was in a very different place. Alain had decided to *allez* and for the first time in my life I was in contention for the World Championship. I was trailing Michael by thirty-seven points and there were ninety to play for. Although I was having a few issues with the written press at the time, when we arrived at Silverstone I was being portrayed as the hero and Michael, whose team, Benetton, were the subject of a plethora of rumours regarding skulduggery, was the villain. But I'd rather made a rod for my own back by slagging off certain members of the press, Prince Edward style. I'd sort of torn them a new orifice because they were stirring it up so much.

**Johnny:** He was Dick Dastardly and you were Penelope Pitstop.

**Damon:** Yeah, kind of, Johnny. Not sure about Penelope Pitstop. But do you remember what Michael did during the warm-up lap? This was very strange. The rules state quite clearly that you're not supposed to overtake the polesitter on the warm-up lap, but shortly after setting off Michael did exactly that. He sped up, overtook me and then slowed right down again and allowed me to pass. To this day I have absolutely no idea why he did it and I was straight on the radio just to let them know, thinking not much of it. Michael wasn't done, though. When we lined up for the start DC stalled, which meant another parade lap. So off we go once more and to my amazement, Michael repeated the move and did exactly the same thing again. It was very fishy. Why on earth would he do it twice? Unless he had to for a technical reason? I mean, if he was trying to psych me out, why do it again? The element of surprise was rather lost the second time. It just left me thinking, *Something's not right here.*

**Johnny:** Didn't he go for the hat trick?

**Damon:** He didn't just go for it, Johnny. He got it! During the race he decided to ignore the official instructions to take the stop-go, which was an even more serious offence! Talk about saving the best for last. It was a hat trick of yellow cards. So he got the red card. I mean the black flag. As well as losing second place his team were fined a cool $500,000. Oh well, you know what they say, 'There's only one rule; don't get caught!'

**Johnny:** Come on then, take us over the line. What was it like for you, Hill?

**Damon:** You know what it was like! That's why I love you. We are both in the realm of the British GP victors! My inner Penelope Pitstop, as you so aptly put it, had prevailed and I was the hero of the day. The jubilation on my slow-down lap had to be seen to be believed. No track invasion this time, because they had outlawed them, but they couldn't stop the marshals, one of whom handed me a huge Union flag attached to a stout piece of two by four about ten feet long. This time it was my turn to break the rules, as we weren't technically allowed to pick up anything that might be added to the weight of the car before clearing the post-race scrutineering. *Oh, sod it,* I thought, *if they think this is part of the car then they shouldn't be in the job!* Had my dad ever won the British Grand Prix, he'd have stopped, got out and nailed the bloody thing on! I'm not kidding. After the presentation, by Princess Diana no less, there was a big cheer and she skedaddled before she got a good soaking with champers. I wasn't quite borne aloft like Nigel, but I was moved, not just by the number of people but by everyone seeming so happy. A British driver winning the British Grand Prix seemed to transcend things like the Championship. Or at least for that moment. After a couple of hours I finally returned to the Williams motorhome. Back then the paddock at Silverstone was not the concrete enclosure it is today, and the Williams motorhome was bordered by a lawn and a picket fence.

**Johnny:** How very twee!

**Damon:** Wasn't it lovely? Like an English country garden. Frank and I just sat outside the motorhome with the trophy, watching the sun go down and soaking up the atmosphere. A perfect ending to a perfect day. Well, almost. A few weeks later during the hearing into Michael's black flag episode, the FIA tried to do us for carrying too much weight!

**Johnny:** What, the flag?

**Damon:** Yes, the bloody flag! But there's a postscript. Many years later I was crawling along in traffic in London and this guy next to me in a van started trying to get my attention. *Oh no*, I thought. *More bother.* But he persisted so I thought I'd grasp the nettle and wound down the window, expecting some abuse. I couldn't have been more mistaken.

''Ere,' he said. 'Do you remember that flag you were handed after winning the British Grand Prix?'

'How could I forget,' I said.

'Well, that was mine. That was my flag and my bit of two by four.'

'Good God,' I said. 'You don't want it back, do you?'

Fortunately, he saw the joke. But that was nice of him to say hello. Just goes to show, be nice to people on the way up and don't ever throw anything away!

Back then, all me and Frank could do was sit there with silly grins on our faces, the trophy next to us, and a steady stream of fans turning up asking for autographs and photos, with the sun slowly setting and a lovely warm feeling of satisfaction inside. After a couple of hours of that I decided it was time to have some fun. As was the tradition, Eddie Jordan had parked his flatbed truck in the paddock and his rock band were in full swing. Actually, some people might not know about this, so we'd better fill them in. In the late '80s or early 1990s, Eddie started hiring a huge flatbed truck, which is basically just a mobile stage containing lights and amplification. Every year after the British Grand Prix this mobile musical monstrosity was parked in the paddock and throughout the evening a plethora of musicians and non-musicians take to the stage and make idiots of themselves.

These days the truck has been swapped for a huge purpose-built stage and the impromptu jam is now a proper gig, featuring a host of renowned bands and musicians. Eddie and his band still make an appearance, I think, but it's all very corporate these days and is now an official part of the proceedings. Over the years we've all been up there – even Brundle – and in 1994 Eddie had asked me a few days before the race if I'd like to bring my guitar along and have some fun. When the autograph and photograph hunters finally began to head home, I decided to pop off and perforate a few eardrums, and after retrieving my axe I made my way stagewards. I was loitering by the stage just chilling before chilling was even a thing, minding my own business and coming down from a bit of a whopper of a day, when this guy couldn't help himself and interrupted my reverie.

''Ere, Damon. I know you're probably relaxing but could you just come over and meet my guests?' he asked in an ever-so-emphatic way.

'Do you mind if I don't?' I began. 'I'm really sorry but I'm absolutely whacked and I've been signing autographs for two hours already.'

Almost before I'd finished my sentence this chap was on at me again. 'Oh, come on, Damon,' he said. 'It won't take long. Just a minute, tops.' It's safe to say that this chap was in what you might call an advanced state of refreshment, and the thought of having to sit with him and his buddies was not too inviting.

'Look, I'm really, really sorry,' I said, trying to both look and sound genuinely apologetic. 'I'm sorry but I actually need a bit of peace and quiet right now, if you don't mind?'

'All right, all right,' he said, a bit put out. 'It's been a lovely day. Don't spoil it.' So there you have it, Johnny. You really can't please everyone.

Anyway, that's almost enough about me, Herbert. Let's move

on a year and bring you into the equation. I think I can say without fear of contradiction that the result of the 1995 British Grand Prix is one of the most popular there has ever been. Not just with the great British public, but with everybody in F1. Apart from Flavio, perhaps. You see, dear reader, this annoying little man who is sitting next to me in his highchair defied the odds every day of his entire career, and even though the circumstances of his win were not conducive to a happy afternoon for yours truly, or for a certain Michael Schumacher, I was absolutely over the moon that this diminutive giant of motorsport had won his home Grand Prix.

**Johnny:** At first I didn't realize I was in the lead. In fact, it wasn't until I got to Stow that I found out. Ross Brawn came on the radio and said, 'Right then, Johnny, you're in the lead. Try not to mess it up!' It was at that moment that I started noticing the flags in the grandstands. I still had five laps to go, of course, but it was a very, very emotional moment. I was brought back down to earth again by the toes on my right foot. From about the middle of every race my right foot used to get really sensitive and on this day it had been especially painful. Because it was almost severed in the accident, there's a lot a callus underneath the toes and it had been playing up for the last fifteen laps. What I always used to do was use my left foot to brake for one lap and then use my right foot to brake for two. It was all about concentration and I had to make sure the pain didn't divert my attention away from the drive. In my entire career I think there were three races where I didn't feel any pain, and unfortunately this wasn't one of them.

**Damon:** I'm really sorry I put you through that, Johnny. If only Michael and I hadn't collided.

**Johnny:** I forgive you! What made it easier that day was that I didn't have anyone on my tail, so I could relax and take in a bit of that famous atmosphere we've both been talking about.

**Damon:** I genuinely had no idea you had to go through that during every race. Is that why you laugh at drivers these days who drop out of free practice because of a cold? I bet it is.

**Johnny:** Yes! 'A cold,' I cry incredulously. 'Get in that bloody car and drive you great steaming Jessie!' Getting back to the fans for a second. You've made this point previously but the knowledge of the fans at the British Grand Prix is of a very high standard, and although they obviously love to see a British team or driver win the race they'll cheer whoever's up there. They just love F1. When Sebastian Vettel won in 2018 the team principal, Maurizio Arrivabene, said that he wanted to thank the British fans for cheering Ferrari. I don't think he'd been expecting such an enthusiastic reception but that's a mark of the people who go there.

**Damon:** Come on, let's talk about your big day.

**Johnny:** Like you, Silverstone had always been very dear to my heart, not least because it was the venue of my first win in F3. In fact, you came third that day and there's a photo in my autobiography of me and Gary Brabham, who came second, looking rather pleased and you looking rather fed up.

**Damon:** I obviously must have felt inadequate.

**Johnny:** Obviously. In 2019 our employers sent us off to a cinema to watch and discuss the 1995 British Grand Prix and you described it as one of your darkest hours. Not the cinema bit, the Grand Prix. You were obviously only joking but it was certainly a peculiar moment. I was asked many times just after the race if I'd thought I could ever win the British Grand Prix, and people seemed to be surprised when I said yes. Perhaps they knew something I didn't? You see, despite all the hoo-hah going on with Michael and Flavio I was still in a competitive car and had qualified fifth that day. I was still about a second and a half behind you and Michael but from fifth and with a good chance of rain absolutely anything can happen. So yes, I genuinely did believe before that race that I was capable of winning the British Grand Prix. All I needed was a little bit of luck and for the two cars on the front row to collide and let me through!

I was on a two-stop strategy that day and Michael was on a one, so I wasn't expecting any interference from the team. I was lying third after my first stop and just seconds after rejoining the track my visor was absolutely covered in bugs. You get days like that at Silverstone, when the clouds are heavy and low, and that day was bugtastic. By lap forty-five I was still lying third and, barring any disasters, which was obviously still very possible, I thought I was potentially on for a podium. At that point I'd never won a Grand Prix. In fact, my best result so far in my career had been second in the Spanish Grand Prix a few weeks before. I'd also had a couple of fourths in Argentina and Monaco, so it had been a good start to the season. Then, as if by magic, my old pal and sparring partner, Damon Graham Devereux Hill, OBE, generously drove into Michael Schumacher, which gave me the lead. After watching it back, which I have a few million times, as you and Michael go off Murray says, 'They're both out; Johnny Herbert is leading the British Grand Prix.' The second half of the sentence, as in, '*Johnny Herbert* is leading the British Grand Prix', is said with a not inconsiderable amount of disbelief, as if somebody has just told him that some Martians have been found at Club Corner. He wasn't the only one!

**Damon:** At first I was pretty pissed off with Michael and the thought of watching it back would have been unthinkable. The only thing, genuinely, that has made it easier to talk about and watch is the fact that it has such a happy ending. Had anyone else won the race then it probably would have remained an unwanted memory, but watching Johnny Herbert win a Grand Prix is like seeing Lassie come home.

**Johnny:** What a lovely thing to say. If a bit weird. Not only do you gift me a Grand Prix win, but you pretend you don't mind! Seriously, though, that is nice to know. When they were filming us watching and discussing the race you made the point of what an honour it was having Murray Walker – the great Murray Walker – commentating on my last lap as I drove to victory at the British Grand Prix. You were absolutely right. Murray was always one of my biggest supporters and, after I'd been chatting to Steve Rider before the race, Murray went on to tell the viewers at home all about my accident and referred to me as being a very brave young man. He's one of the dearest men you could ever meet and you making me appreciate the fact that he was commentating on that win has made it all the sweeter. That's yet another one I owe you!

**Damon:** Talk us through the final lap and the presentation then.

**Johnny:** I don't want to keep harking back to the negative stuff, but as I was being waved towards the chequered flag by that incredible sea of Union Jacks all I could think about was what had happened since the accident. I'm known as being a very happy-go-lucky kind of chap, and generally I am. You'd be surprised by the amount of people, F1 fans included, who have absolutely no idea it happened and that's partly because I used to go out of my way to avoid talking about it. Being Mr Cheerful used to help me to come to terms with it, and adopting that persona came naturally to me. The only problem with that was that I probably became a bit too happy-go-lucky and lost a little bit of my competitive edge. It was essential, though. It was either be miserable and damaged, which would never have worked, or happy and damaged, which fortunately did.

I think if you interviewed every British driver who has won the British Grand Prix over the last forty or fifty years – that's John Watson, Nigel, you, me, DC and Lewis – we'd all say pretty much the same thing about that final lap. It's one of the most amazing things you can experience. The only thing I can compare it to is England winning the World Cup, except that, rightly or wrongly, everyone at Silverstone is cheering for one person, and that's you. Just try imagining that for a second. A hundred and fifty thousand people cheering you on and celebrating the fact that you – and your team, of course – have done them proud. When I finally crossed the line I felt this enormous surge of relief.

It was obviously a day of firsts for me. I'd never had the team there going bonkers as I finished a race before. That was good. One of the first people to come up and congratulate me after the race was Michael, and he seemed genuinely pleased for me. Again, it was a day of firsts! Only joking. The next person after him was Jean Alesi, who finished second. He told me that I deserved it after everything I'd been through and gave me a big hug. Jean had recently won in Canada after God knows how many seconds and thirds and I was pleased he'd broken his duck. My favourite part of the post-race proceedings, apart from being on Eddie's truck, was the presentation ceremony. Being short, I often need all the help I can get finding a decent view and the view from the top of that podium at Silverstone is like no other on Earth. After receiving our trophies, Jean and DC lifted me up and put me on their shoulders. That was definitely a first and according to Murray, as far as he knew, it had never been done before. After then it was off to the race interview.

The only song I remember singing (if you can call it singing) afterwards on Eddie's truck was 'Johnny B. Goode'. We did do some other ones but I can't remember what they were. Somebody handed me a tambourine, which was a mistake, as I have the natural rhythm of a dead elephant. Eddie was on the drums, as was Nick Mason from Pink Floyd, if I remember.

Incidentally, I also talked to Steve Rider after the race. He was live on BBC1 and as we talked I started getting a bit emotional. I thought to myself, *If I'm not careful I'm going to burst into tears here.* He asked me a question which I just managed to get through without blubbing and then fortunately he had to go back to Murray. Had he asked another I'm afraid that would have been it. Funnily enough, when I spoke to Steve on the grid prior to the race he finished off by saying, 'You're owed a good British Grand Prix. Have one today.'

**Damon:** So now Steve Rider gets all the credit? What about me! Talking of Steve Rider, he also spoke to me before the race. He asked me what I thought was going to happen, and I predicted that I should be able to convert my pole position into a win. To once again quote our mutual friend, Murray, 'I don't make mistakes. I make prophecies which immediately turn out to be wrong!' Incidentally, who presented you with your trophy at the British Grand Prix? Bet you can't top Princess Diana.

**Johnny:** Prince Michael of Kent. It's almost an allegory (please note that's the second time I've used that rather impressive word) for our careers really. Yours is a tall blonde icon who was idolized by millions, and mine is a bloke with a beard who nobody can remember.

# CHAPTER SEVEN

## Whither Ferrari and whither Williams?

**Johnny:** Far too many whithers for my liking. I take it we're supposed to discuss whether these two teams can return to glory? Well, you obviously drove for one of them and both of us could have driven for the other.

**Damon:** How very intriguing. Do go on.

**Johnny:** Well, I was supposed to meet Enzo Ferrari during the 1988 season but unfortunately I crashed and he died.

**Damon:** Are the two incidents unrelated? It's odd, though, that they happened roughly at the same time. Perhaps Enzo gave up the ghost after learning you'd had an accident?

**Johnny:** He was ninety years old, but that probably pushed him over the edge. I broke his heart.

**Damon:** Where else might you have gone had you not crashed at Brands? I know you were supposed to have seen Frank about this time.

**Johnny:** That's right, and I would definitely have seen him first. McLaren and Williams were the ones to beat and they were also British. Regardless of how big or prestigious a team is, if a car's not up to scratch and/or the team is underperforming, which Ferrari were at the time, you don't want to go there. They actually finished second in the Constructors' Championship in 1988, but the year before Williams had won it. Their drivers, Nelson and Nigel, had also finished first and second in the Drivers' Championship.

**Damon:** If there had been, in some parallel universe, a situation where a driver could have raced alongside Michael Schumacher with parity then I probably would have signed for Ferrari. Then I'd have had Mansell, Senna, Prost and Schumacher as teammates. And DC and Jacques, of course. Let's not forget them. I think Jean Alesi and Gerhard Berger played an absolute blinder at Ferrari. They really had the best of both worlds. They never did too badly that they attracted too much pressure, and they never did too well. They were obviously remunerated handsomely and the team never blamed the drivers. Absolute bloody genius! There's been all this talk recently about Lewis ending his career at Ferrari. Well, it would certainly do that! If you want to destabilize a team, though, that's the way to do it. Ferrari already had two drivers who were at each other's ankles. What better way to calm the waters than to come out publicly and say, 'Ooh, it'd be nice to have Lewis here, wouldn't it chaps?' You would then have had to go back into the garage and the drivers would have said, 'OK then. Which one of us two will be going if Lewis decides to join?' It's destabilizing – obviously – and a bit unnecessary. All academic now with Carlos Sainz confirmed for 2021 at Ferrari. The worry for Lewis is a 'free-floating' Vettel.

**Johnny:** That's the way the sport works, though. It's not just Ferrari who do things like that. We're back again to what you said earlier about the unequal way in which teams often treat their drivers. It's about keeping them on their toes, ultimately, and it works. The reason Michael Schumacher went to Ferrari was to return them to winning ways and regardless of what methods he used, which were roughly the same as the methods he'd used at Benetton, he was incredibly successful. Michael was also just twenty-seven years old when he signed for them, so he was relatively young. Lewis is in his mid-thirties. To be honest I don't think that would make much difference, though, as he's still at his peak. It'd be a question of how long he'd need to achieve the goal.

**Damon:** He'd probably have a bus pass by the time it happened! What certainly would make a difference is if Ferrari gave him a bad car. If that happened the fizz would go right out of it. It wouldn't matter how much money they were paying him. If Lewis Hamilton was in an uncompetitive car he'd be out of that team faster than a scalded cat.

**Johnny:** I think Sebastian Vettel was trying to emulate Schumacher by going to Ferrari.

**Damon:** And how's that worked out? Seb's failure to emulate his friend's success is probably one of the things that would prevent Lewis from going. Here's a scenario for you, though. Say Mercedes were dithering about staying in F1 and Louis C. Camilleri, the CEO at Ferrari, decided to bring in both the design and management teams from Mercedes, or whoever was available. Under that circumstance I think Lewis might go, but he wouldn't go on his own. He'd be mad to. Michael did something similar at Ferrari, of course, when he took most of his team from

Benetton. The difference being that in those days you were probably talking about a handful of people whereas today you're probably talking fifty or sixty. It's not unthinkable but the task of moving that many people to another country with their families would be Herculean. It took Michael several years to get everybody he wanted over from Benetton. It didn't happen overnight.

**Johnny:** So, over to Williams.

**Damon:** Modesty should really forbid me from making this point but it started going wrong at Williams roughly around the time I left.

**Johnny:** Really?

**Damon:** No, not really. Jacques won the Drivers' in 1997 and Williams won the Constructors'. That was the last car Adrian Newey built for them before he left and they've never won it since. When Jacques Villeneuve arrived at Williams in 1996, I'd already heard a rumour that I might be out of a job. The rumour was that I wouldn't be driving for them that season, but as it turned out I did. What Williams didn't tell me, and probably already knew, was that I wouldn't be driving for them in 1997! Incidentally, I became the fourth driver in nine years to win the World Drivers' Championship for Williams and not drive for the team the following season. Anyway, as opposed to letting the rumour mill get to me, I just got my head down and carried on. There are certain things you can't control and that was certainly one of them. The other is the choice of your teammate. I was conscious when Jacques arrived that he was trying to destabilize me, the naughty minx. Whatever he was asked to do he did the opposite and seemed to go out of his way to do things to annoy me, like trying to nick my lunch. Childish things like that. I took the view that we would sort it out on the track. Frank and Patrick were, I think, scrupulously fair in giving their drivers equal equipment and treatment. I sometimes got slightly better treatment but only because I'd been there longer and was a known quantity. My point being, I never had to deal with the kind of situation you had to at Benneton. Patrick Head would never have stood for that nonsense so it would have been interesting to see how Michael would have fared at Williams. Not as well as he did at Benetton or Ferrari, I'd wager.

Speaking of Ferrari, in 1996 when I was dropped by Williams – sorry, when Williams decided not to renew my contract – I was approached by Jean Todt about racing with Michael. It was obviously very unlikely that I'd want to race alongside Michael Schumacher but out of curiosity I went along for a chat. All the way to Italy. We were invited to his company house and sat outside, all very cosy. The first thing Jean said to me was, 'You know you'd have to be the number-two driver to Michael, don't you, Damon.' So I came home straight away! Recently a journalist asked me if I'd spoken to Ferrari about a drive so I said yes. 'Funny that,' said the journalist. 'We asked Jean the same question and he said it never happened.' I actually went to his house, for heaven's sake! But maybe they drugged me to believe it happened? Can you do that?

**Johnny:** Yeah, yeah, yeah. We believe you. You're delving into the realms of fantasy, Hill, although it does remind me of the afternoon I went to see Ron Dennis. It was the end of the 1995 season and after shaking Ron's hand I sat down and the first thing he said to me was, 'I need to change you, Johnny.'

**Damon:** What, for another driver?

**Johnny:** Yes, yes, very funny. I think he wanted to mould me into something else but as soon as he said that I knew I could never work for him. Rightly or wrongly (probably wrongly in terms of ambition) that was the way I felt so after going through the motions I got up and left.

**Damon:** The world of a team boss or team manager is based around negotiation. Who comes in, who goes out and who gets what, etc. It's a different world. The last thing a team boss wants is a driver who becomes bigger than them and when a driver does become bigger than them things start happening that could potentially pull the rug out from under them. The driver, that is. Not the boss. You have to say that Michael was extremely compliant in that respect and knew that he could basically get anything he wanted providing he didn't challenge or interfere with the prevailing political situation. Which is exactly what Ayrton did. Ayrton challenged the whole concept of Formula One, which pissed off the folk at the top. In that respect you really have to hand it to Mr Schumacher. He'd be an exceptional politician. When I left Williams I got the shock of my life, really.

**Johnny:** So what was it like moving from Williams to Arrows?

**Damon:** I'm going to have to be quite careful here. Let's just say it wasn't always straightforward. For instance, I found myself being challenged by them quite a lot, and especially when it came to money. It felt like they were forever trying to catch me out about something I'd said in the media. Breach of contract stuff. And I'd say to them, 'Why have you got me here if you don't want me to be myself?' I wasn't saying anything contentious. I was just geeing up the team maybe, or the engine manufacturer. Perhaps it's cultural. When you run a smaller team like Arrows or Jordan, which was the team I went to after Arrows, you have to fight for every penny, so I don't think it was personal. It was just their way of doing things.

**Johnny:** Then again, it could have been an ego thing. I hark back to what you just said about signing a big name. When you joined Arrows after Williams you weren't just the biggest name in the team, you were also the biggest voice in the team – as in the media would want to speak to you more than they would Tom Walkinshaw or anyone else there. In that respect, Damon Hill was a far bigger deal than the team he'd just joined, so if he was ever critical of that team it would obviously hurt.

**Damon:** Yep. Good point. There's a lot of sensitivity, I suppose. What happened to Williams after I left is that they went chasing after BMW and, in the age when banks were allowed to spend lots of money on sponsorship, they also went huge with Royal Bank of Scotland. Don't forget, when I won the Championship in 1996 there were 150 people working at Williams, which was one of the biggest teams at the time. Then it went from 150 to about 800 in no time at all. From what I understand there was then a break-down in the way things were done. They moved to a different factory and the dynamic of the team changed.

You can almost say the same about McLaren. McLaren moved from where they were in Woking to this spectacular new facility that's impressive but a bit cold. Once again, the dynamic of the team changed and they're yet to recover. That said, they're definitely closer than Williams. Williams did have some success after moving from Didcot with Juan Pablo Montoya and our mate Ralph Schumacher, but after that everything started going south. They went from winning podiums and challenging for championships to winning points and then nothing at all.

**Johnny:** But for Williams to become the whipping boys of F1 is something nobody envisaged. The question is, can they ever come back? Personally, I'm not sure. In fact, even getting back to mid-table has to be doubtful. It hurts me to say that, but I just can't see it happening. I hope I'm wrong. Look at Manchester United. In the Alex Ferguson era they won everything. And then, just as he retired, a lot of money started being invested in other teams. The equivalent to Manchester United in F1 terms is probably McLaren, in that they're not too far away from being able to make a challenge. Williams, on the other hand, have dropped right out of the division.

To be at the front of F1 these days you have to invest an inordinate amount of money. And, as we've seen in recent years, names such as Williams mean less and less. It's such a huge task that I have difficulty seeing the attraction sometimes. You think to yourself, is it really worth that amount of money and that amount of effort? Mercedes have to do the same thing and more every single year just to stop themselves going backwards. When you've had six seasons of success that's a long run, but is it feasible to keep on doing it? To keep on improving and investing year in, year out. What if they manage to do ten seasons? Total domination in a major sport for an entire decade. It must be tempting.

**Damon:** The thing is, there will be people within that organization who will already be exhausted. I guarantee it. All these teams eventually burn out – I saw it happening at Williams.

**Johnny:** I'm not sure about that. Not that long ago you would have had a mechanic who was on the left front, a mechanic on the right front, and so on. These days you've got somebody looking after every nut and bolt and nine times out of ten they'll be straight out of university. I'd say that for the majority of the team it'd be impossible to burn yourself out these days. And even if they did, they'd be easily replaced. Anyway, half of them don't even turn up to every race. I'm not denigrating them, by the way. It's simply the way a team is structured these days.

**Damon:** I'm thinking more of who would be referred to as the key personnel. People like Andy Cowell, who runs the AMG High Performance Team. It's up to Toto to keep on rejuvenating the team and I'd wager that that's one of his biggest worries and responsibilities. The pendulum can still swing, regardless of whether Mercedes are investing. That's because Red Bull are throwing everything at taking Mercedes' crown. What was it Helmut Marko said at the end of the 2019 season? 'Next year, no more excuses.' He'll be expecting his team to challenge at every single race. But this just highlights the disparity between the top teams such as Mercedes, Red Bull, even Ferrari, and Williams. If Mercedes are at the top of Mount Everest and the other two are a few metres further down, Williams aren't even at base camp. In fact, they're somewhere in Kathmandu.

**Johnny:** Everyone was expecting Paddy Lowe to elevate them back into that mid-table pack but instead the decline just continued. For me, as a racing fan, that was hugely disappointing, but for Williams it must have been devastating. I'm not singling Paddy out here as I have no idea about the ins and outs but it was one of those moves where you thought, 'Great! Williams have finally found somebody who's going to take them forward.'

**Damon:** Unfortunately I don't think Paddy is an F1 team leader in the same vein as someone like Christian Horner or Toto. Brilliant in his own way, but on the technical stuff. I didn't quite have the same enthusiasm for his appointment. He's a similar character to Rory

Byrne. Stick him in a back room with a wind tunnel and a bunch of boffins and he'll work miracles, but he's not a front man – nor do I think he really wants to be. Over the years the roles of technical director and team principal have evolved and these days you're far more likely to have motivators like Toto or Christian in place. People who can stand up to the press and talk publicly. That's certainly one of the problems with Ferrari at the moment. Nobody there is in a strong enough position to represent the team publicly, partly because you've got this iconic company behind you going, 'Get this right next time, otherwise!' Nobody's indispensable but I think both Toto and Christian have had enough success over the years to buy themselves some time, should they need it. Ferrari, on the other hand, have put their trust in a former engineer who spent two years as their Technical Director. Mattia Binotto will have the enormous task of creating some success and then trying to hang on to it. Far be it from me to doubt Mattia's ability as a communicator or a motivator, but I'm not convinced a former engineer is the right front man. Let's hope I'm wrong, because he's a very cool and charming man. I like him a lot. But the team principal at Ferrari should be the biggest character on the grid, as the team they're representing are the biggest and most beloved. I wonder how many casual F1 fans can name a Ferrari team principal who has been in place over the last ten or fifteen years. I doubt there'll be many. Seems like no one wants to grab the 'Ring of Enzo'.

**Johnny:** Would Toto or Christian ever bring somebody in from the factory floor at either Mercedes or Aston Martin and then put them on the F1 team for a Grand Prix weekend? No, of course they wouldn't. Sebastian Vettel's number one mechanic from 2018 told me that's exactly what Ferrari did. I forget which car he worked on but they brought in a guy from the factory floor in Maranello who'd been to four Grands Prix in ten years and put him on the F1 team. That's the mentality of the team, unfortunately. It might have worked years ago but not today. I understand why they'd want to bring in somebody from the factory floor. It's because they want to keep everything in-house. They want to keep it Ferrari. Nobody else does that.

It's obviously very easy for us to sit here in front of our nice log fire (which isn't actually burning at the moment because somebody with a beard hasn't bothered to put a log on) and pontificate about where Ferrari and Williams are going wrong, but to go out and actually try and shoulder that burden and effect some change takes an awful lot of courage.

Do you lament the passing of the Minardis of this world, Damon? The small teams who were in it purely for the sport. I most certainly do.

**Damon:** Times have obviously moved on but yes, I do. You're talking about small groups of people who simply loved motor racing and who didn't see it as part of their 'global marketing strategy'. They were there because they wanted to race. For those racers of our generation and older, that was the case with the majority of F1 teams. Even Bernie, who was often accused of being in it just for the money, was a former driver who adored motor racing. Yes, he liked a deal and enjoyed making money, but he also had a knack for knowing what the fans wanted and that came from the fact that he both loved and understood the sport. The removal of owner-principals – people like Frank, Bernie, Ken Tyrell and Eddie – has been to the detriment of Formula One, and if they ever made a comeback I think it would rejuvenate the sport. I know that Toto owns a 30 per cent stake in the Mercedes F1 Team but it's obviously not the same. I don't know for sure – in fact, I intend to ask them – but if Toto and Christian had the opportunity to own a team outright and be the principal I bet they'd at least consider it. Can I say the same for Mattia at Ferrari? Of course not. He's an engineer, first and foremost. Would Zak Brown at McLaren want his own team? You bet he would! He is the happiest man in the world at the moment because he's living the dream. In fact, the only thing that would make Zak Brown happier than he is at the moment – apart from winning a Grand Prix with McLaren – is winning a Grand Prix with his own team. I guarantee it. That man lives, breathes and sleeps motor racing and I think he knows enough about the sport to make a success of it. I hope we've planted a seed here, Johnny, I really do.

**Johnny:** Perhaps that's one of the problems with Williams? Look at Eddie, though. If somebody offers you a shedload of money for 40 per cent of your team when you're in your late fifties, what are you going to do? Eddie, together with the likes of Tom Walkinshaw, Giancarlo Minardi and even Flavio, was one of those who took over from the likes of Ken Tyrell. The thing is, who's taken over from them? Huge corporate organizations who installed well-meaning front men. In just a few short years owner-principals became a thing of the past. What we've seen since then is a steady stream of very wealthy companies who've tested the water in F1 to see, ultimately, what they can get out of it. In fact, if it hadn't been for the likes of Red Bull and Mercedes sticking at it and showing some real commitment to the sport, I'm not sure how many teams we'd recognize. You'd have Williams, McLaren and Ferrari, but that would be about it.

**Damon:** Something else this corporate revolution has brought to our sport are the job descriptions of its staff. For instance, if you were part of the Lotus F1 team in the 1960s and you wanted job security and some guaranteed time off you'd have been sadly out of luck. You were there because you were doing something you loved and everything else in your life – marriage, friendships, social life – was secondary. Things like job security didn't even come into it. These days you might have a thousand plus people working at a team – or two thousand if you're Mercedes – and although a proportion of these will be fans of F1 that won't be their motivation. And why should it be? In 2018, over 4,500 people attended the Mercedes F1 team's Christmas party. Four and a half thousand! That's the population of a small town, for heaven's sake! Well the COVID thing has forced their hand. The budget cap has finally been ratified, which cuts the spending weapon in F1 for the bigger teams from $145 million in 2021 to $135 million by 2023. We shall see if that works how its meant to.

**Johnny:** With an operation of that size ruling the roost you're not going to get a chancer like Eddie Jordan coming in and trying to have a go, are you? It's just not feasible anymore. Do you know what I miss most about those little teams? The reaction when they had some success, like the time when Mark Webber won a point – a single point! – for Minardi on his F1 debut in 2002. Financially it probably meant survival for the team but for sheer sporting endeavour it was colossal. Bigger than big! I think a better example, certainly in terms of the effect it had on the sport, is obviously Jordan. Thanks in no small part to you, that team started winning races and at one point they even led the Constructors' Championship. That ain't going to happen again, is it? I could never understand this push to get manufacturers involved in F1. Yes, they have a bigger budget, but ultimately they're going to be there for other reasons – namely to support their core business and sell road cars.

**Damon:** Absolutely right. And because it's ostensibly there to com-plement something else, it has to be as uncontroversial and as dull as is humanly or mechanically possible. Ferrari are always the exception. Don't forget that Enzo started off building racing cars until somebody suggested he build road cars to fund the racing. The cart was in front of the horse, or the other way around. Anyway, you know what I mean. At the other end of the grid you have Renault, who are the polar opposite to Ferrari. They are never going to get there in F1 because, as a manufacturer, they won't fully commit. It's so, so obvious. If the management are expecting the rug to be pulled all of the time, how on earth can they operate? It's ridiculous. Here's a question for you, Johnny. Would you buy a Renault because of their association with F1, either now or in the past?

**Johnny:** No, I would not. Because in my mind, there's almost no connection. It's a shame, because that V10 they created for Williams was a work of art and was by far the best on the grid. In that respect, Renault were actually a force in F1, but that never ever translated to their road car offering. Ferrari are the exception, a) because they manufacture sports cars; and b) because the racing came first. The only other manufacturer I believe have benefited from being involved in F1 are Mercedes. And wadaya know, they're the ones who've invested in the sport over a long period of time – lock, stock and barrel. Mercedes used to be seen as being an old man's car, whereas today they're sexy, modern and aspirational. It's difficult to gauge the amount of influence F1 has had on that transformation, but it's certainly no coincidence that the two entities are very much aligned. Unlike Renault. Somebody from Mercedes once told me that if being in F1 helps to open just one door in one major country it will more than pay for itself, and that's obviously happened.

**Damon:** To be fair to Renault, they did exactly that with Fernando Alonso in Spain. We used to have a house there years ago and nobody was interested in F1. It was great! It was all rallies and motorbike racing at the time and I had complete anonymity, which was very much appreciated at that time when I was winning a lot. Incognito hols! When Fernando came to prominence, the interest in the sport rocketed and Renault's market share went through the roof in Spain. (We sold the house not long afterwards, but not because of Fernando!) It was more about their association with Fernando, of course, but who cares? It worked, so good luck to them, and now he's back! *Viva España!*

**Johnny:** Hang on, you drive a bloody Volkswagen! But how much of the reluctance on the behalf of manufacturers to get involved in F1, on the scale of Mercedes, say, is down to how it's perceived? Not too long ago F1 had all the worst kind of sponsors and it was seen as being a very dangerous sport. It was also very acrimonious at times, which is another thing that's changed. Perhaps that reputation hasn't been eradicated yet.

**Damon:** Perhaps. Do you know, for the budget of one of the top teams you could run an entire championship in another sport for a year, and probably something quite entertaining. Entertainment's more important for F1 now than in any other decade, for the simple reason that there's so much competition.

**Johnny:** About ten years ago, Julian Jakobi, who used to manage Ayrton and now has his own sports management company, did a survey in America about which motorsports people found easiest to engage with. He included Nascar, F1, MotoGP, Superbikes, Monster Trucks, rally and Red Bull X-Fighters, which is the indoor motorcycle sport where they perform incredible tricks. He included the lot. The people they surveyed were sports fans as opposed to motorsport fans and the one that came out on top was the freestyle motorbike stunt competition, Red Bull X-Fighters, which is something short, quick and snappy. I don't think F1 performed badly in the survey but because you can have long periods in F1 where not a great deal happens – or at least nothing dramatic – people lost interest and ended up staring at their phones.

**Damon:** If you're eleven years old and you happen upon a Grand Prix while flicking through the squillions of channels on your TV, what are you going to think? It all depends on what's happening, of course, but if the safety car's out or there's no racing going on the chances are their opinion will be negative. The ardent fan obviously accepts this as being part and parcel of the sport, but if somebody who is new to the sport believes it's indicative of what happens at a Grand Prix then you've lost them, and potentially forever. Do you know what floated my boat as an eleven-year-old? Downhill skiing – Franz Klammer was my favourite skier – and then Evel Knievel on his bike. Then, if I was watching *World of Sport* with Dickie Davies, it would be either surfing from Hawaii or lumberjacking. I found them all really exciting, unlike football and car racing. I'm afraid they used to bore the socks off me when I was a kid.

**Johnny:** Thank God we're not writing a book about car racing, eh Damon! I think F1's constant search for improvement, and ultimately perfection, is definitely part of the problem. After all, imperfections are what make the sport interesting.

Although they're in very different positions – one's fighting for the Championship and one for survival – the next couple of years are going to be crucial for Ferrari and Williams. Ferrari will be OK, I think, but I fear for Williams.

# CHAPTER EIGHT

## Safety

**Johnny:** The original discussion for this chapter was going to be whether it was fair to compare different eras in F1 and, despite it looking interesting on paper, it simply morphed into a discussion about safety.

One of the first questions we asked ourselves while discussing the original question was, if you took a top driver from the 1950s and put them into modern-day F1 car, would they be quick, and vice versa? Well, in my opinion – and I think Champ agrees with me on this – if you put a top driver from the 1950s into a modern-day F1 car they would definitely be quick. Not so the other way around. In fact, I think the majority of contemporary F1 drivers wouldn't even give it a go. And who could blame them? Lewis once told me that he wishes he'd been able to race on some of the tracks the likes of you and I raced on back in the 1980s and 1990s, and I think that he has a genuine interest in F1 history. That's a lot different, though, to jumping into Fangio's Mercedes-Benz W196 circa 1957 and going hell for leather around the Nordschleife for twenty laps with the likes of Stirling Moss on your tail. This isn't a criticism, by the way. The mindset of the modern F1 driver is quite different – not just to the likes of Fangio and Stirling, but to us too. This only became apparent to me shortly after we lost Jules Bianchi at Suzuka. The following race was Russia, and after arriving at the circuit I saw Jean-Éric Vergne, who was very close to Jules, on his mobile phone. He looked really upset so I hung around and waited for him to finish his call so I could speak with him.

'Are you OK?' I asked.

'Johnny,' he said. 'I don't know if I want to drive again. I don't feel anything.'

'Come on Jean-Éric,' I said, putting an arm around him. 'Jules knew there was a risk, the same as I knew there was a risk.'

'No, no, no, Johnny,' he said. 'That's not the reason. When I'm going to go off the circuit, I know I'm going to be OK. As I said, I just don't feel anything. I feel numb.'

Jean-Éric obviously regarded Jules's accident as being a one-off freak event, as opposed to something that was symptomatic of the sport, and he still had total confidence in the safety of his car. *Wow!* I thought, because that wasn't always the case. The generation we grew up around, and learnt from, accepted the possibility of death as being part and parcel of the sport, which resulted in a certain kind of person taking part.

**Damon:** The death rate in my dad's era was truly frightening. Usually about two drivers a year would be killed, so with twenty-four cars on the grid you had a one in twelve chance of losing your life. The thing is, these drivers kept on coming back year after year, and they were all well aware of the risks and statistics. How could they not be?

I once saw an interview with the late Peter Revson, who raced Formula One for Tyrell, Lotus and McLaren back in the early 1970s. When asked about the dangers of driving at speed he was philosophical and said that despite the chances of death being high – the rate in F1 in the 1960s and early 1970s was actually about the same as it was for mobilized soldiers during the First World War – he preferred to do this with his life than anything else. He died during a test session shortly after the interview, in March 1974, and was the seventh F1 fatality of the decade.

It wasn't quite as dangerous when Johnny and I entered the sport. Carbon fibre had just come in, although Johnny will attest via what happened to his feet that it wasn't completely successful! Even so, we were all well aware that as a sport and even a profession it was still one of the most dangerous on the planet.

**Johnny:** Not everybody is quite so philosophical. Take the aforementioned Sir Stirling Moss and Sir Jackie Stewart, for instance. About five years ago I had a chat with them both about safety in Formula One and I was surprised by what I heard. Given the era they drove in, which, between them, covers the early 1950s to the mid-1970s, I assumed that both would be philosophical about it and perhaps believe that there should be slightly less emphasis on safety. Jackie less so, as he was an advocate for improving safety when it was still incredibly dangerous, but I was still expecting a consensus of having an element of danger. Well, I was half right. Stirling believed that there should still be an element of danger in the sport whereas Jackie wanted it to be as safe as possible. It's such a contentious issue, although improvements in safety are difficult to argue against. The reason I mentioned the conversation is because it demonstrates just how divisive it is.

I remember Lewis telling me about a GPDA (Grand Prix Drivers' Association) meeting he attended about twelve years ago in which he told his assembled fellow drivers that in his opinion they were all using the run-off areas too much. He suggested implementing penalties, which is what I believe should happen, and then put it to the floor for a vote. Do you know how many drivers agreed with him? Not one. In fact, they said they wanted even more run-off.

**Damon:** They should race at Oulton Park. That's a great track with hardly any run-off so I always knew that if I went off there, it was going to hurt. That definitely focused the mind. But sadly it also claimed lives, Paul Warwick being the one I remember most vividly. But if you've got bags of run-off and there's no penalty you can go as fast as you like, which actually negates the need for courage. Or at least questions it. It's a tough balance. I believe you had a memorable trip to Oulton Park with one Jackie Stewart?

**Johnny:** I was wondering when Jackie would make an appearance. One of the things I remember most about driving for Jackie was that he was always there trying to help. Every year he'd do a day at Oulton Park where he'd take his drivers out onto the track and give them some advice. I talked about this in my autobiography but I have to give it a mention here; if only to give my colleague and me an opportunity to impersonate him.

What he used to do was send the driver out first for a few laps, watch him from various vantage points around the track, and then go out with them and chat. 'I've been watching you, Johnny,' he said to me when I first went out with him in 1999, 'and one thing I'll say is that' – at this point he squinted his eyes and his voice went into a kind of hiss – 'you're veeeeeeeeeeery aggressive with the car, Johnny. Veeeeeeeeeery aggressive. You have to be smoooooooooooth with the car, Johnny. Smoooooooooooth. Treat it like you would a nice young lady. You do like nice young ladies, don't you, Johnny? Remember what I said, smoooooooooooth. I'll be watching you, Johnny. I'll be watching yooooooooooou.'

**Damon:** What happened?

**Johnny:** I did as I was told. When Jackie could see what I was doing. When he couldn't see what I was doing I just went for it. After that he got in with me and when we arrived back in the garage he took off his helmet.

'Are you OK, Jackie?' I asked. 'You look a bit pale.'

'My word, Johnny,' he began. 'That was veeeeeeeeeery aggressive, Johnny, wasn't it now? Not very smoooooooooooth at all.'

We had endured a couple of scrapes while we were out and at one point we'd bounced three times over about a hundred yards before screeching to a halt.

'You almost had us both killed there, Johnny,' said my sensei. 'What on earth did you think you were doing?'

I may be wrong, but I'm sure Jackie had had a little accident. Just a wee one.

Anyway, after delivering the rest of his verdict, which continued along the same vein, Jackie and I swapped places and he took me out for a few laps. Because of what he'd said I'd been expecting – well, cashmere on wheels, basically – but he was worse than me! I did try and remonstrate with him afterwards but he was having none of it. 'No, no, Johnny, that's as smoooooooooooth as you'll get. It's all in the hands, you know.'

Despite the above, which obviously hasn't been exaggerated at all, Jackie could be quite ruthless when he had to be and he was, and still is, a phenomenal businessman. I've got an awful lot of time for Sir Jackie, and at the end of the day we won a Grand Prix together. That was pretty special.

**Damon:** Some of the most successful team bosses have been failed racing drivers. Jackie's obviously the exception! I suppose John Surtees and Jack Brabham are also exceptions. I think the old man was getting there, too. I'm losing my own argument! But look at the rest; Ron Dennis – hopeless. Bernie – hopeless. Frank – hopeless. Christian Horner – OK. Toto Wolff – not bad on his day. Probably better than Christian! But you know the saying, those who can, do. Those who can't, manage F1 teams.

The dream job in an F1 team will always be the driver. I mean, who wouldn't want to be in that car driving around Silverstone or Monaco at 200 mph?

**Johnny:** The engineers?

**Damon:** They don't really count. I'm referring only to humans. Anyway, back on topic; to get into a Formula One car in the early days, which had no seatbelts and virtually no protection, and then drive it around the Nordschleife at well over a hundred miles an hour where there were just trees instead of run-off, took an unbelievable amount of courage.

When Dad first went to Spa, he did one lap, came back in, and said, 'I'm not sure I can do this guys.' He was terrified. The mechanics just said, 'Well, you have a think about it Graham and then let us know.' He had to literally sit there and try and summon up the courage to carry on. In IndyCar, drivers have to find the courage to take corners flat out, which again must be petrifying. I love the story Willy Ribbs tells in his film *Uppity*. He had one more go to become the first black guy to qualify for the Indy 500. So his engineer brings out these 'magic' tyres and tells Willy he's been saving them especially for this moment. Of course they were just like all the other tyres! But it did the trick in Willy's head and he qualified. Big balls. Great story about courage and self-belief.

**Johnny:** How on earth did your mum cope with your dad going racing every weekend and knowing there was a good chance he wouldn't come home?

**Damon:** I have absolutely no idea. She probably didn't cope, Johnny. Not all the time. But she never tried to make him stop. It was something you had to try and accept. Funnily enough, when I was racing, my wife Georgy never once said she was worried about me, whereas now I'm retired I can't even go down to the shops without her expressing concern. 'Are you sure you'll be OK, dear?' she'll say nervously. 'Do take care.'

**Johnny:** I get that. When I was driving a car at 200 mph around a racetrack risking life and limb, my wife Rebecca would just sit there getting bored and twiddling her thumbs. Now I'm a pundit and at home more often it's, 'Are you sure you can carry that on your own?' and, 'Do you need the loo?'

When did we suddenly become so vulnerable, and when did our wives start noticing?

**Damon:** When we started spending more time at home, I suppose. You see, when you and I were racing drivers, Johnny, our friends and families were under the strange misapprehension that we and those around us knew what we were doing and that providence would be kind to us. They probably did worry from time to time, but like my mum they just accepted it. Rather ironically, I think the truth would probably have killed them, or at least done them a mischief.

During the 1950s, '60s and '70s, it would have been at the forefront of everybody's mind. In fact, you might even have been expecting it. Imagine how that must have felt?

**Johnny:** I actually have an example for you. Did you ever drive the old Mulsanne Straight at Le Mans, before they put the chicane in?

**Damon:** Yes I did, in 1989! It was my first and only entry at Le Mans and we retired after 228 laps. But by Jove, missus! That put hairs on your chest!

139

**Johnny:** By the time I drove at Le Mans they'd put the chicane in, more's the pity. How long is that stretch, about 3.7 miles? Pre the chicane, that used to take about a minute apparently, and the average speed would have been about 210–220 mph. A couple of the guys I've spoken to who drove the Mulsanne Straight in that condition say that they were half expecting a tyre to blow, and if a tyre blows when you're driving at 220 mph there's only going to be one outcome. They weren't just fearful about death. They were expecting it.

**Damon:** I remember driving into a bank of fog on the Mulsanne Straight. *Hang on,* you think to yourself, *that wasn't there the previous lap.* The dilemma you face is whether to stay flat or slow down. You're travelling at over 200 mph and suddenly you can't see a thing and you don't know when you will again. In one second? Two seconds? Five seconds?! You can travel a long way in the wrong direction at that speed. The other thing is you don't know if there is something in there that's not doing 200 mph. But you have no choice. If you slow down you could be hit up the arse by the car behind and even if you did slow down you'd still be doing 180 mph! So you just keep it flat and hope. That's probably the longest leap of faith I've ever made.

**Johnny:** Did your bum squeak a bit?

**Damon:** Yes, just a tad. It was certainly an adventure! But for me, the definition of madness in F1 was racing flat out in the wet. It used to produce this intense emotional hybrid of fear, excitement and resignation to the fact that you had no option but to push as hard as possible. It's what keeps you fully concentrated.

**Johnny:** It was fun, though, wasn't it? Racing in the wet? I used to love it. Anyway, in conclusion, and going back to the original question, I think it's impossible to compare different eras of F1 fairly and I think we've proved that. I think a fairer question would be, if the likes of Charles Leclerc and Max Verstappen had been around in the 1950s and had the mindset and mentality of a driver from that period, would they be fast? The answer to that question is undoubtedly yes.

**Damon:** What did we admire drivers like Fangio and Moss for? Take Moss's drive at the 1955 Mille Miglia, for instance. The Mille Miglia ran from 1927 to 1957 and the course stretched from Brescia to Rome and back. It was a thousand miles in total and took in some of the most challenging roads in Italy.

To add a little bit of excitement, as if watching the likes of Stirling Moss and Fangio charging through the Italian countryside wasn't enough, the organizers used to let the slower cars go first, meaning that the faster cars were constantly catching and passing them. You can imagine what this led to. It was often carnage.

That year, Moss put in speeds of up to 170 mph and was confident that his performance would not be over-driving the course. As one journalist for *Petrolicious* put it, 'As spectators, teams, and other drivers discovered, Moss was at his best and began to carve unbelievable amounts of time from his rivals.' At one point during the race, Stirling took more than four minutes from his nearest rival over just sixty-five miles. I believe the rival was none other than Fangio, who was the current F1 Champion. To put that into perspective, it would be like a driver in the Indy 500 pulling out a four-minute lead over twenty-six laps. Absolute madness!

Stirling Moss and his co-driver, Dennis Jenkinson, finished the course in ten hours and seven minutes, and that's a record that still stands as the fastest any driver has travelled on those roads. As *Petrolicious* also observed, 'Moss performed a feat of driving skill that is scarcely believable, even today.' They also commented that it was important for us to remember that the event was an achievement from a time when mankind was pushing the boundaries of speed in every way. 'To go any faster than Moss on May 1, 1955,' they wrote, 'you'd need wings.'

Sadly Stirling is no longer with us, but I heard him talk a few times and he said that their attitude towards risk was totally different in those days, to the extent that they were putting the spectators at risk. The view in those days was, if you want to stand there on that corner and you get hit by a car travelling at 150 mph it's your own stupid fault! The world's changed completely from that point of view. For one thing it's far more litigious, which means that if something goes wrong somebody will be to blame. You articulated it with your Jean-Éric Vergne story, Johnny. The mindset is that somebody else is taking care of me. I've got a roll-over hoop, I've got crash barriers, I've got a halo. I'll be OK.

**Johnny:** Inevitably, it makes me think of the day when Ayrton died. Although I was incredibly upset, I wasn't shocked, as I'd already experienced it happen several times before. Racing at a karting event in the mid-1970s comes to mind, in which a sixteen-year-old girl called Lorraine Peck tragically lost her life. She was considered to be one of the most talented female drivers in the world at the time and during a practice session in Germany she landed in a trailer after a crash and was killed by one of her seat stays. That was probably my first exposure to death in motorsport. The next one was a lad called Pete Rogers. He was killed in the early 1980s while racing Formula Ford. The reason I remember it well is because the car he was killed in was the car I'd been driving the previous year. A few years after that I saw somebody in F3 break their neck. That was bloody awful. Death and serious injury weren't an everyday occurrence, but by the time I reached F1 I'd become conditioned to it happening. It was, as I think we've said before, part and parcel of motorsport.

**Damon:** Then you had your accident, of course. That was pretty serious.

**Johnny:** Yes, but I wasn't killed, and it just conditioned me even more to the possibility of it happening, which is why I wasn't shocked about Ayrton. The only fatality we've had in F1 since Ayrton and Roland lost their lives in 1994 is Jules. As tragic as his death was, that's one fatality in over a quarter of a century. I know we've had them in other formulas and at events, but F1 as a sport has fortunately been able to relinquish its crown as, arguably, the most dangerous sport on earth.

**Damon:** At the end of the day, though, F1 is part of motorsport and every injury and fatality that befalls motorsport is felt by everybody within it.

The only track that used to put the fear of God into me was Suzuka, which is where I had one of my best Formula One wins in 1994. Mark my words, you do not want to go off at Suzuka, and when I first arrived at the circuit I was, for want of a slightly less crude phrase, crapping myself. *Wow,* I thought. *This is a bit manly. A bit butch.* It was always known as being a very technical track and quite difficult, but what I hadn't appreciated was just how fast and scary it was. Half of my brain was saying, this is going to kill you, Damon, and when your brain tells you there's danger ahead, the natural response is to attempt to remove yourself from the situation. Save your skin, basically. The other half of my brain was saying go for it, so I had a kind of mental conundrum to contend with. I had to try and ignore the sensible half of my brain as

143

best I could, and, just as Dad had at done Spa all those years ago, try and summon up some courage.

**Johnny:** That's one of the biggest challenges you face as a Formula One driver, and despite what Jean-Éric said I'm sure there are plenty of drivers on the grid at the moment who experience exactly the same thing that we did. The thing is, the mental conflict we experience isn't confined to just before the race. I remember Nigel Mansell telling me that during qualifying one year – again, this was at Suzuka – his head was telling him to back off and he had to force himself to stay on it. This was happening in real time and at about 180 mph, so the danger was even more clear and present. Without wanting to sound crude, which will make a change, Nigel Mansell has balls as big as planets, so for him to come out and admit that he had to force himself to keep pushing, it must have been bloody scary.

The only thing more difficult than overcoming that dilemma, either before or during a race, is returning to it after you've had a bad accident. The voice telling you not to do it is obviously louder than ever and the only thing that can overcome that is your desire to succeed. I don't know if the Champ remembers this, but you once said during a conversation we had that, when we started out, the people entering Formula One were basically outcasts who would never fit into modern society and part of their motivation was the fact that Formula One was all they had. The reason I remember that conversation is because after my accident I was told I probably wouldn't walk again, let alone drive an F1 car, yet all I could think about was Formula One and all I wanted to do was drive. Everybody who knew me who wasn't in Formula One thought I was either mad or weird, which kind of proves your point. I was not normal! Sorry, *am* not normal. The only mental scars I had were fears that I wouldn't make it back into a car. If that happened today, I would never get the chance of making a comeback as I wouldn't fit into the world of perfection which Formula One has created. That's not a criticism. It's just a fact. Had it not been for Peter Collins having so much faith in my ability, I would never have made it back. These days, though, certainly with regards to the big teams, it would never happen.

**Damon:** Ironically, with the pedal systems they have these days, you might have been better off. Just going back to what you were saying about Nigel Mansell – we keep coming back to bravery, which is what obviously allows the ambition part of your brain to prevail over the cautious part. Courage is the thought and the word, but bravery is the deed. It's a common mistake to believe that Nigel Mansell was just a brute in a car, and we have no doubt about his bravery, but he also had great touch. That said, he was, and is, incredibly strong. If you ever shake hands with Nigel Mansell, just be careful. He's got a grip like King Kong! Very few drivers – or human beings, for that matter – have as much bravery as they do courage, but he's definitely one of them. We're back to Nigel's big balls again, aren't we? Please excuse us. Johnny's very uncouth.

# CHAPTER NINE

## Big Bernie

**Johnny:** I'll start this one, if you don't mind. If it wasn't for Bernie Ecclestone I would never have made it into an F1 car. Finally, the world has somebody to blame! It was actually him and Professor Sid Watkins who gave Peter Collins the go-ahead to give me that drive in Rio back in 1989, and as far as I'm aware Bernie went to a lot of effort. Had it been up to Fabio and Luciano Benetton it would never have happened, so the three people I have to thank are Peter, of course, the old Prof, who will always be a hero of mine, and Bernie.

Did I agree with everything Bernie Ecclestone did while he was in charge of F1? Of course I didn't. Nobody agreed with everything Bernie did. Apart from Bernie. I also think he probably stayed on a bit too long, but that's just my opinion. At the end of the day, though, I believe that the vast majority of what Bernie did during his tenure was for the good of the sport. His rise to the top began in 1972 when he purchased the Brabham F1 team. At the time, F1 races were almost amateurish in the way they were organized and presented and Bernie saw not just a problem with that – which was that everything was fragmented (as an example for instance, teams were making separate deals with event promoters on a race-by-race basis and sometimes there weren't enough cars to fill the grid) – but an opportunity. After forming the Formula One Constructors' Association (FOCA) in 1974, which he did with Colin Chapman, Frank, Max Mosley, Ken Tyrell and Teddy Mayer, Bernie finally seized control of the sport in 1981 after convincing the teams to sign the now infamous Concorde Agreement, which not only committed them to race but guaranteed the sport coverage on TV. The teams controlled the commercial rights to the sport but Bernie negotiated the deals and for doing so he took a share of the profits. The remainder went to the FIA. For the first time ever Bernie turned the sport of F1 into a professional, commercially viable proposition that could be watched all over the world. He revolutionized the sport. Had he not stepped in it would have trundled along at a snail's pace and probably would have remained amateurish. In fact, there's no guarantee it would have survived without his intervention.

**Damon:** When Bernie bought Brabham in 1972, which is when I first met him, my dad was driving for the team. Rather ironically, Brabham were the only team on the grid at the time that didn't have a major sponsor. This was unfortunate, not only financially, but also aesthetically, as the car was a deeply unattractive greeny-blue colour with orangey-yellow front wings and split radiators at the front. It was known affectionately as 'the lobster claw'. After Bernie bought the team, which he did from Dad's very good friend, Rob Walker, who was heir to the Johnny Walker fortune, Dad invited him over to our house one day. I'd have been about twelve at the time, so a bit taller than Bernie, and I remember thinking, who on earth is this guy? He arrived with Carlos Pace, who was another one of his drivers, and as Dad showed them around the place Bernie remained impassive and made none of the appreciative noises visitors usually made. It was almost as if he was sizing the place up and he seemed to scrutinize everything. I'll tell you one thing, Johnny: for his size he certainly left a big impression on me.

I think Bernie influenced the way people approached F1 because his methods always seemed to work. He was able to galvanize the teams to support a common goal – which was ultimately his goal. Bernie benefited, but they also benefited. If he'd presented the teams with an agreement that said, OK, I'm going to get 90 per cent of everything and you lot are going to get 10 per cent, they obviously wouldn't have signed. What he did was generate a brand-new and much-needed revenue stream from the TV companies, or at least a potential revenue stream. Some of the teams weren't sure about the deal, so to ensure that everyone was on board, Bernie said, 'Here you go, teams, here's some money up front.' 'Really?' they said. 'Great, thanks!' None of them asked how much Bernie was getting or how much the deal was worth, but they didn't care. In hindsight perhaps they should have, but at the end of the day Bernie was coming to them with money. Guaranteed money! I think they were just grateful it was there and grateful they were able to race. From Bernie's point of view possession was nine tenths of the law and even though he didn't have a licence to sell the TV rights, he just got on with it. He was playing the long game. The teams were always deep in short-term issues.

A few years ago, during an interview with *Tatler* magazine, Eddie Jordan said of Bernie, 'Anyone who has had a business, sold it four times, has never bought it back, has never lost its control, and still owns it, is pretty special. And do you know the most important thing? He never fucking owned it in the first place!' Basically, Bernie Ecclestone was a very astute chancer who saw an opportunity, grabbed it with both hands and shook the living day-lights out of it. He must have been thinking to himself, *Surely somebody's going to realize that I don't actually own the sport?* By the time they did it was all academic, as he'd made it legal.

**Johnny:** People who weren't around in the pre-Bernie years often assume – understandably, given the way the sport and its protag-onists are remembered – that F1 has always enjoyed widespread coverage and popularity, but that's simply not the case. When we were talking about Monaco earlier you mentioned very few races were televised back in the 1960s and F1 was, not a minor sport necessarily, but it certainly didn't have the cachet or the coverage it does today. I reckon Bernie was a trailblazer when it came to commercializing sport and it wouldn't surprise me if the govern-ing bodies of football and cricket have followed *his* lead.

**Damon:** It was also Bernie's idea to bring in Professor Sid Watkins after the death of Ronnie Petersen in 1978. The safety measures that were then insisted upon by the Prof will have prevented many deaths and many serious injuries through the decades.

In some ways, Bernie contradicts the public image that he him-self created and used to promote while he was running the ship: a nasty, cut-throat businessman who used to win every deal and who never gave a damn about anyone else. In actual fact, Bernie's not like that at all. He's much, much smarter than that and he actually gets the meaning of professionalism and the importance of raising standards and doing things well, to the point where he's probably a little bit OCD. I mean, if you pull a telephone off a wall because the receiver's been put on the wrong way around and the wire's tangled up, you've probably got a problem. What about when ten or twenty trucks turn up at a circuit and you make them all come in again because they're not lined up inch perfect?

As eccentric or as obsessive as that may seem to some people. It was Bernie's attention to detail and his insistence on doing things right that enabled him to sell the sport to potential advertisers and sponsors. If the CEO of a big company is interested in investing money in a sport and you invite them to a Grand Prix you want to make damn sure you've given yourself the best possible chance of winning that investment, and the best way to do that is by making sure everything is exactly as it should be. Bernie's attention to detail is forensic and it obviously paid dividends.

**Johnny:** What about the year when Bernie got rid of the burger bar at Silverstone? Everybody went absolutely ballistic but the stench of the onions and the fat was upsetting the corporate guests and so Bernie said it had to go. All he did was replace it with something better but some of the fans were outraged. Sometime after that Bernie decided to put the kybosh on Eddie's musical trailer. Like the burger van, all he did was replace it with something better, so as opposed to the trailer turning up and being wheeled into position after the Grand Prix we had a professional stage installed that was there for the whole weekend. The thing is, you're never going to be able to please everybody all of the time and over the years Bernie had to make some pretty unpopular decisions. They were his decisions to make, though, and in an attempt at quoting a proverb correctly for a change, you can't make an omelette without cracking a few eggs.

Once again, I am not saying that every decision Bernie Ecclestone made during his time in F1 was right or even good for the sport, but it takes a lot of guts to put yourself in that position. He might be small, but he always wore a bloody big hat did Bernie.

**Damon:** As drivers, Bernie knew us better than we knew ourselves, which is why he always got his own way. Do you remember in 1996 when he was trying to get us all to sign the new Super Licence? There was a clause in it saying that we had to drop everything at a moment's notice and fly anywhere in the world to promote F1. So we had a GPDA meeting and we all agreed we were never going to sign this outrage. But when we excitedly went to get our Super Licences at the first race in Brazil, there was Bernie standing at the bottom of the stairs. 'Where you going, eh?' was all he had to say, and we all signed the bloody contract because we were too scared of not being able to race! He'd made himself abundantly clear; he could prevent me from becoming World Champion. As you rightly said, Johnny, Bernie may be small in stature, but his reputation, personality, and ultimately his power tend to transcend all the physical stuff and it turns him into a giant. Or an ogre, depending on what situation you've got yourself into.

Speaking of which.

Fourteen years earlier something similar happened, but instead of the drivers capitulating they locked themselves in a bus at the South African Grand Prix and went on strike. This was definitely one of the times when Bernie overstepped the mark and thank God the drivers fought back. Once again it was over clauses in the new Super Licence and to be honest they make our cause for disquiet seem unimportant. The first clause said that they wanted to forbid any of the drivers criticizing the governing body, regardless of the circumstances. The early 1980s was a turbulent time for F1, so this seemed ridiculous. The one that really annoyed the drivers was a new clause stating that they would no longer be allowed to negotiate their own contracts, meaning that control over who drove where would ultimately lie with the teams. This promoted fears that drivers would be traded between the teams willy-nilly and would have no say at all in their own futures.

**Johnny:** That still makes me laugh, even today. Can you imagine Ron Dennis walking up to Niki Lauda and saying, 'Look Niki, we know you've won a couple of races for us this year and we're grateful. Thing is, Toleman have offered us £250,000 for you to race for them next year so that's where you're off to. You probably won't qualify for many races, but it's a great deal for us.'

Talk about taking the piss!

**Damon:** Niki didn't stand for any of that crap. He was a blooming hero on and off the track. In fact, the two drivers who were most vocal in their opposition to the new clauses were Ferrari's Didier Pironi and Niki. Niki was returning to the sport after retiring at the end of 1979 and he obviously commanded a huge amount of respect among the drivers. Not just because he was a phenomenal driver, but because he was a very astute businessman. Bernie and Jean-Marie Balestre, who was President of FISA, which was the forerunner to the FIA, were going to have their work cut out persuading the drivers to sign something so incredibly ridiculous. A great deal of negotiating went on between the drivers' representatives and FISA, but in the end Balestre issued an ultimatum. 'Sign the licence, or you can't race,' he said. 'Take it or leave it.' Had Niki and Didier not been there then perhaps Bernie and Balestre might have had their way.

Shortly before the first practice session was due to take place on the Thursday, the Grand Prix Drivers' Association arranged for a bus to be driven onto the circuit, and as the drivers arrived Niki and Didier shepherded them onto it as quickly as they could. They must have thought they were going to the seaside. As the bus left the circuit, an engineer from the March team tried to block the exit with his car but the drivers were having none of it. Quick as a flash they jumped off the bus, pushed the car out of the way and then headed off in the direction of the Sunnyside Park Hotel, which was about five miles away. The media were obviously fully conversant with what was occurring and a throng of them followed directly behind.

The only driver who stayed behind was Didier Pironi. It was his job to conduct the negotiations with Bernie and Balestre et al, and as these negotiations took place he fed regular updates to drivers. The negotiations didn't go well, however, and the most vociferous voice on the baddies' side, which is obviously FISA, was Bernie. He claimed he'd fired his two drivers, Nelson Piquet and Riccardo Patrese, and claimed that every driver who was striking could be easily replaced. After the initial negotiations broke down it was announced that the race would be postponed by a week and that everyone taking part in the strike would be banned from F1 for life. A bit strong, in my opinion, but emotions were obviously running high.

**Johnny:** I think everyone involved was probably compromised in some way (other sports were already boycotting South Africa over apartheid), and that probably clouded their judgement a bit. Take the smaller teams, for example. Regardless of how unfair the clauses were they would have had sponsors breathing down their necks and the consequences of not putting a car out would have been catastrophic. As a result some of the smaller teams tried to bully their drivers into playing ball but every single one said sod off. Apart from the Italian, Teo Fabi. This was supposed to be Teo's debut and so instead of rocking the boat he crossed the picket line and decided to race, which was understandable. Not every driver necessarily agreed with the strike but the rest all stuck with it.

My favourite part of the story is what the drivers did to entertain each other at the hotel. I'm not sure whether it's all true or not

(I hope it is) but apparently Gilles Villeneuve started playing a few tunes on the piano but was completely outdone by Lotus's Elio de Angelis, who was a bit of a concert pianist. The piano was eventually used as a barricade to stop team members from trying to force their way in. Marlboro's Bruno Giacomelli was next on the bill. He was a dab hand with a pencil and paper and did an amusing routine using diagrams to explain exactly how to dismantle an AK-47. As you do. Top of the bill was none other than Mr Niki laugh-a-minute Lauda, who, so legend has it, did a short stand-up comedy routine. Yes, you read that correctly. The Austrian funster did stand-up comedy. Had them in stitches, he did.

The race did eventually go ahead, but only after Balestre promised that there would be no ramifications for the drivers. This meant bugger all in the end as after the race he slammed each and every driver with a $10,000 fine and a suspended race ban. There's a very famous photograph of some mechanics playing football on the track while the standoff was taking place. It was certainly an interesting weekend!

That really is one of my favourite stories in F1. I love it. There were times, I think, when Bernie thought F1 was his and his alone, and they were the times when he came unstuck. It's kind of understandable, as he did, in many ways, establish the sport in its modern form. He's a very complex character is our Bernie, complex and intriguing. He's probably one of the most pragmatic people I've ever met, and one of the most insensitive. I don't mean that in a derogatory way. He's just very, very focused.

I'll tell you one thing about F1 Bernie didn't see, and that's the power of the sport to do good in the world, because F1 could generate tens of millions of pounds a year for good causes, if it wanted to. Unlike the commercial side and the TV rights, there's never been anyone leading the way, so it's always fallen by the wayside. I think Bernie's approach was always, 'Why should we?', or, 'What's in it for us?' To be fair to Bernie, raising money for charity and thinking about others obviously wasn't his strong point. It's a pity, though.

**Damon:** In my opinion that's a side of F1 that suffered under his stewardship, as the sport is seen by some people as being not just elitist, but selfish and a bit self-obsessed. He obviously thought a lot about the commercial side of things, but alas, not the cultural side. He could be kind of crass with his comments sometimes. 'At least Hitler got things done'. That wasn't one of his finest moments. And then there were his inflammatory comments on the Black Lives Matter issues. So no marks for diplomacy and good taste. But it's like that sketch in *Life of Brian*, when they have to conclude that the Romans, despite being a bunch of barbaric tyrants, were the only people who could possibly keep order in a place like this.

It makes me think of that time in 1996 in Spain, when Bernie made us race in a deluge. From where I was on the grid the track looked more like a large infinity pool! I'd qualified on pole with Jacques alongside me and Michael directly behind. Herbert, you were a few rows further back. You know your place. (Sorry. Couldn't resist.) It had been piddling down since morning warm-up and the conditions were worse than they had been at any point during the weekend. I was remembering seven seasons prior, in Adelaide, when the drivers had refused to start the race because it had been too wet. Bernie must have been thinking about that very same race and reading my mind. There was no such thing as a safety car start at the time so with the prospect of there being no action on the track at the scheduled hour, which I assume would have resulted in Bernie losing enough money to clear the national debt of a small country, he decided to take action. Just as I was wondering whether or not to register my concerns with the team, this mop of hair appeared inside the cockpit and its owner, in a tersely unequivocal voice, said, 'Race starts on time, OK?' Before I could reply to the mop of hair it was on its way to Jacques to repeat the same directive.

It was a masterstroke on Bernie's behalf, as with the possibility of protesting now removed we all went back into race mode and sure enough, the race started bang on time. I spun off on lap ten, you spun off on lap twenty, and the race was won by Michael. I should have taken my opportunity and complained!

**Johnny:** Around the same time, I was approached to do a computer game and the guy who was setting it up (and paying me) wanted to have 'Grand Prix' in the title. He was the kind of person who likes doing things first and then asking permission afterwards (or not at all), but when it came to using anything to do with F1 I decided to err on the side of caution. 'Let me just go and see Bernie,' I said. 'Just out of courtesy.' So I went to see Bernie and explained everything to him. 'Don't worry, Johnny,' he said eventually. '*I* won't be coming after you.'

The emphasis was on the I, as in, *I* won't be coming after you, Johnny, but somebody else might be! It felt very strange walking out of his office. I thought I was going to get shot! Nothing ever happened, but every time the phone went after the game came out – at least for the first couple of weeks – my bum cheeks clenched a bit. Incidentally, the description for what became *Johnny Herbert's Grand Prix Championship*, which came out in 1998 on Windows, read as follows: 'The goal of Johnny Herbert's Grand Prix Championship 1998 is to win the Drivers' Championship and become the World Champion of 1998.'

Really? I finished fifteenth.

**Damon:** That reminds me of an interview I saw once with the London gangster, Mad Frankie Fraser. The journalist was asking him about a famous gruesome murder back in the day. The journalist swallows for possibly the last time and pops the key question, 'Did you kill so and so?' 'Well . . .' says Frankie, cool as you like, '. . . they say I did.' Sends just enough of a chill down your spine not to doubt him, doesn't it?

**Johnny:** I know you're not calling Bernie an East End gangster, Damon, but he's very good at creating that nervous doubt! I think there's a mischievous side to Bernie, though. He's certainly got a wicked sense of humour. Here's a scenario for you. Say one of his associates got caught one day being spanked by a young lady in a dungeon somewhere. It's a fanciful suggestion I admit, but if that happened I reckon Bernie would have sent him some kinky boots.

**Damon:** For that, Johnny, you're going to have to have your bottom spanked. Not by me, though.

**Johnny:** I'm always ready for a good spanking. Just like Brundle. In the mid-1990s, the paddock at Silverstone didn't have any of the electronic security equipment it has now. You just showed your pass to the security guards and providing you weren't carrying a gun, you were in. Because of my dodgy feet I used to have a quadbike for getting around but when Bernie put the new security measures in it wasn't allowed. He made me suffer! These days I have a little electric scooter and last year at the Abu Dhabi Grand Prix while I was riding this thing I saw Bernie coming towards me. I deliberately tried avoiding him as a joke before pulling up for a quick chat. As we were talking I asked if I could come and see his car collection one day at Biggin Hill Airport – which he obviously owns. Who owns a bloody airport for heaven's sake? That's just mad. Bernie's car collection, a proportion of which he keeps in Bahrain, so not too far from Abu Dhabi, is, as you'd imagine, mightily impressive. The proportion I wanted to see comprises of the following legendary marques. Get a load of this:

1937 Mercedes-Benz W125, 1937 Auto Union C-Type, 1948 Maserati 4CLT, 1949 Talbot-Lago T26C, 1951 Ferrari 125 'Thinwall Special', 1951 Ferrari 375, 1954 BRM V16 Mark II, 1954 Maserati 250F, 1954 Lancia D50, 1955 Ferrari 555 Supersqualo, 1955 Connaught B-Type, 1956 Lancia-Ferrari D50A, 1956 Vanwall, 1960 Ferrari 246 Dino, 1964 Ferrari 1512, 1966 Ferrari 312, 1975 Brabham BT44B, 1976 McLaren M23, 1977 Ferrari 312T3, 1978 Brabham BT46B, 1980 Brabham–Ford BT49, 1982 Brabham–BMW BT50, 1983 Brabham–BMW BT52, 1987 Brabham–BMW BT56.

To put this into perspective, the legendary Hill and Herbert car collection, which is also kept at two separate locations, comprises two legendary marques that are the envy of everyone in F1: a four-year-old Land Rover Freelander and a five-year-old VW Passat. The Passat's an estate, ladies and gentlemen, and it purrs like a cat.

Get a load of *that*, Ecclestone.

Anyway, after promising to allow me to view his collection in Bahrain, I said my goodbyes and went on my way. Just as I was riding off Bernie said, 'Oi, Herbert! If I was still running this show you wouldn't be riding that bloody thing.'

That was typical Bernie.

Tell us a bit more about when you first met him. Tell us the Roy James story.

**Damon:** I knew you were going to ask that. Oh, all right then. I won't get into trouble because Bernie is quite upfront about it. Anyway, for almost as long as I can remember people have been talking about Bernie and coming up with a lot of myths and gossip, some of it probably true! But I know this is actually the honest truth because it happened to me. Now, I'm not suggesting anything here that hasn't been suggested before, but there always used to be rumours about Bernie and the Great Train Robbery. The rumours were that he had been involved in the planning of the robbery and when he was eventually asked about it in an interview he said, and I quote, 'There wasn't enough money on that train. I could have done something better than that.'

The reason Bernie had been linked with the crime was because of his friendship with a man called Roy James. Roy had won a Formula Junior race at Brands Hatch in 1963 (ironically driving a Brabham BT6 which he'd bought from a man from New Zealand) in which the great Mike Hailwood, who did dabble in car racing, finished fifth. According to Mike, and to many others, Roy showed great promise as a racing driver and had he continued he may well have been destined for great things. Like you, Roy began in karts but as things became more expensive he faced the same dilemma that befalls most up-and-coming drivers. This is where the similarity between you and Roy comes to an end, Johnny, as instead of trying to find a benevolent team manager or a sponsor to help him fulfil his racing ambitions, Roy found another use for his undoubted talent for escaping from his pursuers. He was recruited as a getaway driver for some chaps who were intending to rob a train. The car he used, incidentally, was a Mark 1 Jaguar with lowered suspension, revised brakes and a souped-up engine. He was arrested some months after the robbery after being chased across a rooftop by the police in St John's Wood. Roy was wearing just his underwear and was carrying a suitcase full of money. His lawyer tried to claim that this was perfectly normal behaviour but the jury didn't buy it.

Because he'd been part of the tight racing fraternity prior to being collared, most people knew him, including Bernie and Dad. Nothing suspicious about that. So while he was doing his porridge Roy used to write to Dad. In his plentiful spare time, Roy was learning a couple of more honest trades; calligraphy and silversmithing. His handwriting was absolutely immaculate and the reason he was writing to Dad was to see if he could help him get some work when he was released. So it came to pass that, by and by, one day in 1975, I was at home doing nothing interesting and the doorbell went. When I answered it there was a man who said, 'Hello. My name is Roy James. Is your dad home?' Now, I happened to know who Roy James was, having read a very exciting book about great crimes. How could you forget a name like Roy James? Too like Jesse James. So what my brain was telling me to shout at that moment was, 'Muuuuum! There's a Great Train Robber at the door!' But I was in a state of shock, so just said, 'Hang on. I'll get Mummy.' I think I shut the door just to be safe before getting her to deal with it. I wonder what she said to him? He never darkened our door again.

The rest of his story is rather tragic. He tried to make a comeback but broke his leg and never competed again. He then went back to his bad old ways and was arrested for a VAT fraud involving melting down gold coins, for which he was acquitted. But he then was put back in gaol for attempted murder in 1993. He died just after being released in 1997. But his marvellous silversmithing talent is celebrated every year when they present the FIA F1 Constructors' Trophy, which he made. Sad, eh Johnny?

**Johnny:** Next time I see Bernie I'm going to ask him if he has in his collection a 1960s Mark 1 Jaguar with lowered suspension, revised breaks and a souped-up engine. I bet he has!

Whatever you think about Bernie, he's one of the few characters within F1 who has the status of people like Ayrton and your dad have without being a driver. With drivers it was all about talent and endeavour whereas with Bernie it was about endeavour and vision. He created the platform that allowed the likes of McLaren and Williams to produce some unbelievable cars and create what became a golden era for the sport. Imagine F1 without Senna, Prost, Mansell and Piquet. It's unthinkable. I'm not saying Bernie was responsible for realizing their talent but he allowed the teams to flourish, which meant they were able to produce the equipment, which allowed the likes of Senna, Mansell and Prost to go into battle and show the world how exciting and exhilarating the sport of Formula One can be. They in turn inspired the likes of Schumacher, Häkkinen, Hill, Alonso, Hamilton, Räikkönen, Button and Vettel.

Before I had my accident in 1988 I was invited to do a test for Lotus in between the Hungarian and Belgian Grands Prix. The aforementioned Nelson Piquet was driving for the team at the time, *and* he was the reigning World Champion. Can you imagine what that was like? It was just a couple of weeks after my twenty-fourth birthday and there I was at Monza about to do a two-day test alongside the current World Champion. To me he represented that golden era, and just being in the same garage as him was a massive thrill. I was driving Satoru Nakajima's car at the test and when I arrived at the track I introduced myself to the mechanics and went to look at the car. After a few minutes Nelson arrived. I tried my best to look cool and unaffected but I don't think it worked. 'Who are you?' he said with his chin in the air. He was strutting around the garage like a peacock. 'I don't know,' I replied. 'Who are you?' 'That's none of your business,' said the World Champion. 'Now, come on young man, who are you?' 'Why should I tell you who I am before you tell me who you are?' I asked. 'Because of who I am!' 'And who are you? You still haven't told me yet!' Although I'd never met Nelson before I already had the measure of him. He could be severe when he wanted to be but he had a great sense of humour and boy, was he competitive!

**Damon:** Bernie loved Nelson. Couple of bad boys together. But it's interesting that it's not always all about money with Bernie. No, really! When Bernie owned Brabham he had an approach one day from a pizza company who were interested in sponsoring the team and he turned them down. Why? Because he didn't want a pizza company on the side of his car. Like the burger van at Silverstone, it didn't form part of his vision. When he was at Brabham all of his sponsors had to have blue and white logos on the cars because they were the colours of the team. And conveniently enough, his prime sponsors' corporate colours just happened to be blue and white; Olivetti and Parmalat. He didn't mind the cheese, he just didn't want the whole pizza! Bernie somehow always got what he wanted. Clever, clever man. When he was up in front of the parliamentary select committee who wanted to find out more about the fabled 'Bernie Bung' of £1 million to the Labour Party, which many felt was linked to the decision to make F1 exempt from a ban on sport sponsorship by tobacco companies, they started questioning him about some of his companies. It went something like, 'Mr Ecclestone, could you tell me about this company you own called All Sports.'

'Never heard of it,' said Bernie as quick as a flash.

The MP looked a bit stunned, 'Never heard of All Sports?'

'Nope. Never heard of it.' The MP starts shuffling his papers and looking a bit flummoxed and eventually gives up, thinking he's been given duff information. But Bernie was right. He'd never heard of All Sports. He'd heard of All Sport, though. Because it's a company that used to own all the trackside advertising and hospitality for F1. And he part owned it with Paddy McNally. He should have been a barrister. The nerve. Quite brilliant, though.

When Bernie was investigated for allegedly bribing a member of the Bayern Bank so he could get a 'sweet deal' on buying back the shares in F1, the German judge let him settle the case with no admission of guilt for €100 million ($1 million of which went to a local children's hospital). Quite an unusual outcome by all accounts, to be able to buy your escape mid-trial, but you get used to being amazed with what Bernie gets away with. That was probably Bernie's closest call, though. Anyway, when they asked if he could get the money within one week, Bernie comes back with 'Would you take dollars?' 'That'll do nicely,' said the judge. The cheek of the man! Got to laugh, though. If that had happened to you or me we'd have fainted first and then wet ourselves. He's got more front than that big shop down the road from his offices. But to add his own bit of spin on it, he comes out claiming to be a philanthropist who gave €1 million to a children's hospital! Forget the punishing €99 million he had to cough up to stop the trial from getting any further.

But even that was a masterstroke, because, by hook or by crook, he'd bought back control of F1 for $100 million. Add that to the $350 million it cost him for the hundred-year lease from his old friend Max and he'd bought something eventually valued at $8 billion for $450 million. 'Do the math,' as they say in dollar land.

Since retiring he's invested in his Brazilian wife's coffee plantation. You can now buy 'Celebrity Coffee' without having to be one. I'll bet it's not cheap, though. He's like a cat. He always seems to land on his feet. And he's also just become a dad at eighty-nine! Bet he doesn't change the nappies.

# CHAPTER TEN

## How important is fitness?

**Damon:** Fitness is a funny one. These days F1 drivers are recognized as being among the fittest athletes on earth, so staying in shape is a prerequisite as opposed to a choice. We don't know this for sure, but as far as we're aware it was Jackie in the 1960s who was one of the first F1 drivers to take fitness quite seriously, which would certainly fit with his uber professional approach to driving. One thing's for sure, it certainly wasn't James Hunt, Alan Jones or Keke Rosberg. Let's go back a little bit further, shall we. I've got a photo of Jim Clark on a beach somewhere and without wishing to be rude, it's clear to see he didn't work out. Or at least not often.

In those days exercise meant lifting a few dumbbells in the bathroom and the only reason my dad was fit was because he used to row an awful lot. It gave him very good leg strength, which is absolutely pointless for racing cars. It's the worst thing you can do, really, as you put mass on. What rowing did give him was stamina, and that's possibly what gave him the edge at races like Monaco. The bit that makes me laugh the most when comparing then and now is diet. Dad would have a small bowl of chicken noodle soup before a race, as he was always too nervous to eat.

Years ago I spoke to Barry Sheene about this and he and his contemporaries would never drink water before a race, through fear of it making them sweat! How incredible is that? The knowledge that they had in those days was almost non-existent so imagine how well they could have performed had they been fit, eaten well, and kept themselves hydrated. My dad could have won six Monacos had he had a bowl of porridge and a banana before the race. He'd have been like Superman. Barry Sheene, had he drunk some water, could have won five World Championships.

When did you start taking fitness seriously?

**Johnny:** I'm still waiting! It'll happen one day. Without wanting to sound arrogant, I always had quite a high level of natural fitness and it was only when I got into F3000 that I had to start working on it. When I did karting I used to see people wearing neck braces and I'd think, *What the hell is wrong with these people? I could do another fifty laps.* Formula Ford and Formula Three were the same but after that things started to change. The difference wasn't extreme. I just knew I had to work at it a bit. The big wake-up came during the test I did for Benetton at Brands Hatch. That almost ripped me apart. After ten laps my neck was almost falling off, so the difference between F1 and the junior formula with regards to how fit you had to be was massive, and I don't mind admitting that it took me completely by surprise. I was way off. I think Ayrton had a similar experience, in that, despite being relatively fit, he was caught unawares by the level required in F1.

**Damon:** Perhaps we should go into a bit of detail about the effects that racing a car at speed can have on the body. The problem with us mammals is that we don't tend to have muscles at the front of our necks. They're always at the back. Therefore, when it comes to deceleration, our necks can usually handle it. It's acceleration that's the problem. Combine that with cornering load, which is the force produced by a car turning, and you're doing things to your neck that the human body isn't quite built for. I know astronauts are put in a centrifuge but even then it's vertical, as it is with acrobats. You're either being stretched or crushed. F1 drivers are probably the only people on earth who experiences these kind of movements. The closest equivalent in real life is probably that fairground ride called the waltzer. The one that spins you around and throws you from side to side. Imagine something about five times as powerful as the waltzer that lasts about two hours and you'll be halfway there. Some people assume that in reaction to the g-forces or cornering load you'd tense your neck up or put your head on the headrest, but that isn't what happens. You actually use your head to balance during an F1 race and to gauge how close you are to the edge of what is possible. If you tried to tense up, which would probably be impossible, you'd lose all sensation. If you tried to keep your head on the headrest you'd get bashed about all over the place and you wouldn't be able to see where you're going.

As well as being generally very fit, you obviously have to have a super strong neck and shoulder muscles, and in order to achieve that you obviously have to do lots of neck exercises. I've still got a crash helmet at home with weights on that I used to do a lot of mine with. Something you could probably try at home that will give you an idea of how heavy your head can feel is simply to lie on your back, flat on the floor, and see how long you can hold your head off the ground for. I guarantee that after a minute or two your head will feel like lead. Don't injure yourself, though!

**Johnny:** I used to have an old crash helmet, and after strapping a weight to the top of it I'd put on a very thick jacket, jump on my exercise bike and pedal like hell. I also used to lie on my bed with my head hanging over the side and see how long I could keep it vertical. You see, it was very, very high-tech in those days. I did used to jog a bit before my accident but after that it was impossible, so I just used a bike. Until we got personal trainers, which I did in the early 1990s, you used to go to the gym and just play it by ear. You obviously did a lot of neck and shoulder exercises but there was no schedule, so to speak. No regime. You just did what you thought was right. I was probably at my physical peak in the mid-1990s. I was quite literally a mighty atom.

**Damon:** When I started racing bikes I was horrendously unfit. You used to have to push start your bike at the start of a race and my heart rate must have been about 250 from doing that. Then I'd do about five laps and I'd be absolutely knackered. After a few of these races I thought to myself, *I'm going to have to do something about this.* It was appalling. I started off by taking up jogging and when I first went out I couldn't even go once around the block. It was a genuine rude awakening for me and I look back on it with a certain amount of horror. Being quite competitive by nature, I took my rehabilitation rather seriously and I didn't just want to be fit, I wanted to be the fittest person on earth.

Like you, Johnny, my first experience in an F1 car was testing the Benetton in 1988 and also like you, it almost bloody killed me. I was warned beforehand to get myself something to protect my shins because there was so little room for a fully grown human (you'd have been fine, Herbert) and the steering rack went right across your legs. So I went down the sports shop and bought some Gary Lineker shinpads. After fifteen laps my shins were bruised to hell and my neck was totally knackered. The test took place at Circuit Paul Ricard – the part of the track I found most challenging was the horseshoe; a double right-hander which seemed to go on, and on, and on. As you come out of the horseshoe you obviously have to accelerate and the problem I had was that due to the cornering load going through the horseshoe my head was facing the wrong way as I came out. Had I been required to decelerate then it would have been fine, but with no time for my head to adjust I just had to crack on. I was literally looking out of one eye! The steering on that car was quite light and unfortunately that lulled me into a false sense of security – when I went to Williams I got the shock of my bloody life! I tried driving Nigel's car at Estoril once. I was going around the final corner flat out when I started to realize that I could barely turn the wheel. Nigel's steering wheel also measured about a centimetre less in diameter than most others, which meant you had less leverage. You didn't turn it, as such. You just applied pressure. A lot of pressure! I'm telling you, that man is an absolute bloody animal.

Getting back to my test at Paul Ricard. Afterwards I thought to myself, *I'd be absolutely fine at this, if only I could hold my head up and see where I was going!* Subsequently, the first place I visited afterwards was the gym. When I started doing F3000 I also got a bit of a shock. I remember halfway through my first race, I was sweating, dehydrated and exhausted. The cockpit of a racing car is a violent and bruising environment. Driving is far, far more physical than anyone realizes.

**Johnny:** You remember what I said about lying on the bed with my head over the side? Well, I used to put a bag of sugar on my forehead too, just to add a bit more pressure. Whatever you do, don't try that one at home! Last thing I need is a load of sugary lawsuits. I'll tell you what, though, the environment we used to work in, as in the cockpit of a car, was actually quite violent, yet within that you had to be very precise and quite delicate. I have a theory, Mr Hill. See what you think about this. Because of what we went through during a race, by the end of it I reckon we were slightly concussed. Think about it for a second. Take Hungary, for instance. That race was basically the same as two hours' head-banging, and if you headbang for two hours you're going to be at least a bit punch-drunk. I'm being honest here. It used to take me two days to get over a race. It used to take about a day for the adrenalin to get out of my system, so on the night after a race it was often quite hard to sleep.

One year I came home from a race at Magny-Cours. We were living near Henley-on-Thames at the time and after landing at Heathrow I got in the car and drove home. When I was about halfway there I caught sight of the speedo and realized I was doing about 70 mph in a 30 mph area. I had absolutely no idea I was travelling that fast but because of what I'd been doing all weekend my brain was still in fast mode. It was hardly surprising. It made me think how lucky I was not to have received a ticket, or even worse, run somebody over, as I'd probably been doing the same thing since the start of my career. As a consequence I started watching my speed after returning home from a race, but I bet I'm not the only driver to have done that. In my experience the people who perform best in F1, and I include Champ in this theory, are the ones who, despite the frenetic nature of what happens during a race, can slow everything down in their heads. Do you see what I mean? Not everybody can do it. I certainly can't. It's a real gift, though, as it obviously buys you more time.

**Damon:** It's very interesting hearing you talk about your experiences after a race, Johnny, as it's not something you hear drivers talk about very often. But even before a race we are still racing. During the weeks leading up to races I noticed when I was training that if my mind wandered off to thinking about the upcoming GP my heart rate monitor would start climbing by about 10–20bpm!

I had to try and teach myself to hold off and conserve not just my energy, but my adrenalin. It's actually quite easy to burn yourself out before a race. You can feel the adrenalin and the energy starting to build up and although this is only a theory, I'd say one of the reasons racing drivers often appear quite calm during pre-race interviews is because they're deliberately conserving their energy. It's a psychological strategy, and it's not just about the drive. The race itself is a culmination of a thousand different jobs and conversations and it starts the moment you leave your house. Then, after it's all done you go home, empty the dishwasher and put the bins out.

I think there's something in your theory about us all being slightly concussed after a race, or at the very least punch-drunk. I used to be like a zombie for days. The kids would go, 'Hi Dad, how did it go?' and I'd just stand there trying to register what they just said. It's probably the opposite of what you experienced on the roads, Johnny, in that instead of my brain remaining in fast mode for a few days it would develop a delay. The race that used to take it out of me the most was always Monaco. For a start you have to be there on the Wednesday instead of the Thursday and the entire five days are loud, unrelenting and stupendously frenetic. To me, being right in the middle of all that, your brain circuitry is being burnt out and until at least the following Wednesday I'd be good for bugger all.

In 1994 I was required to go testing on the Tuesday after the Monaco Grand Prix and it's safe to say that I wasn't really at the races. I was there physically, but not mentally, and after a few laps I came into the garage, got out of the car and said, 'Sorry, Frank, but this isn't working. I'm no use to you.' To which he replied irritably, 'Michael Schumacher will be doing a hundred laps around Fiorano today!' 'Well go and get Michael bloody Schumacher then!' I said, before getting into my car and finding somewhere to cool off. A weekend at Monaco is a mental marathon.

**Johnny:** I'll tell you who's got the whole conserving your energies thing down to a fine art – Lewis. He's got it written into his contract that he only has to do a certain amount of appearances and interviews per season, which makes sense, and he doesn't even do the simulator anymore, and why should he? He's saving the maximum amount of energy for the part of his job that really matters, and that's the race weekend.

One thing that really helped me when I was coming back after my accident, physically and mentally, was being able to simulate an entire race weekend – from a driving point of view – by having a monocoque from the previous year's Benetton sent over. It was Peter Collins who suggested it and it had been fitted with a seat, pedals and gear change. To make it more authentic and to enable me to build up my strength he made everything spring-loaded. I'd do two free practice sessions on the Friday – one on the morning and one in the afternoon. I'd do qualifying on the Saturday, a warm-up for half an hour on the Sunday morning and then I'd do the race, and all from the cockpit.

Before that I'd been sent to Austria by Benetton to work with a chap called Toni Mathis. He was basically a sadist masquerading as a physiotherapist and he spent months giving me exercises to do that would invariably have me crying my eyes out. One of the worst experiences I had there wasn't even an exercise, and happened when the Mercedes DTM team, complete with five-time champ Bernd Schneider, arrived to do a fitness course. We all went into Feldkirch one night, which was the local town, and to get where we wanted to go we had to scale about 600 steps. I'd only recently stopped using crutches and my left foot in particular felt like a lump of steel. To this day it won't bend backwards at all which means that in order to scale steps I have to bend my hip out. The DTM team scaled the steps in no time at all and by the time the last one made it to the top old Hopalong Herbert had done about five. It was agony!

Unfortunately, I had to leave the boys to it and go back to Toni's and when I arrived I made the fatal mistake of telling him what had occurred. *Aha!* he must have thought. *Here's an opportunity to inflict yet more pain!* The following day he marched me back to Feldkirch and made me scale the steps three or four times. The pain was so bad I almost vomited but Mad Mathis wasn't done there. The following day he took me to a forest on a steep hill and made me march up and down for an entire day. My entire left ankle was red raw and at one point I thought the wound was going to open. Unfortunately my right foot was in an equally bad state. It had been bent around so badly that the ligaments had been torn, meaning that my toes were pointing downwards, like talons. Each toe was hypersensitive, which made walking up steps a nightmare and walking up or downhill purgatory. Every step I took with the right foot felt like I was smashing already fractured bones against a brick wall. I've never cried as much in my entire life. Crying when you're sad is often followed by a spell of feeling better whereas crying when you're in pain is something you do because you're at the end of your tether. Neither are particularly nice but the latter of the two is more concentrated.

You know what they say, though: no pain, no gain. As much as I jokingly call him a sadist, Toni was one of the reasons I was able to be lowered into my car in Rio for that first Grand Prix, so I've a lot to thank the mad sadistic bastard for.

**Damon:** God, that sounds awful, Johnny. Poor little Herbert. Did you ever suffer from depression during your rehabilitation?

**Johnny:** Yes, but only in short bouts. In fact, I'm not even sure you could categorize it as depression. Once a month for about twenty-four hours a voice in my head would start saying, *I can't do this anymore, I want it to stop*, and for the time it was there I'd be an absolute wreck, crying and stuff. The following morning I would invariably feel better so it was probably just a release.

Getting back to the physical stuff. When we were driving, the standard of fitness instructors and physios in the UK was nowhere near as good as in Europe. We were years behind. It's only in the past twenty years or so that we've started catching up and now we must be on a par. We can't afford not to be. What did footballers do in the 1960s and 1970s in order to keep fit? Apart from smoking and drinking pints of beer. They used to run and wave their arms a bit. That's certainly what we did at school on the football team.

**Damon:** I can't imagine you playing football. Tiddlywinks, maybe.

**Johnny:** I was brilliant, in a crap kind of way. Because I had a blond mullet, the stock-in-trade refrain from whoever was picking the teams during the games lesson would be, 'But sir, he looks like a girl!' I did score two goals in my first game for the school, though. Because I was very nervous I kept on passing the ball back to the goalkeeper and one time he wasn't there. That was one goal. The next one, which I scored against the opposition as opposed to *for* the opposition, was just a mistake really. The goalie tried to clear the ball and it hit my left bum cheek and went in. That's me to a tee, that is. Doesn't know which goal to score in and is ultimately a bit of an arse.

**Damon:** That's what upsets me about you, Johnny. Always going on about how brilliant you are. After Jackie, the next driver to start taking fitness seriously was probably Niki. After his accident he brought in Willi Dungl to help him, who until then had been working with the Austrian ski jumping team. Niki's work ethic was amazing, so despite the circumstances being unfortunate he was the perfect person to start championing the cause of improved mental and physical fitness in F1. The only thing that surprises me slightly is how long it took to filter through the rest of the grid. It obviously did eventually, but given the difference it made to Niki's recovery and career in general, you'd have thought every driver would have been running to the gym and booking an hour on a psychiatrist's couch. Then again, F1 drivers can be quite stubborn creatures, so it doesn't surprise me too much. The next driver who springs to mind on this subject is Michael. He always took fitness very seriously indeed and while striving for world domination it would have been an important part of his arsenal. Nobody covered as many bases as Michael Schumacher did. Eddie Irvine, on the other hand, always used to claim that he had no time for fitness regimes and that his condition, which was obviously at a fairly high standard, was just because he had special 'fit' genes.

All together now, Johnny! One, two, three, four – WHAT A LOAD OF BOLLOCKS! Jordan reckoned that Irvine could have been World Champion if he could only have been arsed. He said he was the laziest driver of all time. Apparently, he never got up before noon. But you never really know. Especially with Irvine. He was apt to say stuff just to wind everyone up.

You couldn't have driven five laps in those days without having a very high standard of fitness. It wasn't possible. Moving on to the present day, it's almost a badge of honour now for F1 drivers to be supremely fit, and that's an incredibly positive message. I'm not sure they need to be as fit as they actually are, because they're not always required to drive to the limit. That's something I still find very odd.

Do you remember a programme called *Superstars*, Johnny? A judoka called Brian Jacks is the chap who is perhaps most associated with the show, and it was presented by David Vine. For those who never saw it, the show would pitch athletes from different sports against each other to see who was the fittest, and it ran from the early 1970s until the mid-1980s. They did revive it a few years back, but it wasn't a patch on the original.

In 1981 they made an international version of the show called *World Superstars* and who should pop up in the field of ten but the 1979 F1 World Champion, Jody Scheckter. Given F1's reputation at the time, which didn't exactly scream healthy living, it's fair to say that Jody wasn't the favourite. After all, he was up against the likes of Edwin Moses, the celebrated American Olympic hurdler, the rugby players Andy Ripley and Keith Fielding and a famous American football player called Russ Francis, to name but a few. Motor racing drivers weren't even considered to be athletes in those days so Jody's inclusion was actually met with a certain amount of derision from some quarters. Understandably, to a certain extent. After all, to the uninitiated what did F1 drivers actually do, apart from sit down for a few hours? The events comprised of a tennis knockout, which Jody won quite easily, a gym test, in which he came second, two heats and a final in swimming, weightlifting for max, rowing, hundred yard dash in heats (Moses won that one, not surprisingly), a bike race, a half-mile run and finally an obstacle course.

The modern-day equivalent of this would be the American-invented competitive fitness sport, CrossFit, which incorporates elements from a variety of different sports and exercises, including high-intensity interval training, Olympic weightlifting, gymnastics and strongman, to name but a few. The all-encompassing nature of CrossFit has to be matched by the fitness of its protagonists, and as a consequence its most talented athletes are considered to be among the fittest human beings on earth. In order to win *World Superstars* you also had to be supremely fit and Jody surprised everyone, although probably not himself, by winning the competition and also a cheque for $35,000. Apparently, in the gym test, he applied motor oil to his shoes to help him do squat thrusts. He finished second, so it must have helped. How many times have we said it, Herbert? You have to read the regulations!

**Johnny:** I used to absolutely love *Superstars.* Jackie Stewart took part in the very first series of the show in 1973 and finished joint third with Joe Bugner, behind David Hemery and Barry John. More surprisingly – in fact this is incredible – in 1976 James Hunt took part in the show and finished third behind David Hemery and John Conteh. He wasn't tied with anyone either, so technically speaking James's performance on *Superstars* was marginally better than Jackie's. Jackie won't like that. Beaten by a womanizing cad? Good heavens no. I think James was a freak of nature, and as far as I know the heart attack that killed him wasn't caused by his lifestyle – it was genetic. His brother, David, who also raced a bit, also died of a heart attack and he was only in his mid-fifties. It's very sad, because we knew both of them. David Hunt was responsible for bringing the biggest sponsor of F3 into the sport, the mobile phone company Cellnet.

**Damon:** I'll tell you one thing we haven't touched on yet, and that's hobbies. Despite the frantic schedule of F1, there are times when there is nothing to do, so you need something to fill your time. I usually have a guitar nearby. I'm obviously highly untalented because I still can't really play, but it fills time and helps me think. The best example I have of an axe relieving boredom took place back in 1997.

After I won the Championship but was kicked out of Didcot, I went to drive for Arrows. People thought I was mad because they had never won a race and never even looked like winning one. But they had a couple of aces up their sleeve. The first was an exclusive tyre deal with Bridgestone, and the second was John Barnard, the genius behind McLaren's domination of F1 with Prost and Senna in the late 1980s. They had also offered me the one-year contract I needed to keep open the chance of driving for McLaren the following year, which was where I knew Adrian Newey was going. It was a perfect plan and it nearly worked, but that's another story.

The point is, while Arrows were trying to get some speed out of their car, they had one really weak link in the plan; the engine kept blowing up. If it was the most powerful engine in F1 and kept blowing up, that would have been a tolerable frustration, but it was probably the least powerful engine in F1. It was badged as a Yamaha, but really it was a Judd. Yamaha have a great reputation for making excellent motorcycles. Some people thought they should have stuck to that. This was their first attempt at an F1 engine. The only thing that was reliable about it was that you could rely on it to blow up. In winter testing in Barcelona at the start of 1997, I'd get in the car, do a few laps, and it would detonate or just break down. I spent many hours just hanging around waiting for another engine to be ripped out and a new one put in.

There I was, the newly crowned F1 World Champion, just kicking my heels and loafing around the paddock. Fed up and frustrated with wasting my time doing nothing. *Sod this*, I thought, and jumped in the hire car. At least that worked! I went to a guitar shop and bought a lovely cherry-red Washburn acoustic. I spent most of the rest of the test learning to play 'Don't Think Twice, It's All Right' by Bob Dylan, which has an apt line about someone wasting your time.

**Johnny:** Heck! You haven't got it here, have you? I can feel my inner Dylan coming out.

# CHAPTER ELEVEN

## Driving by the seat of your pants

**Damon:** Strange things can happen when you're driving an F1 car, and both Johnny and I have experienced what many would term as being an out-of-body experience. Has anybody reading this ever slipped on a bit of ice, expected to fall and then found themselves standing up rather than lying on the ground? Well, that's the kind of thing we're talking about here, only it goes on for a lot longer.

My own experience happened at Suzuka in 1994. I was chasing Michael for the World Championship and was just five points behind him when we arrived in Japan. The race started in torrential rain and by lap twenty-seven there were just thirteen runners remaining. By this time Michael was 6.8 seconds ahead of me, which would end up being crucial as the race would eventually be split into two after being red flagged and the result would be determined by the aggregate times from both parts of the race.

Anyway, as I went into the final lap I'd completely run out of ideas. My tyres were worn and Michael had driven out of his skin. I described it in my autobiography as the highest level of driving I'd ever experienced and I'd taken myself to the edge of my ability.

Now, though, I had nothing left and I knew that Michael would have me unless I could find something extra. But where from? Even my inner voice appeared to have thrown in the towel and I remember saying to myself, 'Ayrton, if you're up there, I could do with a bit of a hand down here.' The only way I can describe what happened next is that from the exit of turn one to the hairpin halfway around the lap I was possessed of an ability to drive way, way beyond my normal limits. I distinctly remember watching my hands move the wheel but I was completely removed from what was happening. I was a passenger in my own car and appeared to have surrendered control to something paranormal. It still makes the hairs on the back of my hand stand up.

The experience wasn't completely alien to me as in junior formulae I'd sometimes reacted to situations so fast that you were left thinking, *Who the hell did that?* It's like slipping on ice but staying upright, as I said. It all happens too quick to be able to say, 'I did that.' But in those situations instinct had been like a stabilizer, whereas this time it appeared to be actually driving the bloody car! To cut a long story short I ended up winning the race and in all of the eighty-seven Grands Prix that followed in my career I never came close to driving like that again. Never. Not even close. When I got out of the car I had to hide in the stairwell for a while before taking to the podium as I just couldn't get my head around what had just happened. I didn't tell anybody about this for years, by the way, because I can see how people might think I'm making it up just to sell a book or something. But I don't have to convince anyone. I'm just telling you what happened to me. You can take it or leave it. But next time you slip on the ice and don't fall, ask yourself how you managed to stay upright. You didn't think about it, I can tell you. It all happens too fast. Welcome to the world of the racing driver. We are constantly slipping on the ice.

**Johnny:** Stirling Moss used to call it driving by the seat of your pants. Had you wanted to, would you have been able to take back control of the car while it was happening?

**Damon:** I'm not sure. It was almost as if conscious thought was holding me back from interfering. It's a paradox, as when a driver concentrates on getting a quick lap what they're actually doing is letting go. I'm sure you've experienced it, Johnny. The quickest laps you do are the ones where you think less and feel more.

**Johnny:** Absolutely. My own experience, which isn't too different to yours in many ways, happened in Sepang at the 1999 Malaysian Grand Prix. It was the race following my win at the Nürburgring and I arrived in Malaysia on a bit of a cloud. It was a new circuit, which was exciting, and the win in Germany, not to mention Rubens's podium, had put everyone in a really good mood. The big difference between our experiences is that mine seemed to last all weekend and after qualifying fifth behind the two McLarens and the two Ferraris, I jumped back on my cloud and just revelled in what was happening.

Like you, I honestly felt like I'd been possessed by something, as although I felt at one with the car – more so than I ever had done at any time in my career – I honestly don't remember lifting a finger. Like you, I've thought about my experience long and hard and the only explanations I can offer are the cloud of euphoria I'd been travelling on and/or the fact that we were driving a new circuit. What makes me doubt these theories somewhat is that when I've watched the coverage of that weekend back there's an urgency to my driving that I don't think had been there since before my accident.

The only time I experienced something similar in F1 was at Adelaide sometime during the 1990s. I remember aquaplaning down the Brabham Straight at about 200 mph and the next thing I knew I was arriving at the hairpin. It was almost as if I lost consciousness for a moment and the dilemma that had been going on in my head as I started to aquaplane just disappeared. I think that experience was more 'driving by the seat of your pants' as opposed to being possessed by a poltergeist.

**Damon:** Or in your case, by somebody who can actually drive.

**Johnny:** You really are a \*\*\*\*. Anyway, you remember earlier when I quoted Rory Byrne? He said that he could design the best chassis and get the best tyres and the best engine, but at the end of the day there's just one weakness, and that's the driver. I think that relates to what we both experienced and what we experienced was us letting go of what prevents us from putting in a perfect drive. Or as near perfect as we're able. Drivers are always checking and double checking what they're doing and what we lack is faith – not confidence – faith, in our own abilities. In Malaysia, I had faith not just in my own ability, but in everything and everyone around me and I was able to let go. Like you, I'd had glimpses of it once or twice in my early days but that was the first and only time it happened to me in F1. I read this magazine on a plane once—

**Damon:** What colour was it?

**Johnny:** Less of your cheek, Hill! The article was saying the human brain is wired to doubt and ask questions, so that's going to be the default position for every F1 driver. If the doubting ever stops for a while, like it did with us, your abilities have to match your faith, otherwise you're screwed! Fortunately ours did.

One thing we haven't mentioned yet as a possible explanation is that both of us were going through a pretty emotional time.

Especially you. My emotions were a bit more reflective but the theory still stands. There was a lot going on in our heads at the time.

**Damon:** I've been thinking about your question as to whether I would have been able to take back control of the car and the more I think about it the more convinced I am that I couldn't lift my foot off the throttle. In fact I'm adamant I couldn't have. After the kink at turn one the car suddenly took off through the chicanes and I remember thinking, *What the bloody hell's going on? It's not slowing down!*

**Johnny:** I never experienced that, for the simple reason I was always flat out. There was never any conflict going on in my brain, such as it is. It was pedal to the metal, every lap, every time.

Talking of brains, drivers spend half their lives in a state of hyper-awareness that can often be quite useful in real life. Damon, how many times have you pulled somebody out of the way of danger without even thinking about it? I bet it's loads. I certainly have. F1 drivers constantly anticipate danger. It might be subliminal sometimes but if and when it occurs the reaction is instantaneous. I'm not saying we're cleverer than other people (well, *he* is), we're just a bit more present. That said, it does all change when you stop racing.

**Damon:** It most certainly does. You tend to fall to the back of the grid a bit when you stop racing. Like when you go live on Sky Sports. I must admit, I've been taken by surprise more than once in this situation.

'What did they just say? Say that again. What lap is it?'

'Too late. We're live.'

'Bugger!'

Not so much an out-of-body experience. More an out-of-touch experience!

Do you remember that Formula Three race in 1986, Johnny, the one with the geese? He's looking at me quizzically, ladies and gentleman, which means he's either forgotten or he wasn't there. If memory serves me correctly, I don't think you were there for some reason. Anyway, the venue was Zandvoort and on the first lap Paul Radisich's back wheel fell off. Coming out of the hairpin at Hugenholtzbocht, this wheel just flew over the top of everyone and it ended up in the paddock. I can remember watching it fly high over my head as I came out of the turn and thinking, *What the bloody hell is that and where's it going?* It's a wonder nobody was killed. But no one lifts off, and we race on over the fabulous dunes. As we crest the hill at the back of the track and start descending on this fantastic rollercoaster-ride of a circuit, a family of seemingly deaf and blind geese decide to walk across the track.

Maurizio Sandro Sala, who was leading the race, tried to avoid them and went left onto the grass. The following pack, of which I was one, sort of did a Red Arrows manoeuvre and fanned out all over the place, while the rest had absolutely no chance of avoiding these geese, and what followed must have resembled a pillow fight between the cast of *Reservoir Dogs*. We pressed on, of course, but as we came to the start line this jalopy comes out of the pit lane with flashing lights on the roof, so we all dutifully line up behind it thinking it must be a pace car – or safety car as we call them now – for Paul's accident. For a couple of seconds we all sat behind this car wondering what to do, then Julian Baily just makes a break for it! So we all dither for about one second before concluding, *If he's going then so am I!* So off we charge and race on through the carnage. Turns out it was a doctor's car not a pace car and Julian could read the sign! At the end of the race we were all so stoked. It was epic. But our cars were all covered in blood and white feathers! Tragic really. For the geese, I mean.

Have you hit anything during a race, Johnny?

**Johnny:** Yes. Cars, usually. I've hit a lot of them over the years.

**Damon:** Nice work.

# CHAPTER TWELVE

## Has F1 lost a bit of its soul?

**Johnny:** Personally I think the soul of F1 is still there. It's just partly obscured. The Champ and I are on the same page with this, and I think part of the goal has to be taking away the things that prevent drivers from being themselves in a race situation. We want to know what makes them tick and at the moment that's kind of hidden away. Sure, we get glimpses occasionally, but it's not enough.

We understand the team's anxieties. Teams these days are multi-million-pound operations and they have responsibilities, not only to sponsors and advertisers, but to thousands of employees, suppliers and their own brand. Some would argue that that in itself is responsible for part of that soul disappearing, but that's progress for you. If you want to blame anybody then blame Bernie. I appreciate we're going over old ground slightly but the soul of F1 will only truly return when the teams both realize and accept that they are in the entertainment business. The 'win at any costs' attitude has been part of the sport since day one. What's changed is the fact that the 'costs' are no longer carried by the drivers and the risks they take. In fact, they could be carried by any one of about a hundred different people. Perhaps more.

So, let's get onto Liberty Media, who I understand paid Bernie $4.6 billion for F1. Not a bad return of investment, is it? Especially if you bear in mind he never bought it in the first place. I've actually been quite impressed with what Liberty Media have brought to the table so far. At Abu Dhabi in 2019, for instance, the grid after the race was absolutely rammed with spectators. It was awesome. There was a time in Bernie's era when that wouldn't have happened and if I had one big criticism of his stewardship, one I believe was partly responsible for taking away the soul of F1, it would be making the experience of attending a Grand Prix too remote and too corporate. In 2019, Silverstone opened up the pit lane to the public for the first time in donkey's years and it made the weekend very special indeed. Part of the soul came back! Under Bernie's watch I don't think it would have happened. That privilege would have been reserved for the corporate guests. Allowing the general public on there as well, even at a different time, would have made the experience less attractive to the VIPs, and therefore less valuable. The public absolutely loved it, of course, as did we.

I think Bernie's idea was always to tease the fans and give them just enough contact with the sport to make them want to come back. In other words, the bare minimum. Like access to the pit lane, over-delivering on what you'd promised was a luxury reserved for the corporates and the VIPs. The big money, in other words. I think one of the problems is that F1 has changed so quickly over the years and nobody's had time to breathe.

**Damon:** Bernie's tactic was that if you take things away from people they'll give you a lot of money to get them back again. As long as they've been improved slightly or there's at least a noticeable difference, generally they'll cough up. I think that probably worked for a certain amount of time, for the simple reason that so much needed to change. Things have calmed down a bit now and the race-going public have started to demand more, as well they might.

But it's not just contact with the cars that the public yearn for while they're wandering up and down the pit lane. They want contact with the drivers, too. You talked earlier, Johnny, about going to Silverstone and seeing James Hunt signing autographs for an hour or two. That kind of driver interaction was all but eradicated under Bernie. Once again, it was a privilege reserved for the high rollers and not the hoi polloi. Sadly, and rather unfairly. The 'hoi polloi' are the genuine enthusiasts of the sport – they are the ones who would appreciate that kind of interaction the most and for many years it was restricted to the drivers' parade lap and little else. As with the pit lane, this is now starting to change too, slowly but surely, and thank God for it.

In 2019 I attended the Indianapolis 500 to see if Fernando could emulate my dad's Triple Crown and boy, do the Americans know how to put on a show. The razzamatazz takes up at least half of the proceedings and regardless of whether you're a fan or not you can't help getting swept up in it. They've got marching bands, cheerleaders and God knows what. The crowd can also wander around the paddock and talk to the mechanics. It's a cornucopia of motorsport, a carnival, and the entire event screams inclusivity. That's what I loved about it.

I watched a video recently of Dad winning the race back in 1966 and even then, everything was geared towards entertaining the 275,000 people who had made the journey. Americans just get it. They really do. I'm hoping that because Liberty Media are an American organization and own the Atlanta Braves they'll appreciate where F1 has been going wrong and bring us in line a bit. It certainly seems like they're trying to. I read an article recently about Tottenham Hotspur and their new stadium. Instead of the fans just turning up for a pie and a pint half an hour before the game and then leaving straight afterwards, they're looking for ways to get their supporters to come for the entire day. After all, how else are they going to pay for the stadium? In order to make that happen they're going to have to rethink the way football is presented in this country, and that's exactly what we're having to do with F1. In fact, I think we're slightly ahead of the game in that respect.

**Johnny:** Many years ago DC and I got off a plane in Tokyo and went straight to the Tokyo Dome to watch a baseball game, and it was shocking. Baseball can certainly be exciting, but it can also be as boring as hell and if that's the case, in America at least, you can guarantee there'll be plenty going on to take the onus off the game. Unfortunately, the Japanese had adopted the sport but not the philosophy to entertain the fans, and subsequently I fell asleep in the grandstand. To counter that, when I was racing out in the States I brought the family over and we went to see the San Francisco Giants. It's like you say, Damon, the entire day was filled with entertainment and the game itself, which was actually quite good, was just part of the proceedings. What really sold it for me was being able to get popcorn and beer at my seat. I'm a simple man really, with simple needs, and as long as I'm fed, watered and entertained, which I was, then I'm good. I remember leaving the stadium thinking, *That was bloody brilliant!* Not just the game but the entire experience.

**Damon:** Can you imagine an F1 version of the Indy 500? They sort of tried it at the US GP a couple of years back with Michael Buffer, he of the famous 'Let's Get Ready to Rumble!' shout before big boxing fights. It kind of backfired, though, with a lot of the drivers looking a bit self-conscious. Maybe they should have had Nigel? 'And now, all the way from Beeeeeeeeeermingham, Ingland, it's "Il Leone", Nigeeeeeeeeeeeeeeeel, MANSAAAAAAAAAAAAAAAAAAL!' Nigel then runs out of the garage waving like a contestant on *The Price is Right* and leaps into his car headfirst.

Every F1 driver worth his salt has a nickname. Fangio was known as El Maestro, Dad was Mr Monaco, Jim Clark was Mr Smooth (same for Jackie in our book), Mike Hailwood was Mike the Bike, Vittorio Brambilla was the Monza Gorilla (one of my favourites), Mike Hawthorn was Papillon (I suppose because of his bow tie?), Niki was the Rat, Alain was obviously The Professor, Mika was the Flying Finn, Fernando was Telefonso, which may or may not have had something to do with the spygate and crashgate controversies, and Kimi, of course, is the Iceman.

What was yours again?

**Johnny:** It was The Imp when I was in F3 and Little 'Un in F1. Mark Blundell's was Mega, but I think that was down to his size more than his ability to drive a car. JOKE! Brundle's was Billy Bob, which I believe has something to do with his proficiency on the banjo, and yours was Secret Squirrel, because you always kept your cards very close to your chest. Thinking about it, we actually do nicknames quite well in F1. Generally speaking, they actually tend to mean something in our sport and there's usually a story behind them.

Never truer than when Nico Rosberg was christened Britney. We have Mark Webber to thank for this and the story, which I read in full recently in a piece written by the BBC's Andrew Benson, is an absolute cracker. It really highlights Mark's fabulous sense of humour, not to mention Nico's gorgeous blond locks. During their final race together at Williams, which was in Brazil, Nico rammed into the back of Mark's car on the opening lap, breaking the nose on his car and Webber's rear wing.

Because it was going to be quicker for the team to repair Nico's car than Mark's, a message went over the radio giving Nico priority. Annoyed at his teammate's mistake, Mark was determined to get back to the pits first, and so they began to race, despite Nico suffering from a lack of front grip and Mark with his dodgy rear. As they came onto the pit straight Nico was just ahead but lost control going through the flat-out kink just before the pits and crashed heavily into a concrete barrier. Mark was right behind him and, as he passed his stricken teammate, the team came back on the radio issuing another message about Nico having priority. After pausing for a second, probably for comic effect, Mark said in his languid Aussie brogue, 'Don't think so, mate. Britney's in the wall.' To me that was absolute genius and ever since then I've never been able to look at Nico without humming, 'Hit Me Baby One More Time'. Perhaps he will if he reads this? I wonder what he looks like in a school uniform?

**Damon:** For heaven's sake! Going back to Michael Buffer again – because it's fun – I couldn't quite imagine Ayrton receiving the Buffer treatment, could you? 'From Sao Paulo, Brazil, it's Ayyyyyyyyrton Sey-naaaaaaaaar.' Ayrton wasn't exactly a Daniel Ricciardo, was he? He'd probably have walked out backwards with his arms folded, looking moody yet magnificent. James Hunt would have made the best entrance, and for very obvious reasons. He'd have had at least two girls on each arm, one of whom would have been dragging an intravenous champagne drip on wheels, and a Marlboro sticking out of the side of his mouth. What I wouldn't give to see that.

So, what about the new guard? They haven't really been around long enough to have earned themselves a nickname yet, or at least one that refers to either their style of driving or their hair. It appears that Lando Norris was known, for a time at least, as the Meme King of F1. Not knowing what a meme is, and being confident it has nothing whatsoever to do with aesthetics or driving, I think we'll move swiftly on. As Johnny has just informed me, George Russell is yet to be issued with an appropriate sobriquet, so you've got one for him, Johnny, haven't you? But after he went driving in the Styrian GP perhaps we should just call him St. George!

**Johnny:** If I had to give George Russell a nickname it would be Mr Tumble. Not because he crashes a lot, but because he looks like a children's television entertainer. It's that huge smiley grin of his. In fact, just to complete the effect I think he should learn to make dogs using balloons and should have a huge red 'G' sewn onto the front of his overalls.

Because he's incredibly rich and has lots of famous friends in America, Lewis has two nicknames: The Ham and the Billion Dollar Man. In respect of the fact that we're supposed to be consuming less these days, I've decided to amalgamate the two and knock off a few quid, so from now on Lewis will be known as the Million Dollar Ham. Imagine that. A million dollar ham. It'd be absolutely enormous! Then there's Max, of course, who was nicknamed Mad Max by Esteban Ocon a few years ago. Apparently young Max didn't take too kindly to this, so in the interests of keeping everyone happy might I suggest we change it to Moderately Mad Max instead. His father, Jos, who is a good friend of mine, was known as either Jos the Boss or the Dutch Devil. To me, the latter sounds like a cross between a vacuum cleaner and a porn star, so for that reason and that reason alone I think we'll plump for the former.

The fact that many of the new guard don't yet have nicknames doesn't mean they don't have big, interesting personalities or individual styles of driving, because they do. Fortunately, they didn't start their careers in F1, otherwise that might be the case. They need for them to be able to express those personalities on the track, and the fact that we are getting glimpses is certainly encouraging. I suppose one of the advantages of social media is that the drivers are able to interact with the public any time they like. To me that's also a potential disadvantage, as it makes the prospect of seeing them in the flesh and at close quarters at a Grand Prix less attractive. After all, when there's always biscuits in the tin, where's the fun in biscuits? I'm hoping it works the other way and fuels people's interest.

Lewis recently articulated the importance of having so much young talent coming through. He said, 'The core of what I do is that I love racing. I love the challenge. I love arriving knowing I have got these incredibly talented youngsters who are trying to beat me and outperform me, outsmart me, and I love that battle that I get into every single year.' Without discounting the importance of the car you're driving, that's an extremely positive message for the sport as a whole, and I think the balance on the grid between youth and experience is as good as it's ever been.

**Damon:** What was that about biscuits in the tin again? Where do you get this stuff! Getting back to characters and fan interaction for a second, I think Dad used to treat every Grand Prix like a show, basically, and he used to enjoy transforming himself into the man who the fans believed was the real Graham Hill. In truth, Graham Hill the racing driver wasn't too different to Graham Hill the husband or dad. Not day to day. But there was definitely a change. Something came to life. He wasn't the only one, of course.

An F1 event is like a play, in a way, featuring an array of unique and distinctive characters. The greatest example of a character transcending their sport is undoubtedly Muhammad Ali. F1 was always an ensemble piece, in that the soap opera that surrounded the sport and created quite a bit of interest relied on each person playing their role effectively. With boxing it was effectively a one-man show. Other 'characters' followed, but Ali was so talented, engaging and entertaining, that you couldn't help thinking to yourself, regardless of whether they could box or not, *You're no Ali*. F1, like every sport, has turned in on itself occasionally and there have been periods where the characters within the sport either haven't been very interesting or haven't been allowed to be. You don't expect every driver on the grid to be able to hold the audience on their own. What you always hope for, though, are a couple of villains, a joker or six, somebody who is evidently unhinged and unpredictable, and a slightly hapless underdog with a mullet. Or you could have Herbert here, who is all of the above! If you could bottle it, Herbert, you'd be a billionaire.

I know I'll be accused of being anti-Schumacher but one of the least entertaining periods F1 experienced was probably the early noughties. At that time, the disparity between the amount of respect F1 seemed to expect from its public and the amount the public were willing to give it was absolutely huge. It almost became a kind of religious ceremony going to an F1 race, in that you were always expected to believe that what you were watching was really significant and if you ever dared to criticize it you were branded a heretic. I remember thinking to myself one day, 'This really has gone too far now.'

I come back to the original question of whether has F1 lost a bit of its soul since becoming more corporate. If you stripped away all the TV coverage, and the sponsors, and the VIPs, the people who turn up to watch a Grand Prix will still be the same people. They, together with the cars, the drivers and the teams, are the soul of F1 and regardless of how much money is thrown about or how much a hamburger costs or a pint of beer, that will never change. I agree with you, Johnny. The soul of F1 hasn't been eradicated, it's been obscured a bit, and I dare say F1 isn't the only sport with the same issues.

**Johnny:** I know we must sound like a couple of grumpy old gits sometimes but this conversation has actually made me feel quite positive. We have a great crop of drivers, young and old, and attendances rose almost 8 per cent in 2019. The Australian Grand Prix attracted 102,000 fans on race day and over 324,000 over the entire weekend. That was an increase of over 30,000 on the previous year. Not surprisingly, Silverstone attracted the biggest crowd of the year, with a massive 351,000 people descending on Northamptonshire over the weekend and 141,000 on race day. Our goodly employers, Sky Sports F1, also saw an increase of about 2.2 million viewers in 2019, and it can't all be down to Brundle.

What's really been driven home during this conversation is, yet again, the importance of the driver. If you go to a circus, the people you're really in awe of are the acrobats. You admire their skill, their strength and their tenacity, and that's ultimately what sells the show. It's not the candyfloss or the clowns. You go there to watch a group of highly trained and highly talented individuals performing acts that you could only dream of performing. However fantastic they look or however technologically advanced they are, the cars in F1 aren't going anywhere without the drivers, so exactly the same thing applies. Regardless of how many people it takes to make a Grand Prix happen, and there must be tens or even hundreds of thousands in total, the drivers *are* the show and one of the reasons

I'm feeling so positive is because I think we're finally starting to remember that. I want to know what their emotional state is both before, during and after a Grand Prix. I want to know what their flaws are and what they think of the other drivers. I want *Gone with the Wind* on wheels! I want scandal, intrigue, speed, suspicion, danger, wealth, nice dresses, champagne, parties, unrequited love and lots and lots of lovely sex. You name it, I want it!

**Damon:** I think you need to start going to a day centre during the off season. I agree with your films analogy, though. Or was it just a plea? Either way, it all relates back to what you said about the circus. In the background you have lots of very talented people beavering away but the magic will only happen when Clark Gable and the actress whose name I can't remember walk onto the set and start acting.

**Johnny:** They'd have a job now. Hattie Jacques?

**Damon:** No. Vivien Leigh. Hattie Jacques? You've got *Carry On* on the brain. I thought the Netflix series *Drive to Survive* was like a breath of fresh air. Or in the case of Guenther Steiner, foul air! It allowed people to connect with the effort that goes into being part of an F1 team and I'm glad it got a second series. In fact, by the time this book comes out most readers will have seen the second series, which was even better than the first, I thought, partly because you had Mercedes and Ferrari in there too. But the old favourites Haas and Guenther Steiner were classic. I think it lets people into the real stress and drama of the game.

At the 2019 United States Grand Prix, which attracted a combined audience upwards of 300,000, both Johnny and I noticed that, not only did there appear to be more people, but the atmosphere there was buzzing with anticipation and you got the feeling these people knew a lot more about F1. I just got the feeling that *Drive to Survive* was responsible for attracting at least some of the extra people, and if F1 can build on and maintain its popularity across the pond – which, let's face it, it's never really been able to do – then who knows what might happen. Putting the Yanks in charge, you see. That's been the masterstroke. God Bless America.

# CHAPTER THIRTEEN

## Favourite F1 driver(s) of all time

**Damon:** Johnny Herbert.

**Johnny:** Ditto.

# CHAPTER THIRTEEN (PART TWO)

## Same question again, only serious this time

**Johnny:** When I was a young whipper-snapper my favourite F1 driver was Gilles Villeneuve. I'll tell you for why, shall I? Well, I forget when it was exactly – probably 1981 – but at Zandvoort during the Dutch Grand Prix Gilles got a puncture after having a rub against somebody. He'd only just passed the exit to the pit lane so had just under a lap before he could come in. In order to protect their wheel and prevent an accident, most drivers would have slowed right down until reaching the pits, but not Gilles. If anything he sped up! The TV cameras stayed on him while this was going on and slowly but surely the tyre began unravelling itself from the wheel until it finally rolled off onto the grass. Or what was left of it. Surely he'll have to slow down now, we all thought. He did slow down a bit, but he must still have been going at over a ton. I was transfixed! After losing the tyre completely the rim started making contact with the track and for what must have been about a quarter of a mile the rear side of Gilles car resembled a mobile foundry!

To a lad in his teens who'd been karting for a few years and who hadn't been completely averse – unintentionally, of course – to losing the odd wheel here and there, this was manna from heaven. I wouldn't have been aware of the word then but the endeavour Gilles showed by trying to stay in the race was mesmerizing, and it completely changed my mentality. What it said to me was, it doesn't matter what situation you're in, you've got to get yourself back into the race as soon as you possibly can no matter what. When it came to Gilles racing, I'd already seen his now fabled duel for second place against René Arnoux at the 1979 French Grand Prix, and to me the Zandvoort lap merely consolidated his position as the ultimate racer. Whenever I got into a kart, I was just pretending to be Gilles Villeneuve. Every time.

The thing is, you didn't have to be a racer or even an F1 fan to appreciate the mercurial talent of a driver like Gilles. It was fruitcakes like him who used to make kids like me run into school on a Monday and start yapping away to anyone who'd listen about how fantastic the previous day's Grand Prix was. There's no doubting that definitely rubbed off on a few people. Today, probably thanks to the glamour of the sport and perhaps to a certain extent the technology, I think F1's actually quite fashionable, which isn't doing its cause any harm whatsoever. In those days F1 most certainly wasn't fashionable – not among the young, at least – and so the only way you could convince a non-believer that F1 was worth watching was to present them with someone like Gilles. Unfortunately, we never saw Gilles win the World Championship. Partly because he died, of course, after an accident in the final qualifying session at the 1982 Belgian Grand Prix at Zolder, but also because he flatly refused to compromise his style of driving. This is simplifying things a bit, but with Gilles it was all or nothing every single time. To a young racing enthusiast like me, or even an interloper who had heard me wax lyrical on a Monday morning but who had hitherto only watched football matches, it was like watching a magician on wheels.

After doing that test for Lotus at Monza in 1988 I was approached by the assistant to the Ferrari team boss at the time, Marco Puccini. Ferrari had also been testing that day and just as I was leaving the circuit he stopped me. 'I've got a message for you from Marco,' he said. 'He's been chatting to Enzo about you and they've agreed that you and he should have a chat about next season.' Benneton already had an option on me at the time and they're ultimately who I ended up driving for after my accident. But to be approached by Scuderia Ferrari was immense, not least because Gilles had been a Ferrari legend and I'd heard rumours that Enzo had a photo of Gilles on his desk. I thought to myself later that evening, *I could be the next Gilles Villeneuve!* That was what potentially racing for Ferrari meant to me. It was all about Gilles.

**Damon:** Not sure red is good on you, Johnny. Makes you look pasty. This one is a difficult question, though. My decision may have to be an arbitrary one, as if I think about it too much you may never get an answer. The first driver I was conscious of other than my dad was Jim Clark, and the reason I was conscious of him was because he spoke with a Scottish accent. Daft, isn't it? This man was lauded for being one of the biggest talents ever to grace motor racing and I thought he sounded quaint.

But it's hard to have a favourite racing driver when a) your Dad is one and you're surrounded by them, and b) you're not really that interested in motorsport, which I'm ashamed to say I wasn't. Not when I was young. I started showing more of an interest when I was about ten, I guess. Then Dad became my favourite, not surprisingly. The difference between your hero and mine, though, was that you learnt about Gilles from newspapers and the television but I learnt about Dad as a dad. I suppose you can't see the legend when you see them doing mundane things like mowing the lawn and brushing their teeth.

Even if he hadn't been a racing driver I think he'd still have been my hero, though, because he was an exceptional human being. His philosophy was always to work hard, get stuck in and make life as fun as possible. He also rarely complained about anything. When Dad died I didn't want to have anything to do with racing at all, so I'm afraid I rather missed out on the career of Gilles. I was aware of him, obviously, but I wasn't engaged at all. My heroes were bike racers. People like Barry Sheene and Kenny Roberts. Giacomo Agostini was a little bit before my time but he was the one everybody used to talk about; 122 Grand Prix wins, fifteen World Championships and ten wins at the Isle of Man TT. Incredible! Freddy Spencer was another rider who used to amaze me. My hero, though, was Barry Sheene. By the late 1970s Barry's talent on and off the bike had made him the most famous racing motorcyclist in the world. He was chirpy, cheeky, extremely like-able, good-looking and had bucketloads of talent. Bit like yourself, Herbert! Who wouldn't want to be like Barry Sheene?

He'd paid the price, though, as after a tyre blowout at Daytona in 1975 he'd had to be pinned together like an old ragdoll. Like my dad, who, when asked if he had a message for my mother after breaking both his legs at the 1969 United States Grand Prix at Watkins Glen, said, 'Just tell her that I won't be dancing for a while.' Barry also made a spectacular recovery and as well as winning many more races he also won the 1976 World Championship. In fact, it was his crash that actually launched him into the big time. My dream of wanting to become Bazza was cemented during the epic Sheene–Roberts British Grand Prix when Bazza overtook King Kenny and gave him the 'V' sign behind his back as he did so. 'One day,' I remember saying to myself. 'One day!'

I'm proud to say that many years later Barry and I became good friends, but attempting to emulate the great man, which I did rather too often working as a despatch rider, used to bring me to the attention of people who, shall we say, weren't appreciative of my efforts. One day I was going round Hyde Park Corner, giving it a bit of lean and dangle as I peeled off through Belgrave Square and fantasized about making this a section for a London MotoGP track, when a large gentleman on a white motorcycle pulled up alongside at the inevitable traffic lights.

'Do you want to know what I think you are?' the policeman asked me after telling me to pull over.

'Er, OK!' I said, but thinking, *This should be interesting.*

'I think you're a c**t!'

He tried to charge me with reckless driving, which is about as serious as it gets, so I had to defend it. I managed to convince the magistrate that hanging off the bike like Barry Sheene made the bike more stable! Meanwhile, my mum had written a letter of complaint to the Met about the foul language, so they had to respond to that and instigated a so-called 'independent' enquiry, which involved a whole bunch of them coming round to our house. I can remember it like it was yesterday. I was about eighteen. My mum told them off for using abusive language as we had tea and Jaffa Cakes. They sat there like naughty school children. Then their leader plucked up courage to say, sheepishly, 'Well, he could have used worse language . . .'

'Like what?' my mum asked.

'Well, he could have used blasphemy.'

With the benefit of forty years' hindsight, I'd say suggesting that the use of a coarse term for female genitalia as an insult was worse than taking the Lord's name in vain, in front of my mother (or anyone's mother!), was courage above and beyond the call of duty. Frankly. They made their excuses and left. What a bunch of . . . men.

**Johnny:** Christ on a bike! A motorbike, even. Let's get back to F1. Who was the first driver, post motorbikes, who tickled your fancy?

**Damon:** It'd have to be our mate with the ginormous 'you know whats'.

**Johnny:** Bollocks!

**Damon:** No, really! Mr Mansell. He made me believe that it was possible for someone from these shores to get out there and do it. He was probably my favourite driver and my biggest inspiration. His feats of derring-do, some of which we've already touched upon, should, more often than not, have been put straight into the heroism category. As a stylist I'd have to choose Alain Prost. When my contract was up with Arrows at the end of 1997 he asked me if I'd come and drive for him. I'd always got on very well with Alain and after he told me all about his new eponymous team I said I'd think about it. After giving it some thought I decided it wouldn't be a good fit and a bit later on I ended up inadvertently insulting not just Alain, but his entire team. When asked by a journalist why I hadn't joined Prost F1, I rather clumsily said it was because it was 'too French', meaning that I would be the only non-French person in a French team with French engines and a French teammate. You know what they say, you can have too much of a good thing! I'm afraid I rather upset them. Me and my big mouth.

**Johnny:** Rubbish. In fact, *honi soit qui mal y pense*! By the time I got to F1 the driver who impressed and inspired me the most was definitely Ayrton. Despite him being a few years older than me I'd known him since my karting days, and even then he used to do things slightly differently. For instance, with a two-stroke engine you'd normally choke it at the end of a straight, whereas Ayrton would always choke it at the beginning. To this day I don't know why he did that and the chances are he might just have got it wrong. But, because he was so talented, we used to watch him like a hawk and we scrutinized everything he did. That was the effect he had on us. He was the only driver whose career I followed from karts all the way through to F1, and you could say that even in the karting days I was a bit of a fan of his. Not many drivers, certainly in karting, have an aura about them, but Ayrton certainly did. Even then he seemed to walk on a higher plane to everyone else. He also had his own karting track, so that may have helped a bit. The driver who impressed me the most during my career, apart from Champ, of course, would be have to be Mika. When did having two pedals become standard in an F1 car? I think it was 1998. Well, Mika suggested that six years earlier in 1992 while I was racing with him at Lotus. By the time it was mentioned again Mika was at McLaren and as far as I know he was the person who, with McLaren's help, of course, drove the idea and brought it to fruition. Clever chap, eh? As a driver Mika was very exciting to watch. Very spectacular. He's also a lovely guy. He was somebody who, regardless of what was happening or where he was lying in the championship, never lost his sense of humour or sense of fun. To have one driver who liked a laugh in a team was rare, but to have two, like we did at Lotus, was almost unheard of. I don't know if it was intentional but more often than not teams would have a fun driver and a serious one, but we were like the Chuckle brothers. When Mika went to McLaren he became more workmanlike. More corporate. That's obviously what Ron demanded of him and it didn't do his career any harm. The humour was still there. It just didn't do to express it. As soon as Mika came out of F1 he became his old self and every time I see him now it's just like being at Lotus again. The difference between Michael at Ferrari and Mika at McLaren is that Michael was very good at getting people to believe in him and give him what he wanted, whereas Mika had to be led by the team. It was all about raw talent with Mika, and he and Ron made a formidable team.

**Damon:** Mika's one of those people who uses his words sparingly yet always has something interesting to say. Finnish drivers often tend to adopt a less is more policy, although compared to Kimi, Mika's a positive chatterbox. What a driver, though. As you said, Johnny, very spectacular. If I had to choose a driver from the past twenty years it would have to be Lewis. Yes, I know we've already talked about him quite a bit but the fact that we're doing it again should mean something. When all's said and done, he has fulfilled every single expectation many times over. You cannot argue with that. He's also far less contentious than Michael was, so although he's not everybody's cup of tea in the GOAT argument, which is ultimately subjective anyway, the case is a lot more straightforward with Lewis than it is with Michael. I can't actually think of one example of Lewis being overly aggressive on track. Can you, Johnny?

**Johnny:** I can't. If we're wrong I'm sure somebody will write in. The address to do so, by the way, is Damon and Johnny, Seaview Cottage, Tibet. Something else I like about Lewis is that he hardly ever uses run-off areas. He likes to race fairly and between the white lines. His racing ethic is very old school in that respect and he's told me several times that he'd have loved to have raced in our era.

**Damon:** I'm bloody glad he didn't!

**Johnny:** Anyway, let's get back to the original question and try and narrow it down. Lewis is my favourite driver from the current era and the most rounded I've ever seen, but is he my favourite of all time? My head's saying yes, but my heart is screaming, 'No, Gilles or Ayrton!' I think it's like choosing your favourite song, in a way. Most people have more than one and it's down to what kind of mood you're in. If I was in a nostalgic mood then I'd definitely go for Gilles or Ayrton. Not a bad dilemma to have, is it? I'll tell you what, sod it. I'm going to break the rules and go with all three: Gilles Villeneuve, Ayrton Senna and Lewis Hamilton. They are my three favourite drivers of all time.

**Damon:** What happened to Johnny Herbert? To be the best you have to accept the fact that being the most successful driver and being the most beloved do not always correlate. I often refer to you as one of our lost World Champions, yet despite never winning the Championship you were always one of the most popular drivers on the grid. Not just with the public but also with the drivers. What the Alain Prosts, Niki Laudas and Michael Schumachers of this world tended to command was respect rather than favour, and I doubt that any of them ever gave a hoot that the two didn't always align.

We're back to your omelette quote again, Johnny. The one about cracking eggs? In order to become the best you have to accept the fact that you're probably going to bore some people, and unless you have the personality to counter that and win them over you're not going to be the darling of the grandstands. Two that spring to mind who broke the mould would be Nelson Piquet and James Hunt. James was obviously a bit on the controversial side but the public, and in particular the British public, thought he was the absolute bee's knees. Nelson, as you've already inti-mated, Johnny, is full of fun and is like a Brazilian version of yourself, but with lots of wins and championships. This is a completely different category, isn't it; the drivers you'd pay to go see, instead of the drivers you think will win all the races. It's, 'think they're going to win' versus 'hope they're going to win', basically. You'd choose a whole different load of people to the ones who win all the time. No disrespect to Jackie but I wouldn't have him on my 'hope' list, neither would I have Michael, surprisingly enough. I think Jackie's often stated that he always did just enough to win races. Being too good and winning everything does not necessarily make you universally popular.

Fangio and Moss are a good example. I wouldn't have paid to go and see Fangio necessarily but I would definitely have paid to go and see Moss – the greatest driver never to win a World Championship. Another driver who I would have paid to go and see is Montoya. He probably belongs in a subcategory of brilliant drivers who were driven out of the sport. Alonso would be another one. Shall we call them bad boys? OK then, let's have two grids, Johnny. One for the drivers we'd hope to see win and the other for the drivers we think would win. We'll call the first one 'Hope' and the second one 'Think'. What do you think? Or do I mean hope? I'm lost.

# CHAPTER FOURTEEN

## The perennial problem of overtaking, or the lack of it, in F1

**Damon:** There are races with very little overtaking and every time that happens everyone goes, 'Oh my God, what a boring race.' The French GP in 2019 was a case in point. You have to have some sympathy with that, but Formula One will always produce, somewhere in the season, an absolute classic. Or two. When the drag reduction systems failed at Abu Dhabi in 2019, drivers were forced into situations they weren't used to. With DRS it isn't really an overtake at all, though, is it? It's a pass. Jacques Villeneuve summed it up perfectly when he said that when the DRS failed it forced the drivers to plan their manoeuvres carefully. 'It wasn't the usual overtaking, like they're on a highway,' he said. 'It was exciting. It was a good demonstration of what's bad about DRS.' If the new regulations achieve their objective, maybe they won't need DRS? I'd like to see overtaking, not passing.

**Johnny:** During my win at the Nürburgring in 1999 I followed Giancarlo Fisichella in one of the Bennetons, and going down the back straight I got no slipstream whatsoever. None. It was yet another example of the competitive aspect of the sport being eradicated by this continuous search for perfection, and if DRS hadn't been introduced I don't know what would have happened. It would have been follow my leader. I'm glad DRS came in, for the reason I've just mentioned, but I can't wait for it to go again, if that makes sense.

**Damon:** A great overtake is as good as a goal in football, especially if you get an overtake and a pass back. Max Mosley once made the point that if overtaking happened all the time you'd get bored of it, so the rarity is part of the value. You also have to ask yourself whether you actually want to see overtaking or you want to see close racing. Two drivers can get very, very close in a race but not actually manage to get past each other. At Monaco in 1992, Nigel was stuck behind Ayrton and was on new tyres. He was about two seconds a lap faster than Ayrton and the battle that ensued over the last few laps was absolutely thrilling. There was no overtaking but everyone was on the edge of their seats.

I'm going to throw caution to the wind here and include a cricket analogy. Johnny looks like he's just been hit by a bus, but I just don't care. There's a common misapprehension among non-cricket fans that if a game can last five days and end in a draw it must be as boring as hell, but actually the reverse is true. Some of the most exciting cricket matches ever played have featured teams desperately trying to snatch a tie from the jaws of defeat. My point is that regardless of how fundamental overtaking is to F1 it is just one factor of many. There perhaps used to be a little bit more overtaking in Dad's era and one of the reasons for that was what I call the fumble factor. Mistakes, basically. There was a lot more mis-shifting in those days and pressuring other drivers into making mistakes was an important weapon in a driver's arsenal.

Mistakes still happen of course, but mis-shifting's a thing of the past. Sometimes there only used to be sixteen cars on the grid at Grands Prix, so despite it often being tempting to revert to the age-old refrain of, 'It was better in the old days', in many ways it wasn't.

**Johnny:** You're obviously going to get better racing when there is the ability for cars to run together more, and in order for that to happen they probably need to do something about the braking distances, which at the moment are ridiculously short. With MotoGP, for instance, the time spent slowing a bike down before a corner is huge – about 150 metres – and a lot of the time they're hanging off like you were at Hyde Park Corner. In that window riders have an opportunity to pass each other, and perhaps that's something they could look at in F1. I'm not sure how they'd do it, but it would certainly create more opportunities, not just for drivers to overtake, but to pressurize others into making mistakes. Unfortunately this flies in the face of what the teams are trying to achieve, so perhaps it's a non-starter.

Here's a curveball for you. In 2019 we actually saw quite a bit of decent overtaking and one of the reasons for that – in my opinion – was because the drivers felt safer and were prepared to take more risks. In the '60s, '70s and '80s the consequences of going off were far greater and although it's still dangerous it's safe by comparison. After the famous Villeneuve–Arnoux race at Dijon that we mentioned earlier, the drivers were up in arms because they thought it was irresponsible. Dijon wasn't a particularly dangerous track but because of what *could* have happened it unnerved them. That kind of racing probably happens more today than it did then and paradoxically it's all down to the sport being safer.

The poster boy for that style of racing is undoubtedly Max

Verstappen. At first the other drivers complained about him, and with good reason in some cases. His uncompromising and aggressive style of driving was always going to create waves but fortunately he stood his ground and refused to bow to the pressure. From his opponents' point of view it was obviously a case of, if you can't beat him, join him, and that's exactly what has happened. Max has almost goaded the other drivers into following his lead and he's been a breath of fresh air. A lot of people dislike him but that just adds to the attraction. He's almost like a pantomime villain, in a way. Charles Leclerc in particular has risen to Max's challenge and it's obviously allowed him to adopt his own style of driving, which, like Max, is tenacious and, if needs be, occasionally aggressive.

There was an incident at Monza in 2019 where Lewis complained that Charles hadn't left him a car's width to pass and had he not ceded the position they'd have crashed. We've talked about this and in our opinion Charles didn't do anything wrong. The moment a driver mentions the word dangerous, however, which is what Lewis did over the radio, the powers that be tend to flap a bit. At the end of the day, that's exactly what you, me and the fans want to see during an F1 race. A bit of elbows out, a bit of leaning on another driver, and a bit of handbags at dawn. Beautiful! We used to do what Lewis accused Charles of doing all the time in Formula Ford. In fact, it was accepted. We'd obviously always *try* and leave car's width if there was somebody trying to pass, but our idea of a car's width and our opponent's idea were two different things, and it's so hard to gauge in that situation – he says, tongue firmly embedded in cheek. I bet you did it, didn't you?

**Damon:** I didn't actually. I was like the Gary Lineker of F1. Not a blemish to my name.

**Johnny:** What's that smell? Is it cow? Is it dog? No, it's bullshit! I know we didn't race very often because we were often at opposite ends of the grid, but you were known as being quite a hard racer. Definitely more of a Bryan Robson than a Gary Lineker.

**Damon:** I was never much good at overtaking, though. I started out on bikes and one thing you don't do in bike racing is muscle your way through the pack, because if you go down you take everyone else with you. Had I started out in karts like you then things might have been different. When my son Josh started karting I was persuaded to take part in a karting race and I did quite a bit of overtaking then. In fact, if you exclude lapping backmarkers, which often made me nervous and didn't always go smoothly, then I probably did more overtaking during that race than I did in my entire career in F1. Had I started off in karts, Johnny, I could have been a contender. I could have made it! I did do a good one on Heinz-Harald Frentzen at Suzuka once. You see, overtaking was so rare for me I even remember the driver and the track. I quite surprised myself. I actually passed somebody without crashing into them.

**Johnny:** The king of overtaking in our era was probably Ayrton, although some would class him as being too extreme—

**Damon:** Hang on, I've remembered another one. Alesi at Monza. Lap one, second Lesmo corner. That was a good pass that was. It took place on 8 September 1996 at exactly 1400 hours and 50 seconds. You see, they're very rare events! On the Saturday I'd taken pole but I'd also just been told I was without a drive with Williams for next year. So a bit emotionally confusing! It was also mathematically possible for me to clinch the title at this race and with Jacques being just thirteen points behind me there was everything to play for. Is the prospect of another Hill over-taking manoeuvre exciting you, Johnny? I know you love hearing all about me, really. The start of the race was dramatic to say the least, as the front two rows, which included myself, Jacques, Michael and Mika, all started terribly. I slipped and slithered, like a slippery slithery thing; Villeneuve spun; Schumacher got bogged down and Häkkinen . . . hesitated. In the first three rows the driver who got the best start was Jean Alesi.

'The start was just magic,' Jean later said. 'Qualifying is not so important because I am with them by the first corner!'

He was that. While Jacques, Michael, Mika, DC (who was in fifth), and I all made hashes of it, the flying Frenchman, who was never one to look a gift horse in the mouth, saw a gap, which I'll come onto in a second, drove through it and took the lead. *Merde!* Or *merda*, as they say in Italy.

The gap had appeared because as Jacques and I dragged down the road I moved to the right to stop him getting ahead, and because Jacques kept his foot in we very nearly touched. So, by the time we got to the first corner Jean was first, I was second, Jacques was third and Mika fourth. It's safe to say that I was not planning on taking this lying down, and as Jean went slightly wide at the first Lesmo corner, leaving me more than a car's width to pass, I took my chance and drove down the inside. The world of F1 was aghast. 'What's this?' they asked. 'Damon Hill overtaking? At the second Lesmo corner? Come on, you're having a giraffe!' Jean didn't make it easy for me. In fact he pulled alongside me as we went into Ascari but I held my line aggressively and came out ahead. It really was a bloody punchy first lap.

**Johnny:** You turn into an absolute potty mouth when you talk about overtaking. Some drivers have this instinctive sense of how

216

much space they have either side of them and they can go through ridiculously tight spaces. Michael certainly had that, as did Nigel and Ayrton. In fact, the majority of drivers I can think of who seemed to have that skill and knew how to use it – Piquet's another one – are, not surprisingly, former World Champions. The only former champion I can think of who was quite risk-averse is Alain. He was certainly capable of being aggressive but that wasn't his natural style, which means that when he did drive aggressively it took you by surprise. On the other end of the scale you have the aforementioned fruitcakes, Gilles and René. They were just off their trollies those two. Imagine Max and Charles being on the same track as those two. The mind boggles! Happily, though.

The person we have to give credit to for allowing this to happen – it's not all down to Max's driving style – is FIA race director Michael Masi. A lot of people reading this won't have heard of Michael Masi but he's the fellow who had the unenviable task of taking over from a man they said couldn't be replaced, Charlie Whiting. And what a great job he's done so far. Charlie often used to err on the side of caution at races, which would sometimes result in drivers moaning, which led to stewards getting involved. Michael has been just a little bit bolder in his decision-making and instead of whinging to the stewards the drivers are sorting out their issues on the track. That's exactly how it should be. To relate this to the original subject, drivers are now being tested in defending overtaking manoeuvres, which is a skill in itself, probably more often than they ever have been.

**Damon:** I think drivers should be allowed to keep weaving as much as they like. At the moment the rules state that, 'More than one change of direction to defend a position is not permitted. Any driver moving back towards the racing line, having earlier defended his position off-line, should leave at least one car width between his own car and the edge of the track on the approach to the corner'.

I assume that the thinking behind the law was to even things up a bit, but to me it's too restrictive. Unless it's to prevent an accident or you're being lapped, nobody wants to see a driver yield to another driver during a Grand Prix. It's anti-racing. This comes back to my argument about mirrors, because if you know that the driver in front of you has no idea where you are or what you're going to do, you're the one who has to get it right, but you have the advantage of surprise.

The driver who was most adept at flouting this rule, or at least taking it to the limits of what was allowable – and often beyond, it has to be said – was Michael. After making his one allowable move he would then provide his assailant with the required width of one car. For a few seconds. That gap would begin to close just as soon as the assailant started to pass and it's fair to say that over the years he was responsible for more than his fair share of near misses. Some were fair, but others were downright dangerous. One that springs to mind is Hungary in 2010. Michael was driving for Mercedes at the time and after providing a much faster Rubens with the required width, he waited until he was alongside and then started to close it. The trouble was that to the right of Rubens was a wall, and as Michael started to squeeze the gap it looked like Rubens was going to hit it. Had the wall been just a few metres longer he undoubtedly would have. Seconds later a clearly shaken Rubens, who is probably one of the least vindictive human beings ever to race in F1, got on the radio and said, 'He should be black flagged for that, black flagged. That was horrible!' Watching back you really do feel for Rubens. It must have been terrifying.

**Johnny:** Like you I'm all for squeezing and weaving, but it has to be done safely. It's what you said about yielding. The reason for squeezing another driver isn't to force them into a wall or onto the grass. It's to get them onto the side of the track so their tyres pick up all the dirty rubber – and to make it difficult for them. As the rule says, you only need to give them the width of a car and it's up to you to make that width as small as you can without taking the piss and incurring a penalty. In other words, try and make it difficult without putting anyone's life in danger. There should be a point, based on you following the rule, when you think, *OK, I can't defend anymore*, and that's when you relent. I, like Damon, would get rid of the bit about allowing drivers just one attempt to defend their position but keep the rest.

**Damon:** It was competitive madness when Michael nearly put Rubens in the wall, though. Eventually (twenty-five days later, to be precise!) Michael apologized to him, saying he realized it was too hard. You can say that again! It's still terrifying to watch today! But I don't think this was a malicious act. More like the competitive demon took over his mind. What happened in Suzuka in 1990 with Senna and Prost was not so clear-cut, but you do have to take into account the circumstances. Not in order to excuse him, but in order to try and understand why one driver would deliberately take themselves and another driver out of a race.

The biggest consideration is what was at stake. In that case it was the F1 World Championship, which then hung by a thread, and if you take into account the rivalry surrounding Alain and Ayrton, which is undoubtedly one of the fiercest and most written about in the history of sport, it's a wonder they weren't trying to ram each other every week! What compounded the situation and made Senna extremely angry was that despite being on pole position he had to start the race on the dirty side of the track, meaning that Alain, despite qualifying second, would have the racing line going into the first corner.

After being refused permission to change the side on which pole position was located by Johnny's fan, Jean-Marie Balestre, Ayrton decided that, should his French foe get the advantage, which he ultimately did, he would drive his McLaren into Prost's Ferrari at the first corner. Again, I'm not excusing Ayrton – anything but – but I honestly can't say, hand on heart, that if I'd been in the same situation as him I wouldn't have done the same thing.

The year before at Suzuka, Prost had pulled an equally audacious move that resulted in him having to retire and Ayrton having to be push-started by the stewards and ultimately disqualified, although not for that, so perhaps there'd been a touch of revenge involved? The backstory to that incident is equally fascinating but a bit more straightforward. With just a few points separating them in the Championship (Alain was marginally in front) and with two races to go there was everything to play for. As they were going into the chicane on lap forty-seven, Senna came through on the inside and Alain squeezed him out – rather unequivocally, it has to be said. Both drivers skidded onto the escape road and their engines stalled. Murray came out with an absolute classic when it happened. Clearly excited, he cried, 'Oh my goodness, this is fantastic!' before realizing that unbridled euphoria probably wasn't an appropriate reaction.

That kind of behaviour wasn't typical of Monsieur Prost, which demonstrates that extreme situations can often provoke uncharacteristic behaviour. Rather ironically, the year before that at Suzuka, in 1988, Senna had pulled off a mesmerizing overtaking manoeuvre – successfully this time – on his diminutive French adversary. What was also quite ironic about that manoeuvre was that Ayrton was only able to get close enough to Alain because he was having trouble overtaking a backmarker. Not Johnny Herbert this time. It was Andrea de Cesaris, or, as Murray referred to him after Senna made the move, and obviously on Alain's behalf, as 'the dreaded' Andrea de Cesaris.

Johnny, put yourself in Alain's shoes in 1989. You've got a points lead in the World Championship, there are two races to go, and your fiercest rival and nemesis, who also happens to be closest to you in the Championship, is about to go through on the inside. What would you do?

**Johnny:** First of all I'd probably let out a couple of cheers. After all, I'm winning the World Championship! Then, I would do exactly the same thing.

**Damon:** As your official legal representative, Mr Herbert, I must advise you that is the wrong answer. The truth is, though, I don't know a single racing driver in the world who wouldn't have squeezed Ayrton like Alain did. Not in those circumstances. What would the alternative have been? To give him plenty of room and cry, 'God speed my Brazilian friend' as he goes charging through and then congratulating him afterwards on a perfectly splendid win. Rubbish! What Alain did wasn't necessarily sporting, but it wasn't illegal either. In fact, Ayrton was the one who was later penalized for missing the chicane.

The same thing happened between me and Michael in Adelaide in 1994, of course. If anything – and I'm being generous here – the pressure on Michael will have been even greater than on Alain because the gap between me and him was just a point, and it was the last race of the season. As dramatic finishes go it was pretty damn epic. For those too young to remember 1994, or those who have just decided to forget, allow me to quickly set the scene.

Because it came on the back of an epic win to keep my hopes alive in Suzuka, and because it was a last-race title decider, and because of Imola, Senna and Ratzenberger and all the other crazy things, like the black flag etc. etc., that had happened during the season, the race newsworthiness was stupendous. But it was about to go off the scale. It was like an England versus Germany 1966 rematch. We had a German and an Englishman, so it was all too easy for the press to make me out to be Douglas Bader and Michael to be Manfred von Richthofen, the Red Baron, which actually became Michael's nickname at Ferrari.

So as not to be left out, Nigel was on pole, with Michael second and me third. We mugged Nigel at the start and left him for dead. We were so pumped-up that even Nigel couldn't stay with us. I stuck to Michael like glue for thirty laps but ever so gradually he started slipping away from me. Just as I was thinking, *Damn him!* I suddenly saw him on the exit of East Terrace and Flinders Street corner, slithering back onto the track after obviously having gone off. This mistake put me right in the mix and I went from going, 'How the hell am I going to catch him', to 'Bloody hell, race back on!' It all happened within a split second and with Michael struggling for traction I decided to make my move. As I approached the next corner, which was only about a hundred yards away, or a short squirt, as we say in the trade (meaning a quick blast of throttle, not you, Johnny!), Michael started to pull over to the left, so I began the manoeuvre. *There you go, Hill*, I thought. *It's your birthday!* So I shut my eyes and launched it towards the gap.

But as everyone could see, the gap that was about two cars' width a split second before suddenly became half a car's width, and the next thing I knew he was on two wheels hurtling towards the tyre wall and I was wobbling down Hutt Street on three, my suspension irreparably bent out of its intended shape.

As ever, Murray was on hand to keep the viewers at home in the picture and his first words after the incident were, 'Damon Hill only has to keep going to become the World Champion of 1994. But *can* he keep going?' To my credit, I made it to the pits! The guys then began trying to bend my wishbone back into shape by hand. Desperate times call for desperate measures. I have to admit to you all that if they had succeeded, I'm not sure I'd have been too happy about going back out with a suspension that had been hand-bent back into shape! As the media and the audience went into meltdown, the question everyone was asking was, would he be penalized? It was a pretty conveniently timed collision, but was it deliberate? Who could tell? Well, obviously not the stewards! It was decided that nothing should be done and as far as I can recall, no one protested, so that was that; Michael had won his first of seven world titles. But the incident remains one of my worst overtakes ever! Many people think he did it on purpose. There is still a lot of discomfort about the way it was all handled. But it's history now and Michael is not in such a good place. There is nothing to be gained by blaming anyone.

**Johnny:** What's your opinion?

**Damon:** Did he see me? I'll never know for sure but he was a wily old fox. Probably, yes. But if I was in his position, I'm not too sure I wouldn't have done exactly the same thing, knowing what I know now. You heard it here first, folks! Herbert dragged it out of me!

# CHAPTER FIFTEEN

## Geniuses in F1

**Johnny:** You made the point earlier that there are very few sports out there that have been devised and developed by genuine technical pioneers, so that has to be our starting point. There's a nucleus of about six or seven people that immediately spring to mind – or at least my mind – but the more I think about it the more people pop up. The thing is, are they actually geniuses? I suppose it's subjective really. Colin Chapman's legacy is still very much alive and well in F1 and he's also credited with transforming the sport from being a pastime for the rich, which is basically what it was until the mid-1960s, into a high-tech global enterprise that large companies were falling over themselves to sponsor. It obviously didn't happen overnight, but by the time Bernie got his hands on the sport a lot of the groundwork had already been done and much of that was down to Colin. But it was no good just being a clever bugger in those days. You also had to have conviction, confidence, and a certain amount of bravery.

**Damon:** Absolutely. When John Cooper and his designer, Owen Maddox, came up with the idea of fitting the motorcycle engine that was powering their car into the back and then running a chain, they had absolutely no idea that it would start a revolution. Or so they claimed. John Cooper was a famously modest man and he always played the achievement down, claiming that it had only been done for convenience. Personally I'm not convinced, and when Enzo Ferrari first sported one of John's rear-engined cars neither was he, but for different reasons. John Cooper used to tell the story that Enzo laughed when he first saw the car and said to John, 'Everybody knows that the engine has to be in the front.' Oh, do they?

**Johnny:** I don't think Colin Chapman was ever laughed at, although not everything he devised worked as well as it could have. He was F1's original flawed genius, in a way. Your dad obviously had a close relationship with Colin. Would he have referred to him as a genius?

**Damon:** Having read my dad's diaries from the late 1950s, which is when he started driving for Colin, he never referred to him as a genius. He referred to him as other things not so flattering, but not a genius! Don't forget he drove for Colin *and* helped build the cars, so he was keenly aware of the shortcomings. Colin clearly *was* a genius, and what made him so was realizing that weight was the enemy. John Cooper realized you could get more balance and a more nimble car by putting the engine in the back and Colin basically expanded this concept by experimenting with weight distribution and moving not only the engine, but also the fuel tank.

The overriding principle was to make cars lighter and therefore faster and when asked to explain the advantages of rear-engined F1 cars, Colin said, 'The rear-engine layout offers several advantages for an F1 car – low frontal area, a low centre of gravity (with no propeller shaft problems) and minimum power-loss problems through the transmission. The chief disadvantage of such a car is that it has a low polar moment of inertia.' I don't understand his last point, as I would have thought it would have been an advantage to have a low polar moment, which basically means it changes direction more quickly, like when an ice skater pulls their arms in and spins faster. But I suppose that's the last thing a driver likes!

When it came to fuel tanks, Ferdinand Porsche had already been experimenting with their positioning for a number of years before Colin started tinkering, but once again he took a good idea and ran with it. So, fuel tanks were moved in an attempt to nullify the effects of their weight loss during races. It's something worth taking a moment to explain because the weight of fuel is a massive factor in understanding the nuances of our sport.

Imagine there was a very large man sitting on the boot of your car. This would have been how a rear-engine car felt in the 1950s, when the fuel tank was over the rear axle, just behind where you sit. Good for traction, because the weight is over the rear wheels, which are trying to put the power down. However, when you go round a fast, tight corner, the back of the car tries to swing out like a ball on the end of a length of rope and throw the man off. All well and good if you can dial out the 'oversteer' with car control. But there is a price to pay when the tyres slide like that – there is a limit to how fast the car can go round the corner if it is also having to go sideways.

Fuel is also a diminishing weight, as it gets used by the engine through a long race. This can be a considerable amount of weight, too. One litre of fuel weighs roughly 0.75 kilograms, but because it expands with heat, you can get less for your money per volume, which explains why fuel these days in our sport is measured by weight, not volume. So, getting back to the 1950s, the Maserati

250F beloved by Stirling Moss had a tank capable of holding 200 litres, which could weigh about 150 kilograms. I don't know about you, but I don't weigh that much! But if me and Johnny jumped on the back of Stirling's car, we would roughly represent the weight of the fuel at the start of a race. This would reduce as time went on, to the point where we would lose either me or Johnny by halfway, and then whoever is left by the end. Stirling would be mighty relieved to have got rid of those idiots crawling all over the back of the car, making it near impossible to control. This hopefully explains the designer's dilemma. The car is not only changing weight throughout the race, but the weight distribution is changing, and therefore the handling is changing. It's basically a moving target throughout the race. So ideally, what you want is for the weight to be as close to the centre of gravity as possible, not sticking out of the back of the car like a pendulum! This way the effect of weight loss on handling is less dramatic. These days the fuel tank is right between the driver and the engine. It seemingly couldn't be better placed, but I bet someone is trying to think of a better spot!

So, back to the 1960s. Colin had his first success after moving the engine, when Stirling Moss won the Monaco Grand Prix driving the Lotus 18. There's an interesting article about Colin Chapman on the website FormulaSpy, in which Aron Day writes about what remains of Colin's legacy in F1. As you've already suggested, Johnny, his influence is still far-reaching. Colin Chapman constantly demonstrated that racing-car design is fluid, and that in order to innovate and transform you have to be prepared to question the norms and challenge convention. This mindset undoubtedly paved the way for modern geniuses such as Rory Byrne and Adrian Newey; the latter openly acknowledges his debt to Chapman.

Other Chapman innovations that are still either part of or relevant to F1 include the introduction of the monocoque and driver position, designing for ground effect, which we mentioned earlier, active suspension and commercial sponsorship.

As the article points out, F1 history is unfortunately strewn with deaths and serious injury and when Colin introduced the monocoque in the early 1960s, not only was it stronger and lighter than its predecessor, but it provided his drivers, and later everyone else's, with a more secure driving environment. Further innovations were required before safety was significantly improved, but it was a definite catalyst for change. What the monocoque also did was to change the position of the driver, from the traditional upright position, which was akin to driving a road car, to the reclined position we are more used to seeing. Jim Clark, who won seven races with the new monocoque in 1963 driving the Lotus 23, took a bit of time getting used to the new position. FormulaSpy quotes him as saying, 'The worm's eye view of the track this position gave meant re-orienting oneself with the features of the track to which one had become accustomed. However, once I had mastered the new position, I wondered how I had ever driven a racing car any other way.' Indeed, if you look at photos of Jim driving he looks like he's looking at the sky rather than the road ahead!

Active suspension, which incorporates the use of computers in managing hydraulic suspension, was something Colin had begun working on at the start of 1982. Tragically, he died that December, which meant he never got around to completing it. Lotus did fit a prototype version of Colin's original plan to a demonstration model of the 1985 Excel road car, but it was removed before the car went into production. That wasn't the end of it, though, and over the next few years the ideas behind active suspension were incorporated into a variety of F1 cars, including the Head and Newey designed FW15c which Alain and I drove in 1993 and in which I managed to win three Grands Prix on the bounce. Just thought I'd slip that one in.

One thing the article doesn't mention is the fact that in 1966 Colin managed to persuade the British arm of the Ford Motor Company to finance the development going on at Cosworth. According to the online Colin Chapman museum, what enabled him to unite the parties were his charm, track record, connections and London base. Colin used to remind me of my dad in many ways. For a start they had very similar voices, not to mention a pencil moustache each. The late Peter Warr, who worked with Colin at Lotus from 1969 until Colin's death, probably knew the great man as well as anybody. 'His most amazing characteristic,' said Warr, 'was that he was always right. When Chapman came in with one of his brainwaves, you'd think *he's really gone off his rocker this time* and nine times out of ten, the bugger would turn out to be right . . . but when he did get it wrong, he made some big ones.'

As you said, Johnny, Colin was a flawed genius, but at least he was a genius!

**Johnny:** One of Colin's most important contemporaries is Gordon Murray, and it'll come as no surprise to anybody to learn that, like Adrian Newey, Gordon's hero and main inspiration is Colin Chapman. Given what Gordon has achieved and is continuing to achieve in the world of car design, you could say that one of Colin's biggest achievements was inspiring a fellow genius like Gordon. My favourite Murray innovation is the fabled fan car, the Brabham BT46, which he designed for Bernie's Brabham team in time for the 1978 Swedish Grand Prix.

**Damon:** The only car in F1 to garner more column inches than the fan car is the Lotus 78. One of the most fascinating facts about the story is that is that Gordon designed the fan car in direct response to the success of Colin's Lotus 78. Innovation's a wonderful thing, but when it's driven by competition it tends to move up a gear. Gordon, like probably every other designer on the grid, used to spend hours and hours reading through the regulations looking for loopholes and when the Lotus 78 came on the scene it almost become an obsession. Then, at last, he found one. The regulations stated that a moveable device primarily used to give an aerodynamic advantage was not allowed, which on the face of it would have made a large fan fixed to the back of the car illegal – had Brabham not insisted its 'primary purpose' was to cool the engine. A wonderful grey area about the size of South Africa!

Gordon had to do the sums several times over when he designed the innovation as he just couldn't believe the amount of downforce he would get. He also had to design a fan that could withstand 18,000 revs, so it wasn't just a case of putting one on and winning. It took several attempts before they got it right. When Brabham unveiled the fan car on the Thursday before the 1978 Swedish Grand Prix it caused a mixture of amusement and alarm.

**Johnny:** Correct me if I'm wrong, but wasn't Brabham's most concerned competitor Colin Chapman? After seeing the car, he immediately claimed it was illegal. Gordon and his team went to great lengths to make the car look like it wasn't going to be fast – instead of putting a bespoke cover over the fan when the car was parked up they used a dustbin lid instead. Despite the team's efforts everybody knew the car was going to be quick and Bernie even made his drivers qualify on full tanks just to give them less of an advantage. The fan car could get as much downforce standing still as it could travelling at 180 mph. This meant that, not only could you get a 2 g standing start, but you could also go around hairpin bends at about 150 mph. That was obviously a massive advantage, so no wonder Colin was angry. The irony of him protesting was that in 1981 they all ganged up and banned his very own radical rule-pushing Lotus 88 twin-chassis. What goes around, as they say.

**Damon:** The biggest complaint from the drivers who had to follow the car, apart from the fact that they couldn't catch it, was the amount of dust and debris that the already infamous fan chucked out. One of the most vocal complainants was, not surprisingly, Lotus's Mario Andretti, who was leading the Championship at the time. According to John Watson, who was driving for Brabham then alongside Niki Lauda, Mario came in after the Swedish Grand Prix claiming that he'd had to dodge rocks and that his life had been in danger. Mario later said that if a car's working better than yours you'll make whatever excuse you can to try and discredit it and have it removed from the grid. Niki Lauda won that race by a whopping thirty-four seconds.

Unfortunately, the other constructors, but in particular Lotus and Tyrell, leant on Bernie to withdraw the car. He certainly didn't have to. After all, there was nothing illegal about it. What I think scared Bernie into agreeing to withdraw it was the thought of what might happen once everybody had started copying them. Gordon had created a monster, basically, and at the time it was just too new, too potent and too unpredictable for the sport to handle. Not surprisingly, Gordon was furious when Bernie told him about the withdrawal. It was obviously hard for the drivers and the team owner, but even harder for the person who'd invented it. Emotions must have been heightened somewhat. Had they run the Brabham BT46 until the end of the season they would almost certainly have won the Championship. To have one revolutionary idea introduced in a season is one thing, but to have two is just incredible. It's showing off, basically. Oh, to have been on the grid in one of those in 1978!

**Johnny:** Over the past few years Gordon's been working on a road car incorporating ground effect and his fan car idea. It's called the T.50 and if Gordon gets his way it'll be out in a couple of years. Gordon recently said in an interview how excited he was at the prospect of being able to incorporate ground effect and his fan car idea into a car that can be driven by the public. Thanks Gordon! How much will it cost? About £2 million.

**Damon:** Do you know what Gordon's all-time favourite sports car is? It's the Ron Hickman designed, and Chapman inspired, Lotus Elan. I've heard tell that Gordon has rather a large collection of them and when asked about designing his fabled McLaren F1 road car he said that he'd attempted to replicate the steering feel of the Elan but had missed it. 'The F1's good,' he proclaimed modestly. 'But not as good as the Elan.' Praise indeed!

Here's another fascinating fact about the South African pioneer. When Gordon, who always preferred wearing T-shirts on the grid instead of overalls and apparently owns about a thousand of them, went to McLaren in 1987, he had it written into his contract that he could wear whatever the heck he wanted. There's a famous photograph of Gordon wearing a Sex Pistols 'Never Mind the Bollocks' T-shirt on the grid, which I assume was taken in the late 1980s. Ron Dennis must have been spitting feathers when he saw it. Imagine if you'd turned up for your interview with Ron wearing a Sex Pistols T-shirt, Johnny. It would have been the shortest driver interview in F1 history. Speaking as an ex-punk rocker, I would have thoroughly approved, though. Spitting would probably have been taking it too far. Just saying, in case you actually go for another job interview with Ron.

**Johnny:** Fat likelihood. But thanks for the interview tips, Hill. Next on our list of F1 genii is John Barnard, who is about the same age as Gordon and who started off as a junior designer at Lola in the late 1960s. Semi-automatic gearboxes, the carbon fibre composite chassis. John is one seriously clever chap. Another visionary. His 'ground effect' or 'fan car' moment, in my opinion, was designing the semi-automatic gearbox. It didn't attract the same kind of headlines as the Brabham BT46 or the Lotus 78, but when Nigel Mansell gave the revolutionary Ferrari 640 its first outing, complete with an electronic gear-shift mechanism operated by two paddles on the steering wheel, he drove the car to victory. It took a while, but by 1995, some six years after that maiden win, every car on the grid was sporting a copy of John Barnard's ingenious invention. I'm not sure John receives quite the same amount of recognition that Colin and Gordon do, but his innovations and overall contribution to the sport of F1, are, in my opinion – and, I'd go as far as to say in the opinion of my learned friend here – up there with the best of 'em.

**Damon:** I'd totally agree with you there, JH. Barnard is one of the unsung heroes of F1. We probably owe our lives to him because of the introduction of carbon fibre in the MP4/1, although Colin would share that accolade if his Lotus 88 hadn't been banned. He's such a nice fellow but absolutely not a showman so maybe that's why he's not so well known. He's not flamboyant like Murray with his crazy outfits or Chapman, who used to run onto the track and throw his cap in the air! But they're mostly like the bass players in a band, designers. Fundamental to how the band sounds but at the end of the day, who on earth wants to listen to a bass solo? Unless it's John Entwistle!

Moving swiftly on then, the next genius on our books is Adrian Newey. There are others, of course, but in the interests of us not sending anyone to sleep I'll attempt to give a character outline of the follicly challenged and unassuming Warwickshire-born Tefal-headed mastermind who designed, among many other cars, my Championship-winning FW18.

Adrian, who came onto the F1 scene in the early 1980s, first with the Fittipaldi F1 team under Harvey Postlethwaite before moving to the March F1 team under Robin Herd in 1981, is a culmination of the talent that preceded him. He is Colin, Gordon, John, and every other clever dick all rolled into one. Adrian has this extraordinary conceptual 3-D brain which enables him to see air moving around objects in his own mind. He doesn't need a wind tunnel! The unexpectedly competitive March 881, which Adrian designed in 1988 and had a Judd V8 engine, brought him to the attention of Patrick Head – yet another pioneer and genius designer, but by his own admission, not the gifted aerodynamicist that Adrian is. Gearboxes were Patrick's thing. Whatever turns you on I suppose!

As Patrick was making an approach for Adrian, Leyton House (March's new name) decided to sack him, so the move was seamless. Surrounded by like-minded people, and with a much bigger budget, Adrian was able to flourish at Williams and he and Patrick formed a formidable partnership that began bearing fruit almost immediately. Within a year Adrian had built a chassis that appeared to be every bit as good as McLaren's, who were the team to beat, and if it hadn't been for some reliability issues then Nigel may well have taken the title in 1991.

In the 114 races that took place during Adrian's six-season

tenure at Williams, the team achieved fifty-eight wins, seventy-eight pole positions, sixty fastest laps, four Drivers' World Championship titles and five Constructors'. Crikey! His record since then is equally remarkable and in terms of respect he probably commands more than anyone else on the grid.

**Johnny:** As much as I admire Adrian, Gordon, John and all the other boffins, the one who resonates the most with me, and who in many ways designed the modern version of the sport, is Colin. He's the godfather of modern F1. He's Zeus. The number of paradigms he created in the sport – I'm talking about game-changing paradigms here – is unsurpassed, especially if you consider the technology that was available to him at the time. Imagine what somebody like that could achieve today? If you took Colin to the Mercedes factory in Brackley I honestly think his head would explode! He wouldn't know where to start.

Your dad summed it up perfectly – when he was asked in the late 1960s what Colin's contribution to motor racing was, his exact words were, 'Original thinking. He set the pace for design and progress.' Unfortunately I never got to meet Colin but from what I've heard he very much fitted into your bass player analogy, as in he was quiet and a bit intense. The thing is, he was also an incredibly successful entrepreneur so he was obviously a bit of a paradox. In 1968, Colin's company Lotus turned over £3 million, which in those days was a big wedge of cash, and in 1969 over £4 million. Colin made one prediction in the late 1960s which sadly didn't come true and it links to what we said earlier about the lack of mavericks and smaller teams. When asked by an interviewer if anybody could ever replicate what he'd achieved, not just in F1 but in business, Colin predicted that there will always be a space for small, virile and adaptable teams and businesses to fill in the gaps that he said must exist when you've got big teams and big manufacturers satisfying a mass market. 'There's always going to be scope for the man who can offer something better,' he said. Today, both in terms of teams and in terms of manufacturers, that's almost unheard of and it's doubtful that we'll ever see their like again. We certainly won't see Colin's like.

**Damon:** I'm not sure Colin and Bernie always saw eye to eye, but that's no surprise really. That said, in my view Bernie is also a genius, of sorts. Something he had that Colin didn't – in fact I'm not sure anybody did in F1 when Bernie came to prominence – was the foresight and ability to be able to massage other people's egos. Why was this so prescient? Because at the time, nobody in F1 – or nobody in power, that is – would ever have dreamt of doing something so weak and feeble as to stroke somebody else's feathers, in particular Jean-Marie Balestre. Balestre had far too much pride to tell somebody they were *magnifique*, and as a consequence, when it came to getting the right people on his side, Bernie had the advantage. During the FISA–FOCA war of the early 1980s, which resulted in the Concorde Agreement, Balestre and his colleagues at FISA were run ragged by Bernie. It was men against boys. Regardless of how brilliant and gifted Colin was as a designer, and to a slightly lesser extent a business-man, Bernie, unlike Balestre, was able to wrap Colin Chapman around his little finger.

During what came to be a crucial point in the FISA–FOCA war, Bernie checked into the same hotel as Balestre in an attempt to find out who he was seeing and track his conversa-tions. The most important of these was going to be Balestre's conversation with Colin. Colin's standing on the grid meant that he would be able to influence the other British owners. After Colin had met with Balestre, Bernie duly called him immediately afterwards. All he had to do in order to convince Colin to stay on his side and persuade the other owners to do the same was to play to Colin's ego by praising his genius as a designer, and wadaya know, it worked!

**Johnny:** Are we including Bernie then? That man would get where water wouldn't get! What about Ross Brawn? He was to race strategy what the likes of Colin and Gordon were to design. He changed everything. I know we weren't going to include drivers in this but the only one who I think deserves the label of genius is Jimmy Clark, for the simple reason that week after week, year after year, people used to stand on the side of the track saying, 'How on earth did he do that?' MotoGP have a genius like that today in Marc Márquez, as do Trials in Toni Bou. Jimmy Clark died over fifty years ago yet people still talk about him in those terms and from what I've seen and heard, which I suppose is quite a lot over the years, despite not seeing him race, I'm really not surprised. One of the most impressive displays of driving I've ever seen in my life is Jimmy Clark driving a Lotus Cortina at Crystal Palace in 1964. It's on YouTube so check it out if you get time. The speed he achieves is just incredible and boy is he smooth. It's Jackie's dream drive.

In keeping with Damon's bass player analogy, and in an attempt to make these people seem a little bit more interesting, we're going to conclude this chapter with a countdown of F1's best ever boffins, or *Top of the Boffs*, as we're calling it.

**10** In at number ten is Big Bernie. You simply cannot ignore F1's very own diminutive doyen of dosh and in paraphrasing Eddie Jordan's summation of his achievements, anyone who can sell a business four times, never buy it back, never lose control, and still own the blessed thing without ever owning it in the first place *has* to be considered a genius.

**9** In at nine we have Mr Chatterbox himself, Ross Brawn. Benetton's two World Championships in 1994 and 1995 had almost as much to do with Ross's strategy as they did Michael's driving and he obviously repeated the trick a further five times at Ferrari and again at Brawn, although in a different capacity. Don't be fooled by the lugubrious voice and the hangdog expression. Inside burns a competitive spirit that could make a dead cat wake up and win a tree-climbing competition.

**8** Patrick Head. The James Robertson Justice of F1 and probably the most terrifying and formidable individual ever to set foot in an F1 garage. It's been a case of weighing up what might happen to us if we *don't* include Patrick on the list, so for that reason, and because he wears a rather impressive cravat these days and headed the Williams engineering team for twenty-seven years, the rambunctious and irascible Mr Head goes in. Congratulations Sir Patrick.

**7** In at number seven is the late and much lamented Jimmy Clark. Yes, we know he's a driver and not a boffin so doesn't really belong, but if you google the name Jim Clark together with the word genius it results in about a squillion different articles. Regardless of whether you're living or dead, that kind of praise is only bequeathed upon those who truly deserve it. Jimmy Clark was the real deal.

**6** In at six it's Rory 'the only weakness is the driver' Byrne. If ever there was an F1 engineer with a talent for showing quiet disdain towards drivers it has to be the Pretoria-born former chemist, who, as well as having the pleasure of working with Johnny at Benetton many years ago, which Johnny reckons will be one of the highlights of Rory's career, although is unable to confirm it, he developed a record with his designs that is, at the time of writing, second only to Adrian Newey and Colin Chapman. Ninety-nine Grand Prix wins, seven Constructors' Championships and seven Drivers' World Championships. Impressive stuff, but what makes it even more so is that Rory received no formal training as an engineer. Wow!

**5** John Barnard went from making light bulbs in a factory to designing title-winning F1 cars, not to mention inventing the semi-automatic gearbox and the carbon fibre monocoque. He's credited as being one of F1's most creative designers and as well as going like the wind his cars always looked fantastic. There was never any style over substance with John's designs. He had both.

**4** In at number four is the record-breaking balding boffin himself, Adrian Newey. Poor Adrian had an appalling start in life. Not only was he forced to attend school with Jeremy Clarkson, but he was then expelled from the establishment after destroying an eleventh-century stained glass window by cranking up the sound mixer at a rock concert. You naughty devil Adrian! In engineering terms that's basically the equivalent of mass murder. Normal service was resumed in 1980, however, when he gained a first-class honours degree in Aeronautics and Astronautics from the University of Southampton and the rest you already know. Like Ross, still waters obviously run deep with this one so don't be fooled by the, 'I'm actually as dull as dishwater' outward persona. The man's quite obviously an animal.

**3** In at number three, it's Ian Gordon Murray, CBE. Gordon's response to Colin Chapman's ground effect was to scour the rule book looking for loopholes that might enable him to exploit the invention and take it to another level, thus echoing Colin's own famous quotation that, 'Rules are for the interpretation of wise men and obedience of fools'. By Jove, Mr Murray actually found one! The reason we've put Gordon in front of Adrian, in addition to him inventing the fan car, is because of Adrian's reprehensible behaviour at school, not to mention Gordon's impressive collection of T-shirts. Never mind the bollocks, here's the fan car!

**2** In at two is the legendary John Cooper. We've barely mentioned John until now and the reason he's so high on the list is twofold: first, for revolutionizing the sport by putting the engine in the back of the car (and more immediately ending the dominance of the Italian teams and winning back-to-back World Championships with Jack Brabham), and second, for being so incredibly modest about the achievement. All this, 'We came upon the idea completely by accident,' stuff doesn't fool us. You'll take second place John, and like it.

**1** No surprise who our Top of the Boffs is. Colin Chapman once said, probably from Mount Olympus, 'A racing car has only one objective: to win motor races. If it does not do this it is nothing but a waste of time, money and effort.' That's a proper dictum, that is.

# CHAPTER SIXTEEN

## Circuits: the good, the bad and the ugly

**Damon:** I think this has to cover the whole of our careers really, as in the junior categories – when we were fighting our way up – there wasn't quite the demand for safety that there is today and we did get to go to some pretty wild places. Did you ever race at Castle Combe in Wiltshire, Johnny? Of course you did. That was pretty wild. Like Silverstone – in fact, like a lot of circuits around the country – it started life as an airbase and the track basically follows the base's perimeter road. When it first opened in 1950 it attracted a lot of big names, including Stirling Moss, Colin Chapman, Roy Salvadori and Mike Hawthorn. My dad had one of his first ever races at Castle Combe. It took place in 1955 and he drove a C-Type Jaguar. As significantly, Colin Chapman gave the Lotus Mark III, which was his first pure circuit racing design, a winning debut at the track. Things started going downhill for the circuit when we arrived in the 1980s (no connection, I hope!) and by 2005 the big events such as Formula Three had been banned for being too noisy. Castle Combe was one of the first circuits that made me think, *Hello, if I'm not careful here I could be in trouble.* It was definitely one of the quickest tracks in the country at the time and if you went off, even in a Formula Ford car, you were going to have a biggie. It also had massive bumps that bottomed out the whole suspension and a tractor that crossed the circuit whenever it liked. You had to time it right.

**Johnny:** I drove at Castle Combe at least twice during the mid-1980s and as far as I can remember I never did very well there. You're right, though, it was bloody fast. Mallory Park and Cadwell Park were a bit more twisty-turny, I remember. My favourite track was the Grand Prix circuit at Brands Hatch. It always felt to me like the track was trying to grab you and chew you up. Proper seat of the pants stuff, as Stirling would call it. One of my other favourite tracks – this was also from our Formula Ford and Formula Three days – was Oulton Park. What a challenging track that was. It was bumpy, close, had a constant flow of corners, plenty of undulations, and boy was it fast. The element of danger always went up a notch at Oulton. The part of the track that used to make my bum squeak the most was Druids. Or the second part of Druids. That probably presented me with one of my first ever mental blocks, as in I had to overcome something mentally in order to get through it. There've been plenty of examples since then, but that was the first that made me take a moment. You and me shared the podium at Oulton back in 1987. It was my Championship-winning season, which is why I remember it, and the race winner was Martin Donnelly. I beat you to the second step by about three tenths, Champ. Looking back, we had a decent grid that day and in the first seven finishers were Martin, me, you, my Le Mans teammate Bertrand Gachot, Perry McCarthy, Gary Brabham and Mark Blundell.

**Damon:** Good old Perry. Apart from you, the only person who pronounces my name correctly is him. It's pronounced Day-mon, as opposed to Day-mun. Yet another scintillating fact from the house of Hill. The first time I raced at Oulton Park was on a motorbike some four years before the encounter you mentioned. It wasn't that long after I first met Georgie, my wife, and I remember us and a friend called Christian Devereux driving up there very late on a Friday night from Clapham. God, that's a long drive, I can tell you. Christian was sort of a volunteer mechanic. I volunteered him. I volunteered him to drive the van, too, which was towing our hospitality unit. I mean caravan. In an effort to try and catch up on some much-needed sleep, Georgie and I decided to travel up there and sleep inside the caravan while Christian drove, which was totally illegal.

Naturally enough, about halfway up the M6 we were suddenly shaken from our beds. Pots and pans flying around, curtains flapping and everything at an unnatural angle, including us. Thankfully, rather than coming to a halt suddenly, the steady reassuring hum of the road rolling beneath us returned and it was as if nothing had happened. It was pretty obvious what *had* happened, though. I peeped through the curtains into the van to see Christian's massive eyes looking at me in the rear-view mirror. He gave me a sheepish thumbs up and we rather less confidently went back to our slumbers.

The reason this story is worth a mention, apart from admitting I was stupid enough to ride in caravans, is that the race itself, after we had eventually arrived intact, was a turning point in my career, providing me with a light-bulb moment that moved me up a level. A few minutes before the start of the race my bike sprung a puncture. Having travelled all that way for just one race, and nearly getting killed in the process, I was dammed if I was going to let it scupper my trip. So after grabbing a spanner and some tyre wrenches I attacked the bike for all I was worth and made it to the grid by the skin of my teeth, still raging. When the flag dropped I was so pumped up with adrenalin that I made the best start of my life and shot into second place from about fifteenth on the grid. It was as if the massive flap before had ignited a hitherto unused part of my brain and I found myself racing on another level of consciousness.

So much so, in fact, that as I swung around Island Bend at the far end of the circuit, hanging onto the leading rider Graeme McGregor's rear wheel, a thought could no longer contain itself and popped into my head: *Hang on, what the hell are you doing up here with Graeme McGregor?* From that moment it was like I had hit reverse and got rapidly eaten up by the pack. But the experience had been enough to convince me that under the right conditions, I could be up there with the best. I just needed my pants to be on fire before the start!

Hang on, didn't you almost lose your private parts at Oulton?

**Johnny:** How nice of you to remember. Yes, I did almost lose my wedding tackle at Oulton. It was my first full season racing Formula Ford, so 1984, and I was up there testing. As I turned into Old Hall, which is a right-hander, I overdid it a bit and in an attempt to regain traction I decided to keep my boot in. Unfortunately the traction was regained just a little bit late, so instead of regaining control of the car and continuing I flew headlong into the barrier. As well as feeling a little bit dazed after the impact I had a warm feeling at the top of my leg, but no pain. And no, I hadn't wet myself! When I looked down the first thing I thought was that one of the suspension links had ripped my race suit but on closer inspection it appeared the wishbone had gone clean through my leg about a millimetre from you know where. I've still got the wishbone. And I've still got my twig and berries. Somewhere. My fondest memories from Oulton, apart from towering over you on the podium in 1987, which was the year I won the Formula Three Championship (did I mention that?), are from when Jackie used to take his drivers up there. He definitely did pee himself you know. Just a spot. I'm sure of it.

One of the greatest tracks we drove on the way up was Macau in China. You wouldn't hold a Grand Prix there – not in F1, at least – although one of the track's most famous races is the Macau Grand Prix, which is a Formula Three event. That race is still one of the most important events on the F3 calendar and I do believe you and I took part in 1987, except this time neither of us made the podium. Martin Donnelly did, though. He won that one too, the swine. Macau is a really tricky street circuit made up of two sections. The top half used to follow the cliff line above the seafront until the Chinese government decided to fill in the sea and make a harbour area, as you do. How on earth do you fill in the sea, for heaven's sake? The higher part of the course is very hilly and very twisty whereas the lower part is fast and flat. We reached speeds of about 160 mph during the Macau Grand Prix, which was the highest speed of any track we'd raced on that year. It was exhilarating. I think Ayrton had won the race back in 1983, which is one of the reasons we all wanted to win.

**Damon:** It's horses for courses. Or in this case, cars for circuits. Tracks such as Macau are perfect for Formula Three, which is why the F3 Macau Grand Prix, and it's better-known Motorcycle Grand Prix, which 'Rocket' Ron Haslam won a record six times, are still such a big deal.

I used to love Enna in Sicily, or Autodromo di Pergusa, as it's officially known. You may not be aware of this, Johnny, but had it not been for an uber-rich Italian gentleman named Alessandro Santin, a race at Enna would have seen you and I become teammates. He looks lost, bless him. Many years ago, when Johnny was driving for Eddie Jordan in Formula 3000, he had a teammate called Thomas Danielsson. Thomas was a crash-prone Swedish driver who I'd raced against in F3 and, unfortunately, during his time with Eddie, he developed an eyesight problem that forced him to give up his seat. As soon as I got wind of this I called up Eddie and asked him, as bold as brass, if I could have the drive. 'Get yourself over to Enna for the next race,' he said. 'And don't forget your helmet and overalls.' So I did. My two young shit-hot contemporaries, Donnelly and Herbert, had already been snapped up by F3000 teams and I was keen not to be left at the altar in F3.

If Eddie was to be believed, and this other guy didn't turn up with the cash first, I was going to be Johnny Herbert's teammate and on the grid. I can still hear EJ's conspiratorial sweet nothings, 'Can you get da money? Surely you can find some money?' I had about £75 in my Post Office savings account, but I think EJ was looking for a more substantial sum. Sure enough, the drive went to guy with more money and better looks. He never did anything, that guy. EJ probably trousered the lire and relied on Johnny to bring him all the glory. We could have been contenders, Johnny! You and me!

**Johnny:** Not for very long. I had my crash the following race! I never used to like Enna. It's flat and just goes on and on. You do have that banked corner, I suppose, which has a touch of the Indy 500s about it. I bet that's why you liked it. You just pretended to be Bobby Unser.

**Damon:** No, it was actually the bus stop chicanes I liked. You used to fly in, hang on the brakes, and just slither through them. You could find so much time there if you managed not to make contact with the tyres. Do you remember them? They were put there in about 1951 and, because they were all tied together, if you made contact with them you'd have this string of tyres following you. The grip consistency was also terrible due to the track breaking up so it was like racing on a worn-out driveway. I can't believe you didn't like Enna, Johnny. Especially that long banked corner. So cool.

**Johnny:** Snakes. I'll say no more. I could be wrong but I think the only track that has had an entire documentary made about is the Nürburgring, or the Green Hell, as Jackie christened it. We obviously never raced on it in F1 – not the Nordschleife – but in 2011 I got the chance when I was asked to take part in the 24 Hours of Green Hell alongside Mark Blundell. Our weapon of choice was a 235GTI Motor Sport Golf, and although I don't really do fear that much I was feeling a bit wary going into the race. The short circuit is only about three kilometres, whereas the Nordschleife is 20.83 kilometres and has about seventy-three turns. Having driven at Le Mans a few times I was no stranger to this kind of race but there were so many more people at the Nordschleife and the atmosphere was more like Silverstone than Le Mans. A lot of the fans camp at 24 Hours of Green Hell, just as they do at Silverstone, and many of them go to the same spot year after year.

Endurance racing is obviously a very different discipline to F1 and one of the biggest problems you have in a long race like Le Mans or the Nordschleife 24 Hour is the amount of traffic. There must have been at least 200 cars on the track, if you count all the different categories. The track itself is like Oulton Park on steroids and it took me about a week and a half to memorize it using a PlayStation. The thing is, when the F1 boys used to race on the Nordschleife they'd turn up without having driven it before and go straight into qualifying. No PlayStations in those days, of course. Just a shedload of horror stories and a mind-numbing amount of deaths and serious injuries. Imagine having to learn the Nordschleife on spec. That must have been truly terrifying.

Despite us having the odd grumble here and there about

technology in motor racing there are a lot more positives than negatives and one of the best examples I can think of – certainly when I first arrived at the Nordschleife – was having been able to memorize the course. Because so much of the track is surrounded by trees it's almost like driving through a continuous tunnel, especially when it's dark. Unfortunately, we had to retire the car about three hours from the end. Would I do it again? You bet I would.

**Damon:** Would it be a good track for Formula Ford cars?

**Johnny:** Probably. Then again, despite doing quite well in Formula Ford I never liked the cars very much. Having come from karting I was used to nippy, responsive drives and the Formula Ford cars were usually quite heavy and docile. Formula Three would work well at the Nordschleife. There are certain tracks, regardless of reputation, that you get a bad feeling about when you race them. My circuit nemesis, if you like, was always Hockenheim. For some reason I never, ever enjoyed racing there. Some of it was to do with how fast the track was, I don't mind admitting that, and the first chicane was especially perilous. The best result I ever had there was fourth in 1995 and every time I left the circuit I used to breathe a huge sigh of relief. It wasn't based on a bad experience or anything. It was just a premonition, I suppose. The flip side of Hockenheim was, as I've already said, Monaco. I just couldn't get enough of that place and instead of breathing a sigh of relief when I left I used to get a bit of a pit in my stomach.

**Damon:** I'm the opposite to you, in that I used to love driving at Hockenheim yet rather disliked Monaco. To me, driving at Monaco was like driving with handcuffs on. Not the pink fluffy ones you use. I'm talking about psychological handcuffs. I found it claustrophobic. It's a great Grand Prix, of course. Just not my favourite drive.

Another driver who disliked Monaco was Heinz-Harald Frentzen. In fact, he used to hate it. Jean Alesi, on the other hand, used to love it and he also enjoyed racing at Macau. There's no exact science to this, though. You loved Monaco, which is a street circuit, yet disliked Macau, which is also a street circuit. Sometimes there are clear reasons as to why a driver takes against a track, and, as you rightly said, Johnny, sometimes there aren't. There are certain tracks that regardless of personal preference are just plain boring. One of the most uninspiring I've ever come across is Barcelona. I can't put a positive spin on it I'm afraid. It's just dull. And so is Jerez for that matter. In some cases it's almost as if somebody buys a map of a plot of land, gets a few protractors and a compass and just joins the dots. 'There you go. There's your racing track.' There is precious little imagination going on. I blame computers again.

**Johnny:** I once blew up three engines in succession at Jerez during a test. It happened just a few days before my debut Grand Prix in Rio and needless to say I was about as popular as a fart in a spacesuit. Or perhaps a race suit. The most boring track I ever raced on – or at least one of them – was Aida, which is in Okayama. I think we only raced there twice during the mid-1990s for the Pacific Grand Prix but it almost sent me to sleep. There's also nothing whatsoever around the track. No hotels, nothing. When everyone moans about Russia or Azerbaijan they should spare a thought for the poor buggers who had to make it to Aida.

**Damon:** My award for most boring would have to be the Autódromo Juan y Oscar Gálvez, which is in Buenos Aires. It was built in about 1952 under President Juan Perón and it was as if after finishing it they said, 'OK, hombres, let's leave the place to rot for a few decades then in 1995 we'll host a Grand Prix on it.' The capacity of the circuit was only about 40,000, which was tiny, and the most interesting thing about the track was that there was a very large bump on one of the corners. One of Bernie's favourite pastimes was parading his drivers in front of the VIPs and when I arrived in Argentina he asked me if I'd like to come up to the control room and meet the President, Carlos Menem. My stock-in-trade answer to Bernie's requests was always, 'Of course, Bernie. I'd be delighted', and so off we went. The fact that this was the first Grand Prix to take place in Argentina since the Falklands War wasn't lost on me so I was interested to see how everyone behaved. Fortunately, all thoughts about the war appeared to have been put on hold for a while and everyone was on their best behaviour. The President especially seemed most amenable and after asking me if there was anything he could do to make my time in Argentina more comfortable, I decided there was. 'I don't suppose there's anything you can do about the bump at turn three, is there?' I asked. 'I'm afraid that's a little bit beyond me,' replied the President. Lovely chap. Awful circuit.

Now we've established which circuits we disliked, let's turn it on its head and talk about the ones we enjoyed.

**Johnny:** Old Spa was probably my favourite. As I said, qualifying at Monaco was the ultimate challenge as far as I'm concerned, but the best circuit was the old Spa. This is when Eau Rouge was still exciting and the run-off was nothing. The flow was also excellent there; from Pouhon all the way round to Blanchmont. If you made a mistake on the way there was a four-storey barrier running along both sides of the track, so if you went off it was like being a ball inside a pinball machine.

**Damon:** I managed to do Paddock flat in an F3 car once.

**Johnny:** I feel like a bit of a wuss then. I never did Paddock Hill flat out. No way. How on earth did you manage to do that?

**Damon:** I had confidence in my considerable talents. And I had a great set-up, I suppose. I was so bloody chuffed.

**Johnny:** I'm very impressed.

**Damon:** Brands is a great track. Loads of great corners and ups and downs. It's a pity it doesn't have the infrastructure to host a Grand Prix anymore but by today's standards it'd be found lacking. Perhaps you and I could hit Bernie up for a few quid. Get the place up to spec and then pitch it to host a future European Grand Prix? When Nigel won the British Grand Prix at Brands in 1986 the cars had about 1100 horsepower and were quite wide. They were beasts. Going into Paddock at 185 mph, Johnny? How do you fancy that? You must have done something like that at your first test.

**Johnny:** Yes, I suppose I must have. Brands is a funny one for me. It's an absolutely fantastic track but because of what happened it makes me wince a little bit. I'm not sentimental or superstitious. It's just a natural reaction, I suppose. Normally you can just compartmentalize everything, so if a track has a reputation for being dangerous, or even a certain part of a track, then you go, well I can't think about that, can I? After that it's put to bed and you can concentrate on getting a good lap time. The golden rule is always the same – do not crash!

For racing, though, Silverstone's hard to beat. In Formula Ford you couldn't get away at Silverstone. You'd get out in front and then everyone else would catch you up. It was mad. What I don't like about today's tracks is that they're all so smooth. There are no undulations anymore. I used to love a good undulation. Dealing with stuff like that used to be part of the skill. Finding grip and finding routes through corners where there were bumps. I'll tell you one track that always produces great races, and that's

Montreal. I doubt it is nowadays but it used to be quite bumpy when we raced there and because of the low downforce we used to move around quite a bit. No architect could ever have designed that circuit yet over the years it's produced some of the best races ever in F1. As a driver it was always very difficult to get right but at the same time it was hugely exhilarating.

One of the modern tracks that I've been to but never raced at is Istanbul Park in Turkey. The Turkish Grand Prix's only been held seven times and not since 2011. It's a bit bumpy, which I love, and among the corners there's one with a fantastic quadruple apex. There's also a bit of a Senna-S towards the start and there's even a downhill section. They had some really good races there.

**Damon:** Never been there, even as a pundit, but you're right about it producing some good races. Felipe Massa won three times there, which is almost 25 per cent of his win tally. One of the tracks I find frustrating at the moment is Baku. I know it's quite highly thought of but for some reason it doesn't really grab me. There isn't really a fast chicane and there's only one difficult corner, which is the last. I could be wrong but I don't think it challenges the drivers much, although it does produce the odd good race. To me the most impressive new track is Singapore. What a spectacle that is. In the daytime the whole thing looks a bit ordinary, but in the evening it really comes to life. Most importantly, that Grand Prix is a proper test. It's a highlight of the season for me.

Did you ever race at Detroit?

**Johnny:** No, but I did race at Phoenix. This was in the American Le Mans Series, which I did for a few years after finishing F1. Driving there was like going over a continuous line of sleeping policemen. I know I said I like bumps but that place was just ridiculous. It was horrible! My feet used to take an absolute hammering there. You know how it can hurt your heel sometimes when you go over a bump? Well, because my feet are so sensitive that was almost constant and with it being endurance racing it would obviously last for hours. The only time I ever go quiet is when my feet really hurt, and at Phoenix I only ever spoke when I really had to.

My favourite track when I was over there – I was there for about four years on and off – was Road America, which is in Wisconsin. JJ Lehto and I won the 2003 Road America 500 driving an Audi. JJ Lehto is a fruitcake of the highest order so you can imagine what it was like driving with him. We were once leading a race over there and during the changeover – I was in and he was out – the rear of the car suddenly went up in flames halfway through refuelling. 'Jesus Christ,' I shouted. 'The bloody car's on fire!' After quickly undoing my harness I attempted to alight the burning car but JJ was having none of it. 'No, no, stay in the car,' he said, and then he began pushing me back in. 'But it's on bloody fire!' I screamed. 'No, no, no. You'll be OK. It'll be out soon and then you can go.' Finns obviously have a reputation for being a little bit unhinged, but until then my experiences of their lunacy had been confined to them either driving or drinking to excess. Pushing somebody back into a burning car was a new one on me, and as the flames began spreading around the side of the car JJ just stood there with his hand on my chest looking a bit bored. In the end he was actually right to restrain me, as about a second later the fire was out and I was on my way, but for a while I genuinely thought I was about to be roasted alive like a chestnut in overalls.

As well as winning the race we actually made it onto CNN's Play of the Day, which was a thrill, and then later that night after drinking a pint of vodka each we broke into the hotel swimming pool, which was locked, stripped off and went skinny dipping. To him that was normal behaviour but to me it was a little bit out of character.

Needless to say, when I woke up the next morning I felt dreadful and vowed never to watch CNN again. If I ever had to describe JJ to somebody who wasn't aware of him, I'd probably say he was like an appallingly behaved version of Mika Häkkinen. What a great guy, though. I did actually get my own back on JJ directly after our win, at Road America, which was the next race. The Champ's sitting here agog. He's never seen me after a pint of vodka, nor has he seen me being restrained by a mad Finn. There's worse to come, though. In fact, this is probably going to make you ill, Damon.

Road America is just a few blocks away from Lake Michigan, and after winning the Road America 500 we decided to go for dip. This was becoming a habit and once again JJ had persuaded me to jump in sans clothes. After swimming out for about ten minutes I stopped to see where JJ was, except he wasn't. There, I mean. I started calling for him and after a few minutes I naturally began to panic. 'JJ,' I cried. 'Where the bloody hell are you, JJ?' We'd had a couple of beers but nothing compared to last time. *The silly bastard's drowned*, I thought. Just then, as I was treading water and calling out his name – in vain, so I thought – the bastard popped up out of the water next to me and shouted, 'Here I am!' According to Wiki-thingy there are 58,000 square kilometres of water in Lake Michigan, so having an accident wouldn't have been much of a problem really. 'You absolute basta—' 'Now, now, now, Johnny,' he said, talking over me. 'Don't get overexcited.' By the time we joined the team, who had holed up in a nearby bar, I was ready for a drink. And I was ready to wreak my revenge. For some reason – I can't think why – there was a big long pole right in the middle of this bar, so when everybody was suitably refreshed I decided to make my move. Or should I say, moves. After borrowing a leopard skin thong from somebody – as you do – I ran to the gents, put it on, made my entrance to rapturous applause – and a fair amount of shock, it has to be said – and proceeded to start my pole-dancing display. To say that JJ was surprised would be a bit of an understatement, and it takes a lot to surprise him. I don't remember a great deal more after that, but I'll tell you one thing, Champ, thank God mobiles didn't have cameras then!

**Damon:** I don't know what to say, really. Please don't do that again? Getting back to the track for a moment – please God – what did you like about Road America?

**Johnny:** There was a flat-out kink, which was good, and it was undulated. The exits out the corners were also a bit muddy at the sides which meant you could plonk your wheels quite nicely. At Old Hall at Oulton Park you always used to dip your outside wheels into the dirt a bit as you came out so it reminded me of that. Road America's also a very dusty track, which isn't to everyone's liking, but I was fine with it. The icing on the cake is the surrounding area, which is beautiful, so to me it had everything. I also enjoyed the Indy.

**Damon:** You never raced the Indy 500.

**Johnny:** No, but I did Bump Day, which is one of the qualifying races. The team ran out of money in the end and the car wasn't brilliant. The fastest I ever did was about 227 mph and I was lifting a bit at the corners.

**Damon:** I see you through different eyes after telling me that.

**Johnny:** Well, you were bragging about going flat through Paddock, so I had to respond.

**Damon:** By telling me stories about you lap-dancing and skinny-dipping with JJ Lehto? I am very impressed, though. About the

Indy thing. I don't care who you are, there's a process you have to go through with every track you visit as a racing driver, whether it be Castle Combe in Cheshire or the Indianapolis Speedway. It's serious stuff we're doing and if you don't treat a track with respect it can bite you. I know we talked earlier about when everything just aligns – like my out-of-body experience – but that doesn't happen for very long. So it's interesting what state of mind the racing driver is in most of the time. I'd guess it was a very concentrated state but also working to deny the fear that must also be there. In fact, the competition is really against yourself. If you can win that one, maybe there are no limits to driving? In the wet, particularly, I just surrender to my instincts. There really is no other way. Discuss, Johnny.

**Johnny:** I've experienced exactly the same thing. And, like you, it was in the wet. It was the 1991 Australian Grand Prix in Adelaide and the rain had been torrential. It wasn't flat down the straight but I'd drive flat until the car aquaplaned, after which it would snap sideways. After that I'd gun it again until it snapped and so it went on. Even now, whenever I sit down and think about that race it still makes me shudder a bit. Not only do you have to be a certain kind of lunatic to be able to drive like that, but you also have to be in a certain frame of mind. I was fearless. Totally fearless. Subsequently, I even ended up lapping my teammate, who was none other than – Mika Häkkinen! I don't like mentioning this fact in fear of embarrassing Mika but it had to come out sooner or later. Fancy being lapped by a fearless Essex boy. Pathetic.

# CHAPTER SEVENTEEN

## Getting the yips and knowing when to quit

**Johnny:** In terms of F1, the yips can often occur after a bad accident but they can also occur during a period of success – i.e., when a loss of form would be most costly. One of the most recent examples of that I can think of is when Jenson almost lost his grip on the Championship back in 2009. The alarm bells started ringing when Rubens, who was Jenson's teammate at the time, won his first Grand Prix of the season at Valencia. Having won six of the first seven races, Jenson had enjoyed an almost unprecedented start but by the time Rubens was presented with his trophy Jenson hadn't won in four and had finished a lowly seventh in Valencia. If ever there was a time to try and ignore the media this was obviously it, because the papers and websites were full of it. Former champions such as Niki were interviewed about Jenson's lack of form and for a time it was a massive story.

Reading what Niki had to say about it was actually very interesting, as in the history of F1 there can't have been too many people who were more adept at overcoming challenges than him. Ultimately, Niki backed Jenson to recover but said it was up to him and him alone. 'The problem must be something within Jenson,'

Niki said. 'Something must have gone wrong in his own mind. He must find the solution within himself and I think he will.' Even Brundle said something vaguely relevant. Speaking from the bar at his local bowls club after an especially raucous Complan binge, he said that, 'After a long stint with a points lead and the end of the Championship drawing nearer, Jenson will have been tightening up in the car.' Probably true, although Jenson never admitted it. According to him, the race at Valencia was the first time he'd had a strong car all season that he hadn't been able to get the most out of. 'I am going to go to Spa and be more aggressive,' he said to one of the newspapers. Unfortunately he had to retire at Spa but after finishing in the points at the remaining five races, and bagging two podiums, he came home with an eleven-point advantage. Not quite a yip, then. More a yipette.

Another more recent example would be Sebastian Vettel in 2019. In many ways his 'wobble' was more serious than Jenson's, as the media weren't questioning whether or not he'd win the Championship, they were questioning whether or not he should still be driving in F1. After a dreadful race in Monza, in which he spun off early on, and with his title hopes long gone, Seb had one opportunity to retain a bit of pride for the season and that was by beating his teammate at Ferrari. Charles Leclerc's win at Monza put him four points ahead of his esteemed German colleague and the majority of the media were suggesting that the reason for Seb's Monza mistake, and others he'd made, was that his touch had deserted him. In other words, he'd got an attack of the yips.

Regardless of whether this was true or not, if you're the person they're talking about it can definitely plant a seed, and the more the media talked about it the more the media and fans thought it might be true. The term they kept on using was 'unforced errors'. Since arriving on the scene in 2008, the name Sebastian Vettel and the words 'unforced errors' had rarely been seen in the same sentence. Ferrari's chief executive at the time, Louis Camilleri, backed Sebastian but others, such as Italy's *Autosport*, were less generous. 'Sebastian is lost and can no longer return,' they alleged. Funnily enough, Sebastian won the next race in Singapore but in the final standings in November he was twenty-four points behind his teammate. No doubt about it. There was definitely a bit of yippage going on there.

**Damon:** But in order to get the yips, you obviously have to have skills in the first place. I take it you've never been afflicted?

**Johnny:** Very funny. Har har. Funnily enough, I haven't. What I think always prevented me from getting the yips is the fact that my ambition just to get a drive far outweighed everything else, and even when I got there the gratitude and relief I felt in actually driving an F1 car did exactly the same job. Also, and Fernando Alonso very kindly reminded me of this a few years ago, because I was never what you'd call a regular on the front row I've never had either the potential or the historical success that's often blamed for inducing the yips. Even if I had, though, I genuinely don't believe I'd have suffered from it. My equivalent of winning a World Championship was just being on the grid and had that ever been taken away from me I'd have been a broken man. My point being that I did actually achieve something big enough – in my own world – to induce an attack of the yips.

**Damon:** You certainly don't get the verbal yips, do you? You always find something to say. Even if I'm not always sure I understand what you just said. I think there's a little bit more to this, as in more to getting the yips – or the motor racing version of the yips, which I think is slightly more experience-led – than just an

261

accident or having to maintain form or saving your reputation. You and I are wired the same in many ways, Johnny, but in others we're wired differently. What separates us is the way we approach things. You're quite happy to throw yourself into a situation and sort out any problems as you go, whereas I will tend to think about it beforehand and weigh up any pros and cons.

The thing that makes me do this is fear of the unknown. The 'what ifs', if you like. I experience anxiety in advance. Kind of 'worry now, not later'. Once I'm actually in a situation I'll then operate in real time and will probably have a similar mindset to you. Also, if a crash, or one of the 'cons' I was weighing up before-hand, actually occurs, nine times out of ten it won't be anywhere near as bad as I feared it would be. The default setting of the human brain – although not necessarily Johnny Herbert's – is to err towards the negative and the reason it does that is to protect you. A cognitive version of forewarned is forearmed, basically. The risk-averse among us will be affected by this more than somebody like Johnny, but we can often take heart from the fact the things that we worry about aren't always as bad as we imagined. Sometimes they're worse!

I think the yips is more normally associated with sports such as golf and cricket. There's an argument as to whether it's primarily a psychological condition or something to do with a loss of fine motor skills where players have a sudden spasm for no obviously explic-able reason. In F1 it expresses itself in more subtle ways. I think Jenson's loss of form was a reaction to his amazing start to the season – both in terms of the opportunity it presented and the pres-sure of maintaining it – and Sebastian's was most likely down to a four-time World Champion being outdriven by a young pretender. Something like that's going to play on your mind, and in Seb's case it led to a few mistakes. It was not in the script, so to speak.

I think expectation can blind us to what is actually happing in the 'now'. Seb expected past glories to continue as always, so this new fast guy thing was not how the story was supposed to go. Whereas Jenson was more a case of the expectations being dramatically different to the new reality of being in with a chance of becoming World Champion. Let's face it, the previous Christmas, he wondered if he'd ever race in F1 again! So he really had to rejig his mind to the enormity of the new reality.

My own version of the yips was the effect certain races had on me psychologically, which made me question not so much my ability to continue racing, but my desire to. The races in question were invariably the ones where I ignored the part of my brain that was telling me to be careful. The most prominent in my mind is the race I mentioned at Suzuka, where I was possessed by some kind of automotive poltergeist. But even before that happened I'd driven the race in a way that I always swore I wouldn't. I hadn't left any margin for safety whatsoever and after the race had ended it hit me really hard. I'd actually survived something I probably shouldn't have and the realization wasn't just sobering, it was terrifying. If I'd been asked then to go testing the following Tuesday I'd have had to refuse point blank. I would not have been able to get into the car. I'd literally frightened myself witless!

The next time it happened was during my final season in F1, when I felt the weight of every bad experience I'd ever had in motorsport, coupled with an appreciation of how lucky I was going to be if I managed to retire in one piece. I didn't end up with smashed feet like you, Johnny, and I didn't end up like Martin Donnelly, or Roland, or Ayrton, or Jules. Bernie once said that when a racing driver sees a red light they should stop immediately, and I didn't stop immediately. I'd seen that red light several times by the time I retired but for some reason I carried on. The fact that I could have stopped but didn't was the part I found hardest to deal with, and it produced an inner conflict which I found hard to reconcile. *Why am I still driving? Why do I need this?* It was pretty disturbing really. Not the state of mind you want to be in as a racing driver.

**Johnny:** My mindset going into a race – this is both before and after the accident, believe it or not – was always that it could happen, but it won't happen. When I did have the accident at Brands Hatch in 1988 my mindset simply reset itself. You're always looking forward as a sportsperson. It's about possibility and opportunity. That's what drives you on. Because of what happened – or at least I think it's because of that, I can't be certain – I was blind to anything other than racing, so even having kids made no difference to me whatsoever. I know it did to you, Champ, but as you said, when it comes to how we approached things our minds were wired differently. I could be wrong, but what probably stopped you from retiring when you first saw the red light was an inability to see anything beyond racing. It's a fear of the unknown, so exactly the same as what you used to suffer going into a race.

I should have left F1 at the end of 1999. Flavio would probably say I should have left at the end of 1989, but you can't please everyone all the time. I didn't enjoy my last season one little bit, really, but without having something else to throw myself into I had to stay put. When I eventually did leave F1 I went into the future looking backwards. I tried turning my head but the problem was I couldn't see anything. There were no races, no press conferences, no tests, no flights, no circuits, no interviews, no drivers, no mechanics. I even missed the bloody engineers!

Before finishing, my wife had tried to impress upon me the fact that when I stopped racing I'd never be as popular again. She was trying to prepare me, I suppose, but it had an adverse effect.

**Damon:** You don't think she meant you'd never be as popular with *her* again, do you? Forget I said that. I shouldn't get involved, really. It's your marriage. But who would you rather be married to; an F1 driver or an F1 pundit? That's not a proposal, by the way. She's a wise woman, your wife, though. Any sports person will tell you that the transition from being 'who you were' to being 'who you are now' or 'who you want to be' is really hard. Especially if you've been thinking and doing nothing else since you were five years old. But trying to discover a new image of yourself is not easy. You have to have an idea of where you want to be in the future. To paraphrase George Harrison in one of his songs, 'Any Road', if you don't know where you're going, it doesn't matter which road you take. I suppose I had the advantage of being ready to leave F1 but I still found the prospect of having to reinvent myself somehow incredibly daunting. I couldn't think what I wanted to do, now I was a grown-up. Still don't know!

**Johnny:** Which is perhaps why the likes of Niki and Jackie did everything they possibly could to stay in the game. As two people who weren't exactly short of a shilling and had multiple World Championships to their names they could have retired and played golf or something. But instead they successfully reinvented themselves within the sport, and not just as pundits. Jackie became a consultant and then a team owner, and excelled in the art of choosing brilliant drivers, and Niki did a bit of everything really before becoming a non-executive director at Mercedes. He and Jackie were both very entrepreneurial, so transferring those skills to F1 will have been a natural step for them. But it's not just about money. It's about getting the best deal for themselves – the best role. Eddie Jordan's another one.

**Damon:** Yep. Eddie also had to transition from being an integral cog in the F1 wheel to something potentially less essential, and by the looks of things he's just about perfected the art. Eddie loves people, and he loves being loved back. Especially if they show the love by paying! But that's a bit unkind. Eddie Jordan is an incredible human being who possesses an unrivalled ability to enjoy life. I'm not surprised he's thrived since selling up, and he'll still have a few irons in a few fires, mark my words. Just like our friend Bernie. You don't suddenly stop being entrepreneurial, the same as you don't suddenly stop wanting to be a racing driver. Although for reasons we've mentioned that can fade quite quickly.

In terms of generating success, arguably the most significant contribution ever made by a former F1 driver within the sport, apart from falling off a hoverboard at Silverstone and delighting tens of thousands of people, is when Niki persuaded Lewis to join Mercedes. I obviously wasn't privy to their conversations but after coming in as the non-exec chairman at Mercedes in 2012 Niki apparently made contact with Lewis, and as well as getting the ball rolling he closed the deal. Lewis himself has gone on record saying that if it hadn't been for Niki Lauda he'd be a one-time World Champion. Not that there's anything wrong with being a one-time World Champion, thank you very much indeed. Ross Brawn was the one who drew up Mercedes' plan, and Niki was the one who took it to Lewis and made him see sense. Sixty-three wins (to date) and five World Championships later . . . probably more since this book went to print. Damn that virus!

**Johnny:** Where on earth did it all go wrong, eh? Success breeds success, I suppose. What a move, though, and what a result. Could you imagine having to live with the ignominy of being a one-time World Champion? It must be humiliating. I don't know how the likes of you, Nigel, Mario Andretti, Alan Jones, Jenson, Kimi and Britney cope. What makes the timing of Niki's approach even more remarkable is when you take into account McLaren's downfall, which began the following season. In his final year with the team Lewis won three Grands Prix and in the seven seasons since then McLaren have had just three podium finishes. That's what you call good timing.

Anyway, let's get back to knowing when to quit.

I made the decision to give up F1 at Monaco in 2000. As I said earlier, I had no idea what I was going to do at the time and what saved me in the end was being invited to race in the American Le Mans Series and have a crack at the Indy 500. Had they not been offered so soon after leaving F1 I'd have been in trouble. I was thirty-six years old and I wasn't ready to become a pundit. In fact, I became almost as busy during my racing career post-F1 as I was in F1, so I was very, very lucky in that respect. In some ways it was like going back to the beginning of my career, as the atmosphere in the likes of the American Le Mans Series, the BTCC and Speedcars was a lot more laid-back than F1, and I felt very much at home in all of them. The team I raced for in the American Le Mans Series, and also in the 2001 24 Hours of Le Mans, were called Champion, and some of the mechanical staff were amateurs who did it for fun. We had carpenters, electricians and car salesmen. They'd turn up at the weekend to mechanic the car and we'd all go racing. Towards the end of my career in F1 I think I'd lost sight of that side of racing and it was nice to be reminded of it again before I gave up.

**Damon:** From the moment you hit F1 you're bombarded by people wanting this, that and the other, and it doesn't stop until the day you leave. By the time I left I was desperate for a little bit of peace and quiet and the last thing I wanted to do was race. Your wife Rebecca was correct in saying that after F1 you'll never be as popular again, and that to me was one of the biggest attractions about leaving. It was liberating. For five or six years I did very little really, apart from the school run. I was effectively an F1 escapee. I'd got out in one piece and was free to do whatever I liked.

The thing is, once you've achieved a certain level of wealth and fame you have to manage that no matter what, so although I wasn't what you'd call active I wasn't completely cut-off either. Around the time I retired, the American team owner Carl Haas rang me up and asked me if I'd like to try IndyCar. 'I've only just stopped doing dangerous things,' I said as politely as I could. 'And I have no desire to start again.' It was nice of him to ask, though. I wanted something more sedate, so I was persuaded to invest in some car dealerships. I had my name above the door of two, one in Leamington Spa and one in Exeter. But it didn't stimulate me and I had no idea how it worked. It was supposed to be one of those businesses that make money while you're asleep. But I soon discovered there is no such thing! Actually, if Sky Sports F1 ever decide to ditch us for robots, we could start our own dealership. Damon and Johnny's Jalopies. Then again, who on earth would buy a car from somebody like you or me? I certainly wouldn't. Not a used one, anyway. Although 'Hill and Herbert' has a ring to it. Bentley dealership?

**Johnny:** What a great idea. All we need now is a billionaire to back us. Is anyone daft enough? Go on Bernie, I dare you. Speaking of billionaires. Instead of doing what EJ and Bernie did, which was to build their businesses inside F1 – or in Bernie's case own the bloody sport outright – some people, such as Lawrence Stroll, did it the other way around. Lawrence is obviously an F1 enthusiast and after making a couple of quid in the big wide world he was able to indulge his passion by purchasing not just an entire team, but a big slice of Aston Martin.

Lawrence used to race a bit in the 1980s, so with Lance flying the flag for him in that department he's covered all the bases. That, my friend, is what you call living the dream. Even so, if I was given the choice of either entering the sport on the very bottom rung of the ladder and working my way up or entering it at a much higher level and in a different capacity, albeit much later in life, I'd still start at the bottom. Then again, had Lawrence been in a position to try and make it as a racing driver I'm sure he'd have done the same. It is good to see somebody so passionate about F1 giving it a go and it kind of puts paid to our earlier gripe about independently owned teams being a thing of the past. There you go, Champ, we've found our hero. Long live Lawrence!

**Damon:** So is there any part of you that yearns for your days as a driver, Johnny? The gym, the exhaustion, the soreness, the interviews, the jet lag, the shunts, the reproachful looks from the mechanics. I have a feeling there is.

**Johnny:** No. Not one little bit. I do like it when I'm asked to jump into a fast car sometimes and go for a spin, as with the Johnny's Comeback piece for Sky Sports. But I would never go looking for it. I know what you mean about being in two minds, though, and if I were able to do the opportunity justice – as in, if I was thirty years younger – then it might be a different story. At the end of the day I'm a ridiculously competitive, shorter than average human being and the only reason that competitiveness has disintegrated is because my ability is no longer there.

**Damon:** I don't think it's disintegrated that much. If you and I went out and did a lap time in a Formula Three car at Snetterton, for instance, and someone went quicker than us, we'd be absolutely devastated. We'd be broken men. You wouldn't get out of the bloody car. 'I want another go!' you'd cry. 'It's not fair!' I'd be the same. We don't lose the memory of being competitive. We just lose the ability to actually *be* competitive!

I'm always reminded that a competitive spark still burns inside Damon Hill when I play golf. What a frustrating game that is. I know you've given up the golfing ghost, Johnny, but I'm still out there fighting the good fight. I started playing golf when I was about ten or eleven. It runs in the family. I've got a photograph of my granddad playing golf in the 1920s when he was the captain of Mill Hill Golf Club, and my dad took it up after breaking his legs. He obviously couldn't run, so it kept him active.

My best ever golfing moment was playing with Seve Ballesteros at the Oxfordshire Golf Club many years ago. Naturally I was in awe of the great man and he was everything you'd expect him to be, only I was a better driver! Golf joke. Sorry. I also played with a French professional called Raphaël Jacquelin at Wentworth in 2016, before the BMW PGA. That was great fun. It's nice to get some appreciation from a few spectators when you hit a decent shot. Makes a change from the abuse I normally get from my friends. Being a golfer is a tough gig. It can be a very cruel game mentally. I remember saying to Jacquelin, 'When you're playing and nothing goes right, what do you do?' I suppose I was expecting him to utter some kind of revelatory piece of golf wisdom. But instead he said, 'You've got to just go with it.' What sort of crazy philosophy is that? That's not something I could do.

Golf does not sit well with a racing driver's temperament. Just ask JH here. You have to have patience and racing drivers have about as much patience as piranha. But one of the reasons I'm so fascinated by golf is precisely because it's so difficult. It suits the obsessive-compulsive part of me. It's also amazing that from one day to the next you can't remember what you did before. You pick up a club and it can feel like you've never held one in your life. It drives me round the twist! If my car driving was that unpredictable I'd have never left the garage. Competitive nutters like you and me, Herbert, need something impossible to tackle, and golf is the most impossible of all. I think you should pick up your clubs again.

Getting back on four wheels for a second, and staying with the subject of competitiveness, I almost got the lap record at Daytona Sandown Park recently, so I'm not 'Hill over the Hill' just yet. I know you're a karting champion, Johnny, so I think you'll appreciate this. In 2006 I helped to found a charity called the Halow Project. We support young people with learning disabilities on their journey into adult life and each year we organize a charity karting event called Damon's Karting Challenge to raise lots of much-needed money. Come to think of it, you've never done our karting event, have you, Herbert? Here's a challenge for you. If you come to Daytona Sandown Park when we've re-scheduled after the evil virus, we'll find out who's the fastest once and for all. Is that a date?

**Johnny:** I might be playing golf that day.

**Damon:** You bloody well won't!

I've just remembered, I did your charity karting event in Dagenham a few years ago, so you can definitely do mine. We'll have a great time. Remember Jesse Owens's famous quote? 'Friendships born on the field of athletic strife are the real gold of competition; awards become corroded, friends gather no dust.'

**Johnny:** Bollocks.

# CHAPTER EIGHTEEN

## How much input does the driver have these days?

**Damon:** When I came into F1 there was next to no input from me. I just did as I was told. Do a hundred laps will you, DH. OK! Think back to the 1993 European Grand Prix at Donington. It was absolutely soaking wet and the communication was almost non-existent. I was sitting there waiting for some sort of advice from the pit wall, thinking, *Give us a clue, will you?* Eventually I plucked up the courage to make a request.

'I think it might be a little bit wet for slicks,' I said humbly. 'If I came in now would you have any wet tyres please?'

'OK, we'll have a look. We've got some intermediates. Would they be any good?'

'I don't know. I suppose so.'

Ayrton just ran rings around everybody that year and put in one of the greatest opening laps ever seen at a Grand Prix. The point being that the relationship between the driver and the pit wall was still arbitrary and the race strategies were basic and haphazard. In 1994 things started to change and by the middle of the season the geniuses at Benetton had turned race strategy into an art form. The rest of us were bamboozled. 'You mean you don't just fill up to halfway and then fill it to go to the end?' As the penny began to drop we started to adapt, but it was still basic compared to what Benetton were doing. They were giving themselves the option to respond to whatever the competition was doing. I remember Patrick getting a sheet of graph paper and a ruler out one day and saying, 'OK, this is what I think we should do.' He was about to work out our race strategy, something Benetton had probably been doing on a computer for months.

In truth, the frustrating thing about it is that you don't get much of a choice. The optimal strategy gives maybe two options, one stop or two, with maybe a couple of laps either side of the pit stop. Only in extreme cases did we need four stops. On those occasions you spent most of the race in the pits! At Monza in 1998, I tried something radical, because I was bored, frankly, and wanted to do something different for the sake of it. The computer said no but it cannot think laterally like we can. I'd qualified way down in fourteenth, so what did I have to lose? The prospect of staying fourteenth was not that appealing.

I was driving for Jordan at the time and the race strategy was supposed to be one long first stint before coming in for about 40 kilograms of fuel towards the end. 'I'll tell you what,' I said. 'Why don't we do it the other way around and put the 40 kilos of fuel in for the start?' For some unknown reason the team agreed. They thought I was mad, mind you. The theory was this: as the cars are more bunched together early in the race, with a lighter car you can make up more places per lap than when they have become further spread-out near the end of the race. This only makes sense if you've qualified poorly. Which I had! So off I went with my light fuel load and, sure enough, I managed to pass the majority of the field like a hot knife through melted margarine. By lap fourteen I was up to fourth from fourteenth on the grid! Which just goes to show how important weight is. The perfect-case scenario would have been a safety car just after I'd pitted, to slow everyone down. No such luck. After emerging from the pits in a car weighing 110 kilos more than all the others I was a sitting duck! But despite that, I finished sixth. Strategy, Damon Hill style.

**Johnny:** So it worked? Knock me down with a feather. Which you could have done after I'd dumped my car at the second Lesmo corner. When the rest of the teams finally got their heads around race strategy the onus was on the driver far more than it is today. For instance, at the European Grand Prix in 1998 I chose to go onto wet tyres against the team's wishes which, *by the way*, eventually won us the race. Please note that I do *not* consider myself to be a master strategist. It was just a hunch that paid off, but it was a hunch based on experience.

The weather had been quite changeable and as well as quite a few incidents there'd been an awful lot of tyre changes. Just after the halfway mark I remember driving up the straight and as I did I saw the strangest thing. When you line up on the straight at the Nürburgring about ninety miles in front of you lies Spa, and what is it always doing in Spa? Raining. What I saw while driving up the straight was a raincloud that looked exactly like a teardrop. I thought, *Bloody hell, look at that!* From then on I noticed the cloud every time I drove down the straight and every time I saw it, it was a little closer – and, it was a little bit darker. It also appeared to be holding the same line so after a few more laps I got on the radio and told the team that I was changing for wets. In hindsight it was a huge gamble but something in my water told me it was the right thing to do. The general consensus in the paddock had been that even if the cloud did arrive and it did start raining it would only be a shower. Subsequently, I think I was the only driver on the track who had changed onto wets and when the rain eventually started, and everybody realized that it was going to be a bit more than a shower, I don't mind admitting that I felt just a smidgen of relief.

**Damon:** Really? Just a smidgen?

**Johnny:** OK, I was mightily relieved! The rain, for as long as it lasted, gave me an advantage of about five seconds a lap, and in addition to that there were cars spinning off all over the place. One of the first drivers I overtook was my teammate, Rubens, who immediately went in to change to wets. It was like taking candy from a baby, really.

'Oh, are you spinning off? You don't mind if I go through, do you?'

The rain did eventually stop, but by that time I'd managed to take full advantage and so immediately went onto slicks. About ten laps from the end the only driver standing between me and my third Grand Prix victory was our mutual friend, the venerable Ralph Schumacher. Ralph and I had never seen eye to eye and I was just in the process of deciding what to do with my magnum of champagne on the podium (both ideas were going to hurt) when Schumacher the younger suffered a puncture. He did manage to pit, bless him, but by the time he remerged he was in fourth place and a good fifty seconds behind the eventual race winner – *moi!*

You finished a very respectable seventh, by the way. Good effort that man.

**Damon:** How gracious of you. As alluring as technology undoubtedly is (especially to engineers), what's even more alluring – to the fans, at least – is the human element. If you asked any F1 fan what they'd rather see, a driver and team working on a strategy together both before and during the race or a team just issuing orders, they're obviously going to choose the former. Or at least I hope they would.

Here's an idea for you. One new set of tyres per team, per race. That'd shake things up a bit!

**Johnny:** I know you're only joking but there is something quite alluring about that rule, or at least the context of it. F1 has to be fun and to me part of that fun is not knowing if a driver is going to be able to make it to the end of a race. Safely, of course. By eradicating these concerns (or even attempting to) you're not only taking the fun away, but you're making the driver's ability to be able to judge whether their car is going to get to the end of a race or not redundant. That's obviously the human element you were referring to and it's what the fans want. It's also what the drivers want. Look at golf. The technology you have in that sport is frightening these days, but it doesn't interfere with the end result. You can have your swing analysed by computers until you're blue in the face, but the moment you step onto that course it's just you, your caddy (if you're a pro or very rich) and your clubs. The human element is king in that sport. Sure, you've got a bit of interaction with the caddy from time to time, and there's obviously technology in the clubs. At the end of the day, though, it's the player who has to perform. Not only is that one of the big attractions about golf, it's one of the things that's missing in F1. Or should I say, evaporating.

Remember we had a laugh earlier about taking away radio in F1? Having thought about it again in the context of this conversation I think it's not a bad idea. The FIA have tried it before, of course, back in 2016 (and to a lesser extent in 2014 and 2015). I remember Charlie Whiting saying that the point of the ban was to ensure the driver was driving the car on his own and was not being told how to do so by the team. At the time many of the team bosses approved of the move, and I believe Toto Wolff actually referred to it as a positive step. It was actually the drivers who put the kybosh on it. Fernando told ESPN at the time that it made no sense to prevent him receiving expert technical information while driving a car that was like a 'spaceship' . He did have a point, but surely that's where compromise comes in? The journalist Matthew Walthert wrote for Bleacher Report at the time that, 'Drivers should be left alone to drive the cars as much as possible, but if there is a simple fix to a problem with the car, why should teams be restricted from providing it?'

I actually agree with that to a certain extent, as the fans want to see as many cars racing as possible and if the technology's there we should use it. I think the most famous example of a driver becoming frustrated by the ban highlights not only the fact that the FIA perhaps didn't think the ban through properly but also the necessity for the teams to be involved in the rule-making process, which fortunately did come to pass. At the 2016 European Grand Prix in Baku, Kimi was having a technical problem and obviously wanted a bit of advice on how he could correct it:

'Is it the same as last race, let's say?' said cryptic Kimi.

'I can't answer, Kimi,' said his engineer. 'Can't answer. I'm sorry.'

'Surely you can say yes or no!' said the frustrated Finn.

'I can't, Kimi. I can't.'

Although I'm all for a radio ban, it's obvious that the one that was enforced in 2016 hadn't been discussed properly, either with the teams or, most importantly, with the drivers. Fernando's point about having a spaceship with no information to drive it really resonates, as does Charlie's original comment that the point of the ban was to ensure the driver was driving the car on his own and was not being told how to do so. There's definitely a common-sense solution to the problem, but F1 doesn't always deal in common sense.

At the moment, technology is making the human element redundant, whereas what it should be doing is complementing it. Personally I used to love that side of things: trying to work out what was going on underneath me and stretching out the life of a tyre a little bit more. DC, for instance, was never very good at managing his tyres, so having that skill gave you an advantage over him. He obviously had a lot more strengths than weaknesses, but at least that was part of the equation.

**Damon:** It's no good saying to teams that they're only allowed to say certain things, as they'd always find a way around it. Do you think, say, that a driver should be able to gauge for themselves what lap times they're doing?

**Johnny:** Yes. I never wanted to know the lap times during qualifying. I thought I'd overdrive if they told me so I told them not to bother. That's obviously down to the individual driver and I'm not saying that just taking away the radio is the answer to F1's problems. Of course it isn't. What I am saying is that putting the driver in charge of the car again will bring their driving skills to the fore, and that is what the fans want. They want to see a driver squeezing everything they possibly can out of a car in the most competitive situations possible.

I recently watched an interview on YouTube with the afore-mentioned legendary Brabham and McLaren designer Gordon Murray, which he did for *Motor Sport* magazine in December 2019. When asked about the current state of F1 he talks about making it a spectator sport again. 'It's a Drivers' Championship,' he says, 'yet at the moment all they do is get in and steer. The team decide where the gear changes are before they leave the factory. They sit in a simulator and pick all the gear change points. They're told when the tyres are going off and when the engine mapping needs to be changed.'

When asked if he's interested in what fascinates today's F1 engineers, Gordon gives a simple two-word answer – 'Absolutely not!' he says, before adding, 'From my point of view it's cobblers, but you can see their point.' I think what Gordon means by that is that the engineers and the drivers don't know any different these days, so to them spending 240 days a year in a wind tunnel is perfectly normal. 'They think that's exciting,' says Gordon, 'and these days if they find a tenth of a second they have a public holiday.' He then says that in the 1970s you could literally have an idea in the bath, make it the next day, put it on the car and go a second quicker. 'And it was visible,' he says.

One of the funniest parts of the interview is when Gordon is asked what he thinks about today's engineers. 'That's almost impossible to answer,' he begins. 'From 1973 to 1977 I knew I was the chief designer [at McLaren] because if I looked behind me in the prefab drawing office there was nobody else there. They [McLaren] now have a technical team of six hundred people and I have no idea how you'd manage six hundred people to design a Formula One car. I don't know what they do!'

**Damon:** You're absolutely right about this, Johnny. We've gone from writing race strategies on the back of fag packets with limited technology to drivers being told exactly what to do lap by lap by a computer, via a group of engineers. Over the weekend each team will gather information and then produce a guestimate as to what pace their drivers have to go in order to get the best lap times. Then, during the race, there'll be thirty people sitting in Woking or wherever analysing every lap of everyone's race and adjusting their strategies accordingly. That, in layman's terms, is what an F1 race strategy is these days. Yes, it's bloody clever, but is it entertaining? I couldn't possibly comment.

Ross Brawn once said that, 'In some ways race strategy is the same as chess. You know which direction you want to go in, and then try to be three or four moves ahead to try and outwit the opposition.'

He's right. F1 these days is basically chess at 200 mph.

The problem now is that computers can teach themselves chess. You just give them the rules and off they go. You no longer need to program millions of moves into them. They invent their own! It's getting close to that situation in F1.

This actually reminds me of the philosophical problem relating to how much we want to know about our lives. Pretty soon we'll be able to find out what lifespan we'll have and what kind of personality. Seriously, how much do you want to know about the future? The whole point about attending a sporting event is that we don't know what's going to happen. Every four years the English press start talking about England winning the World Cup. OK, so we haven't won it for a few years, but could you imagine if we went into the competition knowing not just *if* England are going to falter, but in what round, and against who. Quite often we'll stand there at the start of a race and although we don't say anything, we know pretty much what's going to happen. We don't know exactly what's going to happen, but if we placed a bet on every race as to who'll be on the podium we'd be up a few quid by the end of the season. Foregone conclusions kill sport, end of story.

When the Americans launched the Apollo 11 mission in July 1969 they obviously didn't want anything to go wrong and took every precaution to ensure nothing did. They got to the Moon using, to us, very basic equipment, but somehow they did it. One of the many amazing things to come out of that story is that, when they were within about twenty seconds of landing on the Moon, it became clear the computer guidance was lagging a few seconds behind their actual position. They had to choose whether to abort or carry on. Because the astronauts were all pilots and had insisted on having the ability to fly the craft unaided if necessary, Neil Armstrong and Buzz Aldrin bravely took control. While the computer was playing catch-up and trying to make up its mind where it was – Florida or the Moon – Neil Armstrong had already landed the *Eagle*. They had less than thirty seconds of fuel left. Not enough for another lap! The point I'm making is that the drama is the human drama. What kind of creatures are we? A computer is just a tool for making things easier. We need to challenge ourselves. We need to be impressed and encouraged by what is possible as a mere human. Not just press a button and wait.

**Johnny:** This is another one of your metaphors, isn't it? Formula One needs heroes like those astronauts. People who are *allowed* to be interesting. It puts me in mind of Niki Lauda. Nika was a strategic genius and he used to work out the strategy for a race in his head. He was also very much his own man and not only did the technology work for him – as in he was in charge of *it*, not the other way around – so did the team. The car was his way of expressing himself, as much as it was for driving quickly.

# CHAPTER NINETEEN

## Fame

**Damon:** When I first started racing in Formula Three I became more aware that the motorsport public seemed to have their favourites. The X Factor, if you like. You can't learn it. You either have it or you don't. I would count myself as being one of those who don't, or at least didn't. Who knows what this mysterious quality is? Well, the fans do! But what it is exactly remains a mystery.

The first famous person I knew, before Johnny, was obviously my dad. My close-up childhood observations of what it was like being famous led me to conclude that it seemed to entail a lot of unwanted aggravation. Subsequently, when I eventually started racing and gradually moved into the public arena, I never went out of my way to be famous. Unlike the fame-hungry petite superstar sitting next to me, I just wanted to do my driving and go home. Don't misunderstand me. Being famous can be fun sometimes, in certain situations, but you can't turn it off and you can't choose when you want it on. It's like a bull in a field. Sometimes it will ignore you, other times it puts its horns down and charges straight at you.

You can't really control fame. Some people get really silly about it – like that man at the 1994 British Grand Prix who thought that me not having a drink with him and his corporate guests would spoil his afternoon, and didn't seem to get that I'd already made his day by winning the race. Other people keep their distance, because they don't want to be seen as a hanger-on. When I was in F1, I lost contact with a lot of my friends from the past, and I got the sense some of them were worried about being seen as wanting something from me, that I or others would think they had an ulterior motive. I found both those sides hard back then. These days I'm a lot more relaxed about it, and not only do I appreciate people asking me for an autograph or a selfie, but I get a kick out of the fact that some of them might be excited about meeting me. Being able to make somebody's day is an incredible gift to have and I'm very grateful for it. I guess it takes time to become comfortable with fame.

**Johnny:** I get more of that now than I did when I used to race.

**Damon:** You obviously didn't make their day in those days.

**Johnny:** It is possible to go off people, Damon! At the height of my popularity, which would have been in the mid-1990s, I had a fan club with about 30,000 people in it. Where the heck they all came from I have absolutely no idea, but my mum and dad used to run the fan club and at certain Grands Prix they'd set up a stall and sell Johnny Herbert merchandise. Cups, cars, knickers, Cuban heels. You name it, they sold it, and it was all emblazoned with a picture of Johnny Herbert's famous helmet.

Like you, I'm genuinely touched by the fact that people still know who we are and get a kick out of meeting us, especially the younger generation. The fact that they're even aware of us is interesting.

Actually, it's astonishing! What I like is the fact that they're always full of questions. They're often simple ones, like, 'What's it like being an F1 driver?' but they're so enthusiastic and so excited that you can't help but be moved by it. I certainly haven't had it to the same degree as you have. It's obviously a lot different meeting an ex World Champion than it is somebody further down the pecking order. I suppose my version of that would be the 1995 British Grand Prix. That was my World Championship really.

**Damon:** I never really thought of it like this, JH, but because of your injuries, if we had a para F1 Championship, you'd probably have a gold medal. I mean, I don't think people know quite how debilitated you were by your accident. Which makes what you did achieve even more incredible. Brundle, too, who has smashed feet as well. It's tough enough with everything functioning at 100 per cent. Of course, there is also the remarkable Alessandro Zanardi, who raced with no legs at all, although he didn't race in F1 after his injuries. It's absolutely awful what has happened. We don't know what the future holds for him at this time, but we and his thousands of fans are hoping he'll pull through this one, aren't we, Johnny?

Do people ask you about the accident and your recovery often?

**Johnny:** Funnily enough, no. I don't think many people below the age of forty know about my accident so it never really comes up. I think the kids who come and say hello must have seen me on Sky Sports F1, and whatever information they have about my career has probably been passed on by their parents. It's a shame really as it's something I enjoy talking about. Not the accident, necessarily – although I'm fine with it – but the fact that I still managed to break into F1 after it and have a bit of success. The thing is that when you get to our age you're dragging an awful lot of history around with you and most people are interested in what you're doing now, not what you were doing thirty years ago. It's different when we get to Silverstone. That, for me, is just four days of reminiscing about 1995. I do also do a bit of work, of course, but when I'm not talking into a camera that's all people want to talk to me about. Do I enjoy it? You bet I do! I love it.

**Damon:** That is very evident, Herbert. But every time you go to Silverstone you end up either having an accident – like you did on that bloody hoverboard – or doing yourself a mischief. I am, of course, referring to your legendary attempts at crowd surfing, which take place every year. I genuinely can't think of another current or former F1 driver who, a) would have the balls to do that, or b) would actually end up enjoying it. You're in your element when you're being held aloft and passed along by your adoring public.

Can you imagine DC or Brundle doing a bit of crowd surfing? That I would pay to see.

**Johnny:** Or Damon Hill, OBE? I'd like to see you, DC and Brundle crowd surfing – in formation – at Silverstone in 2021. In fact, I'll even donate five British pounds to a charity of your choice if it happens. I'll let you think about it.

I've always been of the opinion that if it wasn't for the fans then I wouldn't be where I am today, which is why I've always made an effort to engage. What makes it easier is that I genuinely enjoy it so for me it's a win-win situation. If I were a shy, retiring type like yourself, or an introverted extrovert like Brundle, then I dare say things might be different, but having fun with people and playing the fool occasionally suits my personality.

**Damon:** I thinks it's also about chemistry, Johnny. The public get you and I'm quite happy to leave you to it. If I went to the campsite at Silverstone, got on the stage and said, 'OK, everyone, I'm going to go crowd surfing', it'd be like the parting of the Red Sea! No one would want to know. When Johnny gets up it's like, 'Yeah. Come on, Johnny!' I've actually seen Johnny Herbert crowd surfing on an inflatable lilo. That, ladies and gentleman, is what fame looks like. I reckon that if you had enough people – and let's face it, Johnny Herbert's public are legion – he could crowd surf an entire lap at Silverstone. I really do.

**Johnny:** I don't know about that. I never get more than about ten metres. In 2019 somebody shouted that I had BO (which I did not!) and as soon as they said it I was dropped like a sack of mouldy spuds. 'I'm going down!' I screamed. 'I'm going down!' When I first take off I often treat the crowd to a verse or two from 'Walking in the Air', which they appreciate, and then it's away we go. There are some people in F1 who look down on that kind of thing – you know, the hoity-toity crowd – and they probably think less of me for it. Do you know what I think? Balls to them!

**Damon:** Have you ever been asked to sign anything strange, Johnny? I've been asked to sign women's T-shirts when they are still wearing them, which can be a bit awkward! I always make my excuses and move on. Not sure if that's being ungentlemanly or not? A moral conundrum!

**Johnny:** Which is why nobody likes you. If you're going to get on in life and satisfy your public, Damon, you have to learn to say yes to boobs. You have to learn to say yes! Take it from one who knows. Years ago I saw a photograph of your dad. He had his arm around two women and he looked as pleased as punch. One of the girls had a Champion Spark Plugs badge on her chest and your dad was staring straight at it.

Do you know what the most disappointing thing about my public is, Champ? 99 per cent of them are blokes. I very rarely get any female adulation, more's the pity. Not like Brundle. They're all over him and his Hush Puppies like a rash. DC also, but to a far lesser extent. It's Brundle they want, and it's Brundle they get. While we're here, could I make an appeal, to any female F1 fans who aren't interested in Brundle but would still like to shower affection and adulation on a portly has-been? Come along and mother me. I'll be the one falling off a hoverboard or being accused of having BO.

**Damon:** Strangely enough, Johnny, the group of fans I used to have when I was driving were generally made up of mothers. I was what you might call the housewives' choice. 'Aww, look at him,' they used to say. 'He looks a bit shy. Let's go and mother him.' I always had the impression that you were the F1 heartthrob. Perhaps they were just overwrought?

Being serious for a moment, admitting these days that you've signed a part of somebody's anatomy could actually get you into an awful lot of trouble. Especially with Mrs Hill! It's a moral mine-field out there! And that's why I will never, ever say yes to boobs, Johnny.

**Johnny:** These days I rarely get asked for an autograph. Nine times out of ten they want a photo. On the few occasions when I do get asked for an autograph, and this is the God's honest truth, it's always, 'Oi, Brundle, sign this will you!' Apparently he gets accused of being a Herbert occasionally, so it works both ways.

**Damon:** The weirdest thing I've been asked to sign is a shoe. Not a new shoe, but a shoe that somebody was wearing. They literally just walked up to me one day, took off their smelly shoe, handed me it with a pen, and asked me to sign it. How random is that? Actually, here's an even better one. A while back I was out on a bike ride with some friends and we came across this village that was holding a fete. The fire brigade were there raising money for charity and while I was having a drink a fire fighter came up to me and asked me to sign his arm.

'Really,' I said. 'You want me to sign your arm?'

'Yes please.'

I did as I was asked. 'Brilliant,' he said, rolling down his sleeve. 'I'm going to get that tattooed in the morning.' He was being serious!

**Johnny:** I had something similar happen to me in the early 1990s. A girl came up, asked me to sign her arm, and the following year she came back and showed me the tattoo. Thank God you can have them removed these days.

**Damon:** I didn't mention it earlier as I'm obviously sitting next to the doyen of F1 appreciation societies, but I too used to have a fan club. I forget how many members we had but for a couple of quid a year you got a membership card and a newsletter every so often. Like you, I also had an array of merchandise that we used to sell via mail order and at races. The reason I've mentioned it is because I still get people coming up to me today showing me the membership cards and asking for their money back. That is a joke, by the way. They're all very satisfied customers. But you still see DH caps out here. Never mind the quality, feel the stripes.

**Johnny:** We used to send signed photographs out to new members and at least half of these would be returned with a letter claiming that the signature wasn't original! I kid you not. They used to bring them to race meetings and ask me to sign them again. 'Oh, they'd say. It's the same signature!' No trust, you see.

**Damon:** Years ago I used to receive letters from a prayer group who were fans of mine and one day I received a letter saying that they'd had to expel one of the members as they hadn't been praying sincerely enough. I received further letters explaining the difficulties they were having with this recalcitrant worshipper. So, as opposed to them supporting me via the power of prayer, I ended up being their bloody agony aunt!

George Harrison, who helped me a little bit in the early days and was a very lovely man, got a group of Hindu monks in India to chant for me during my Championship year. He got them to video it and send it to me, complete with burnt offerings. I must still have it somewhere. Maybe not the burnt offerings.

**Johnny:** I once read somewhere that George Harrison put up the money to finance Monty Python's *Life of Brian*. So, in addition to being a member of the Beatles he also financed one of the funniest films ever made *and* helped Damon Hill win a World Championship by arranging an all-night chanterthon. What a legacy!

**Damon:** And a whole lot more you'll never know.

# CHAPTER TWENTY

## Whither punditry? Expert analysis, or idiots mouthing off?

**Damon:** Somewhere along the way we appear to have retired ourselves, so now we're no longer racing we may as well move onto our current occupation. Some might say that's punditry and others might say it's talking rubbish at a racing circuit. Either way, some time ago the people at Sky Sports gave us a second chance to make something of ourselves and offered us gainful employment. I think I speak for both of us, and definitely our wives, when I say that we're damn glad they did.

My word, how times have changed, though. Cast your mind back, Johnny, to the 1970s and '80s, when Murray was King. Coverage used to start about thirty minutes before the race then, and as well as delivering most of the build-up Murray would also commentate, together with somebody like James Hunt, and then bring the proceedings to a close. He was, in every sense, the voice of F1. He was the show. Talking of Mr Hunt, one of the most endearing and important ingredients from Murray's era was his relationship with James. The contrast between the two was magical and it's been the subject of many an interview, article and discussion.

Murray always described himself as the commentator and James the commenter, which is another priceless Walkerism. James was the pundit. Some of those comments, though! René Arnoux was a frequent target for James. After taking out Gerhard Berger while being lapped during the 1988 Australian Grand Prix, James described Arnoux (who incidentally called me the worst racing driver he had ever seen, which coming from him was something of an accolade!) as being, 'A man who has no business being in Grand Prix racing with the standard of his driving. He's ruined the race for us.' I don't know if James had an aversion to French drivers but during the 1983 Austrian Grand Prix he suggested that, after a shoddy piece of driving, Jean-Pierre Jarier should receive a short suspension for poor driving, 'and a permanent suspension for being himself.'

James Hunt was as uncompromising and unforgiving in his approach to commentary as he was in his approach to racing and he seemed to have no filter. 'If James wants to call somebody a French wally he can do that,' Murray once said. 'I obviously can't.' Murray's talked about his relationship with James – which, it's fair to say, was a bit up and down – many times in the past and one of the most amusing occasions was when, during an interview conducted at McLaren, I think, he attempted to illustrate the frustrations of working with James Hunt by pointing out how much time he used to have to spend with him. It's almost as if he's reading out a charge sheet! 'There were sixteen races a year,' he began. 'And we would be together for four days at each of them. So, if you multiply sixteen by four, and then by thirteen, which is the number of years we worked together, you get a VERY large number! Those were the numbers of days I suffered with – and enjoyed – the company of James'.

The late, great Clive James, who once followed me around central Europe for two weeks with a film crew while making a TV programme about me, once said of Murray that, 'In his quieter moments Murray Walker sounds like his trousers are on fire.' Juxtaposed with James's occasional laconic insults – sorry, observations – delivered in a voice resembling Brian Johnston's, and you had a partnership the like of which we'll never see again.

**Johnny:** They really were chalk and cheese, which is why it worked so well. Murray obviously found James infuriating at times, which was exacerbated by his excitable nature. James, on the other hand, just sailed through it all and said whatever the hell he wanted. I don't think he tried to wind Murray up, exactly. It just happened! You'll never, ever hear a bad word said about Murray Walker. He's very intelligent, always well turned out, and he knows his F1. He also understands television, which is obviously important. He understands what the viewer wants to know and he's quite happy letting his enthusiasm get the better of him. Sometimes an incident would happen while Murray was mid-ramble and I'd spot it. That used to make me feel a tiny bit smug – the fact that I had and Murray hadn't – but I bet you a pound to a penny it was intentional. He wasn't too proud to allow it to happen, you see, which gave him an instant connection with the viewer. That's Murray's genius. He's a consummate broadcaster and a true legend.

Rightly or wrongly, that kind of commentary wouldn't be allowed now. It would be deemed unprofessional. In that respect, coverage of F1 has gone in a similar direction to the sport itself, which makes absolute sense. People want the coverage to adapt with the sport. And, thanks partly to the way in which the coverage has evolved over the years, your average F1 fan's knowledge is much greater than what it was forty years ago. We've evolved together, basically. That in itself presents a constant challenge to our goodly employers and keeps all of us on our toes.

**Damon:** The fact that we as a sport are no longer willing to tolerate imperfections like that rankles with me slightly. I find it ungenerous and a bit puritan. It's like when you go crowd surfing at Silverstone. I think you've already alluded to this but for every thousand fans who think it's a hoot – and it is a hoot – you'll have a hundred or so stick-in-the-muds further up in the sport who think it's inappropriate. F1 is a serious business to these people and isn't to be messed with. I disagree. As big, expensive and corporately responsible as the sport undoubtedly is these days, you have to enjoy it. And, you have to show that you enjoy it. Otherwise, there really is no point. Those who would like to turn F1 into a club for the terminally elite (and dull) are discounting a very important part of its ethos. Take Daniel Ricciardo. When you listen to him talk he's obviously serious about what he does, but he's not going to do it if it makes him miserable. There was a very, very funny sketch on a TV show called *A Bit of Fry and Laurie* many years ago lampooning this side of F1. A French driver, played by Hugh Laurie, wins a Grand Prix and is interviewed afterwards by a reporter, played by Stephen Fry.

> **Reporter:** *Michael, you must be very thrilled with that result. Take us through the race.*
>
> **Driver:** *Yes, well. I was not very happy with the car. We had a lot of problems and the car was not so good, I think.*
>
> **Reporter:** *Yes, but you won. It's a great result for you. You must be happy.*
>
> **Driver:** *We had a lot of problems with the car. I was not so happy. It was very hard.*
>
> **Reporter:** *[becoming annoyed] Yes, but you won!*

The exchange continues in that fashion until the reporter explodes and then punches the driver. Lampooning something only really works if it starts with an element of truth, and in those days that's exactly how people saw Formula One. A bunch of miserable gits who couldn't even smile when they won. The great Mike Hailwood summed it up when he entered the sport. He said, 'I've never met such a miserable bunch of millionaires in my life.' Like me, Mike came to F1 from bike racing, and when I came over I had a similar experience. I used to think, *What the hell is wrong with everyone?* Everybody was unhappy and everybody disliked everyone else.

Getting back to the coverage, I like to think that Sky Sports usually manage to inject a bit of fun into our coverage, such as arranging an interview with somebody who likes a laugh or by making one of our vignettes. We love making those, and they always seem to go down well. At the end of the day, the sport of F1 should try and lighten up a bit and perhaps rediscover its generosity of spirit. For inspiration, it could do a lot worse than look to some of its younger protagonists. When George Russell, Lando Norris and Alex Albon get together they're like three naughty schoolboys and watching them interact is a joy to behold. And they totally embraced this virtual racing while we were all locked down. Good on 'em.

A lot of it's just waffle, but who cares? It's OK to waffle. There is a ribald sense of humour desperately trying to get out in F1 and on the few occasions it's allowed, it's usually quite funny. George, Lando and Alex – or the Three Stooges, as we should christen them – aren't the only ones who have managed to resist the serious side, and make our lives as pundits, and as fans, that little bit more pleasurable. In Brazil, there's a fifty-metre path you have to take in order to get to the paddock and there are fans everywhere. Some of the more established drivers will be flanked by security guards and people from their team as they make the short journey, but last year Charles Leclerc just wandered up there on his own. No security guards. No PR people. No Ferrari employees. The fans, as you'd expect, went berserk and it's fair to say he received a fair amount of attention. Do you know what, though? I rather think he enjoyed it. And good for him.

When you're in your early twenties and you're in F1, what's not to like? And if a PR person says to you, 'We'd like you to appear a little bit more professional,' they should tell them to bugger off. It's their moment in the sun. Embrace it.

**Johnny:** Not only are we digressing slightly, but you're coming across like a miserable old git who's having a pop at – miserable old gits! It's very entertaining, though. So, let's go back to the beginning, shall we? One of the questions I'm often asked about life as a pundit is how I got the job. Well, there's no screen test. You get the invite and it's basically sink or swim.

**Damon:** It's like a medieval witch trial – chuck 'em in the pond and see if they float.

**Johnny:** Absolutely. When I arrived at my first Grand Prix as a pundit, in China, I did a bit to screen with Simon Lazenby – all fine. Then Brundle glided in and I did a bit with him – all fine. Then, just as I was thinking that this punditry lark was a piece of cake, they asked me to operate the F1 Skypad, which is a touchscreen device thingamajig that helps us with analysis. *What?!* I thought. *I can't do that!* That was absolutely bloody terrifying but it was a masterstroke on behalf of Sky Sports. They must have thought, *Let's test the little bugger and see if he can cope. Make him work for his money!* It certainly made me take it more seriously. Also, despite it not being the chatty walk in the park I'd been expecting I found myself enjoying it a lot more. China was my first ever experience. That's where I lost my pundit virginity. Was your pundit cherry still intact when you were first approached by our goodly employers?

**Damon:** Was my what?! Nope. I lost my virginity while filling in for Brundle, which sounds a bit rude. He decided not to leave the comfort of his own villa in Marbella for Hungary, and ITV asked me to do some commentary. Button's first win! As a young driver you don't necessarily take what the commentators and pundits do seriously. It's not that you don't respect them, you're just ignorant of what their job entails and how much skill is involved. Especially with regards to commentators. When you grow up a bit you start to realize that these people aren't just talking for the sake of it. An even bigger shock is that some of what they say actually makes a lot of sense. What blows your mind is the realization that there are people out there who are actually enjoying listening to it, too! Who said you can't teach an old dog new tricks?

**Johnny:** When I stopped driving, despite not being around much, I still maintained a really good relationship with all of my friends and contacts within F1. Then, when I became a pundit, everything changed overnight. Everyone thinks you're after a story, you see, and their default position when coming into contact with you is suspicion. I actually found that quite upsetting at first, and I know you did too, Champ. I do understand it, though, and the reason I understand it is because when I was a driver I remember how everyone used to dread the journalists or the film crews arriving. Once you go over to that side they see you as a bit of a turncoat.

The default position for a driver when talking to a journalist is also suspicion, as you automatically think they're judging you or holding you to account for something. Sometimes they are, and sometimes they're not. That suspicion not only works both ways, it also transcends the genre. Pundit? Journalist? They're all the same. Personally, I used to have a really good relationship with the journalists and I very rarely received any negative press. It was different for you. Partly because of who your dad was, but also because you were at the sharp end of the sport. Had I been in your position it might have been the same. Then again, it might not. I'm a lot more likeable than you. And, I never used to say no. Fans preferred me because I used to sign their breasts, and the journalists preferred me because I didn't win many races and always gave them what they wanted. Game set and match to *moi*, I think.

What was massively in our favour was that, at the time, we only had Fleet Street journalists to deal with. How many journalists do we have today? There must be hundreds covering F1 and almost everything they produce is instantaneous. Rather ironically, because of our loyalties to Sky Sports F1, we too have to be very careful when speaking to the press, so we probably treat them with the same amount of suspicion as some our old friends and contacts in F1 treat us. What a circus! Formula One is basically an automotive Agatha Christie novel, full of intrigue and suspicion. Dick Francis used to write thrillers based around the world of horse racing, so perhaps we should write one based around F1. *The DRS Murders?* (it's only a matter of time) or *Murder on the Silverstone Express?* You'd make a smashing Miss Marple. A dotty old cowbag with some nice facial hair and a very keen brain.

**Damon:** You're too kind.

**Johnny:** As a pundit, the driver who I find most entertaining is Kimi. For a start, when it comes to members of the press or the broadcast media, he treats us all with an equal amount of disdain.

There's no favouritism. What makes life easier for us occasionally is when the people at Sky Sports, who are a very, very imaginative bunch, come up with an idea that they know will tickle the enigmatic Finn. Something like lawnmower racing or hovercraft racing. Kimi doesn't want to sit down and have a chat about how his season's going, and we can't make him. The man just wants to race! I think he actually looks forward to us approaching him with these ideas, as he knows it'll be slightly off the wall.

Recently I filmed a piece with Lando Norris and Carlos Sainz from McLaren which was even more off the wall. Lando had to drive a car and perform certain challenges while Carlos held a transparent bowl containing two litres of milk. He had to do a slalom, a backward slalom and a brake test. Obviously, the milk went everywhere and a good time was had by all. That, to me, is one of the best things about my job: having fun with the drivers. There are some drivers – and some teams, it has to be said – who would never get involved with a piece like that. They'd consider it demeaning, and, in some cases, it just wouldn't work. Take Lewis and Mercedes, for instance. If we approached them about an idea like that they'd laugh us out of the room, and quite rightly so.

It's all very well watching F1 drivers doing daft things occasionally or things that are out of their comfort zone, but there also has to be an element of enjoyment involved and in the case of Lewis and Mercedes that wouldn't be present. Nor would it be with Kimi. It's horses for courses, basically, and Lando and Carlos were so up for the challenge it was unbelievable. Had we approached McLaren about something like that in Ron's era I doubt it would have happened, and again that's fair enough. It's not up to us to dictate what a team's ethos should be, and the fact that some teams and drivers seem to fit certain events or challenges merely accentuates the diversity that exists within F1 and should be celebrated. That's not to say that McLaren have turned into an automotive version of *It's a Knockout*. Good lord no! In 2020 they just happen to have two young, talented and fun-loving drivers, which seems to have rubbed off on the team's ethos a bit.

**Damon:** I'm going to play devil's advocate here. If you'd been in contention for the World Championship and you had an important race coming up, how would you react if a TV company called you up and said, 'We've got this great idea involving some milk and a transparent bowl.'

**Johnny:** I get that, and you can always say no. It's just really nice when a team and their drivers feel comfortable enough to be able to do something like that. As I said, it doesn't suit everybody, and I'm not saying that McLaren should do it every week.

Anyway, let's get back on subject. How did you become a pundit?

**Damon:** Before I go into that, if I ever do write a thriller based around F1, I know exactly who the first murder victim will be. Rhymes with Donny Sherbet.

I agreed to become a pundit when my son, Josh, took up racing, and for the simple reason that I needed to get back into the sport to find out what was going on. I hadn't watched any racing for about seven years. You can blame the Schumacher era for that. Foregone conclusions in sport don't do a lot for me. Then, when Josh started racing, Sky Sports knocked on the door, so you could say I got into it by accident really. I think Brundle recommended me. So don't remind him. I must owe him a case or ten of shampoo by now. It certainly wasn't premeditated on my part. Like Johnny, I was probably thrown in at the deep end a bit. Over time, though, you get more involved, learn more and want to do a good job. Then you start to miss it when you're not doing it!

The reason I played devil's advocate before was because it sometimes annoys me when we ask drivers to lark around. Some people will be with me on this and some against me, but in my opinion we shouldn't be demeaning the likes of Lando and Carlos and reducing them to being depicted as some kind of comedy duo. Like us, basically! I think I feel this way because F1 drivers are supposed to be the best of the best, which is why they're admired. Regardless of whether they like a laugh or not, give them some respect.

**Johnny:** You're subscribing to the 'elite' thing. Oversubscribing, in my opinion. You said earlier that F1 should lighten up a bit and it should. It's all about finding a balance. Lando and Carlos are at a point in their careers where they can still do something like that, whereas the likes of Lewis and Sebastian – who are the elder statesmen of the sport – aren't. I get where you're coming from, but you have to be able to have a laugh sometimes. Just being great all the time must be downright boring. Not that I've ever experienced it.

Just remember, I know what it's like to fall foul of being taken for a bit of a fool and perhaps I did take it to extremes a bit, in that some people thought I was in it for a laugh, and probably do to this day. As you know, I had my reasons for assuming the role of F1's cheeky chappy and I dare say that if Lando and/or Carlos go on to bigger and better things, which hopefully they will, they'll moderate their behaviour. Yet again, it's horses for courses. F1 cannot afford to give off an air of corporate elitism, not without having something to counter it. Fans would desert the sport in their droves. More importantly, though, it would send me to sleep!

Here's a question for you: was being a pundit ever something you aspired to be? I think I know the answer to this but go ahead.

**Damon:** I'll see if I can answer it on my own, shall I? But thanks for offering. Until I started working for Sky Sports – and for some time after that – I wasn't comfortable in front of a camera, whether that be a television camera or my mum's Kodak. These days I don't care so much, and a lot of my inhibitions have disappeared. I'm also more relaxed about the possibility of saying the wrong thing. Sure, you have to be careful, but if you concentrate too much on that you'll end up making an even bigger mess of the piece.

One thing I will say is that, for all the mistrust that exists regarding pundits and journalists, I feel privileged being able to have my say. I really do. Sky Sports have a lot of experience in covering sport and without wishing to appear like some toadying sycophant I genuinely believe they do it very well. They give the likes of you and me a chance to bang on about our pet hates, our likes and our dislikes, and it's a privilege I value. Something else I've valued is coming back into the sport as a spectator, which is ostensibly what we are. That's given me a whole new perspective on the sport and now I've experienced what it's like I wouldn't be without it. I've actually come full circle when you think about it. I've watched the sport from every vantage point there is. One of the reasons this new perspective resonates is because it's given me an insight into the preparation that goes into covering a Grand Prix these days and bringing the show together. It's a big old job and the people work very hard indeed. Too hard sometimes, such as when we're still rambling two hours after a Grand Prix has finished. We should shut up and let them go and have a rest! Is that a request for an earlier finish time? I suppose it is. Just remember, I'm a bit older than the rest of them.

Should we talk faux pas then? Embarrassing moments? Murray was a regular in *Private Eye*'s Colemanballs and compared to him we're amateurs. Here are a few choice morsels from the great man, including one each featuring me and you:

*'He's obviously gone in for a wheel change. I say obviously because I can't see it.'*

*'With half the race gone, there is half the race still to go.'*

*'Do my eyes deceive me, or is Senna's Lotus sounding rough?'*

*'Anything happens in Grand Prix racing and it usually does.'*

*'Alboreto has dropped back up to fifth place.'*

*'As you look at the first four, the significant thing is that Alboreto is fifth.'*

*'I can't imagine what kind of problem Senna has. I imagine it must be some sort of grip problem.'*

*'He is shedding buckets of adrenalin in that car.'*

*'It's raining and the track is wet.'*

*'And this is the third-placed car about to lap the second-placed car.'*

*'So Bernie [Ecclestone], in the seventeen years since you bought McLaren, which of your many achievements do you think was the most memorable?' Bernie answers, 'Well I don't remember buying McLaren.'*

*Murray: 'What's that? There's a BODY on the track!!!'*

*James: 'Um, I think that that is a piece of BODYWORK, from someone's car.'*

*Murray: 'There's a fiery glow coming from the back of the Ferrari.'*

*James: 'No Murray, that's his rear safety light.'*

*'And Damon Hill is coming into the pit lane, yes, it's Damon Hill coming into the Williams pit, and Damon Hill is in the pit, no it's Michael Schumacher!'*

*'So now you're looking at the battle between Frentzen and Herbert for seventh place. Heinz-Harald Frentzen in the Sauber Mercedes behind Johnny Herbert, and behind him Johnny Herbert in his first race in the Ligier Renault . . .'*

All hail King Murray!

One of the only times I've lost it is during the Greenpeace protest which took place during the presentation ceremony at Spa a few years ago. Somehow they managed to plant a sign behind the podium and after unveiling it – presumably by remote control – somebody from the FIA started ripping it down. Just as he was doing that another one started to appear, so they'd obviously managed to plant two. The dilemma facing our employers was that they couldn't really cut to a pundit who was now wetting himself laughing, so they had to stay with it.

We all thought it was genius. They didn't hijack the event, exactly. Well, perhaps they did at the start. They had a point to make, though, and I thought they were quite inventive. The memory of that second poster popping up as the FIA guy's ripping the other down will stay with me for a long time. The ironic thing about that protest is that F1 is now aiming to become carbon neutral by 2030, and we're all banging on about the environment. Funny how things change.

You pissed Fernando off once, though, didn't you?

**Johnny:** I most certainly did. I still stand by what I said, though. Given the state of the team he was driving for at the time, and the options that were open to him, I still think he should have retired.

I wasn't saying he was past it. I was saying that without the right tools or prospects he couldn't further his career, and I was right. I think I also pissed Mercedes off a few years ago when I accused them of ruining a race. It was the one we mentioned earlier when Lewis was slowing down in Abu Dhabi and I said that Mercedes were attempting to dictate the outcome of the race. There was never any comeback, so to speak, but I think they had a moan.

**Damon:** Accusing a German team of dictating probably wasn't one of your wisest decisions, Johnny, regardless of the context. That said, I know you well enough to know that you would never have meant to cause offence. Things are said in the heat of the moment, though, and if you're the subject of a potentially negative comment – which all of us have had to deal with from time to time – your interpretation of it might be different to how it was meant. And now Fernando is making a comeback! Good luck Herbert! Words can be volatile things and the trick is to try and use them wisely without sounding bland and mealy-mouthed all the time. Like I just did then.

To summarize, being a pundit is an interesting job and we've both loved being there when the sport is showing itself off in its best light. We've also winced a bit while trying to talk up a race that's been a bit disappointing, but that's the nature of the beast. Overall, though, it's been a lot of fun and long may it continue.

# CHAPTER TWENTY-ONE

## The future

**Johnny:** Fortunately, this chapter is about the future of F1 as opposed to the future of him and me. If it were the latter it'd be a pretty depressing affair really. A story of incontinence, forgetfulness and yet more jokes about Brundle and his choice of footwear. One thing we're also not going to do is talk about the new regulations, as anything we say will be out of date in a day or two. Nope. I'm afraid you're going to have to make do with a few words or wisdom from Guru Hill and myself about what we think will happen generally.

One thing that will never change about F1 is its propensity to lead from the front and innovate, and as long as there are people out there saying that something can't be done, that innovation will continue. That, as well as racing, is the lifeblood of Formula One and although I think the two can work against each other sometimes, their default position is to work pretty much hand in hand. That inspiring, ambitious and determined union is what makes our sport unique. Old Bluebeard over there could probably say this a lot better than I could, but this desire to continually move forward and occasionally revolutionize is one of the many reasons I feel proud about being part of the sport. Everybody wants to belong to a club of some kind and regardless of all the niggles we have about F1, there's a lot more right with it than wrong and it's the innovation that keeps it interesting day to day. If that didn't exist it would just be racing and, despite that still being an attractive proposition, if the Chapmans, Murrays and Neweys of this world hadn't happened upon the sport then it – and the world, for that matter – would be a much poorer place.

**Damon:** Hear, hear! That was actually quite eloquent, Mr Herbert. You're coming along. Must be the company you keep these days. You're absolutely right, though. F1 has always shown the world what *can* be done.

You can't have that many races. Yes we can.

You can't go that fast. Yes we can.

You can't make the cars safe. Yes we can.

You can't put races on in the middle of a pandemic. Yes we can.

Success in the field of innovation is what drives the sport and, as the mighty atom rightly said, is what makes it about more than just racing. Other sports offer internal politics, glamour, money, and even sex appeal as enhancements to their offerings – all of which F1 also has in equal measure. What we have that they don't to any great degree, which is the foundation of our sport, is technical invention. The FIA set a technical challenge to restrict development and the F1 teams find a way to defeat it. It is this tension that is what creates the invention. But some really big challenges are heading our way. It's not too dramatic to ask the question as to whether there is an existential threat to F1.

The question facing F1 at the moment is the same one facing every sport, business, and human being on the planet, and that's how to go about the business of improving your lot without destroying the planet. Another problem it has – this was pointed out to me by somebody from one of the manufacturers recently – is that the young people of today are not aspiring to experience the things we did when we were younger, and that could easily have a detrimental effect on the sport. Once upon a time owning your own car was an ambition, whereas now that's becoming unfashionable, or even just not on their radar at all! This chap's worry is that they're either going to want virtual experiences, which are environmentally pretty harmless – or should be – or they're going to want to be seen doing the right thing – which is not having a car. Or, for that matter, not following a sport that does all the improper and politically incorrect things we used to love it for. I suppose he made it sound a bit drastic, but potentially it is.

I used to enjoy disappearing with my mates once in a while on our motorbikes for a few days and I have to say that these days I don't feel good about doing it. In fact, I'm even thinking about getting myself an E-bike. I can have almost as much excitement on a pushbike with a small electric engine on it as I can on a 500cc Kawasaki – and I'm not damaging the environment. In ten years' time will you still have kids turning up outside pubs on motorbikes and revving their engines? I'd be very surprised if you do. This COVID experience has only made it more evident that the things we took for granted may not be set in stone. We can change. It's been tested and found possible.

Even Sky has found itself resorting to broadcasting virtual competitions with, it has to be said, quite a lot of interest. OK, we have a captive audience. But prior to that, the e-sports audiences were already in the millions on YouTube. Would a young Lewis Hamilton today even want to leave his bedroom? The only thing that heartens me slightly with regards to F1 is our track record on making the impossible possible. Once again, we could go into the specifics of this but due to the disparity between how fast the world of F1 moves and how fast the world of publishing moves, we'd end up with more than a little egg on our faces. It's already difficult enough predicting where we'll all be a week from now with COVID. F1 has tended to hide its socially responsible light under a bushel over the years, but it's now finding its voice, and that's partly down to the fact that an issue has arisen that affects the entire planet. And then, of course, there is the campaign headed by Lewis to end racism and push for more inclusion in our sport. I've long felt F1 can do more and now we're just starting to flex our muscles in that direction.

**Johnny:** I bet you a pound to a penny, though, that the politicians and climate experts don't always agree with the F1 point of view. That's a given. The stance of a politician will always be influenced either by commercial factors, political factors, or just toeing the environmental line. The guys and girls in F1, on the other hand, when it comes to innovation, aren't hampered by any of that rubbish. You'll get a straight and honest answer or explanation to a question or scenario.

Take the government's plans to phase out hybrid technology within fifteen years. I could be wrong, but that seems more like a grandstanding exercise than an ecological one and it surprises me that the F1 engineers who developed that technology and remain at the forefront weren't consulted.

Ross Brawn was one of the first people to comment on this and said that picking on a specific technology was crude. 'For me as an engineer,' he said, 'it doesn't make sense. [It should be] this is where we are now, this is where we want to be, what's the best solution in that process'.

As I said, the government are simply playing to the crowd.

**Damon:** The point about F1 is it creates a time imperative. Professor Martin Elliott, the guy who spotted that F1 could teach the medical profession a thing or two about transferring patients from operating theatres to intensive care wards, said that one of the problems in his industry was that they always worked to quite a flexible timescale. In F1 you can't do that. The first race is Melbourne and you have to design and build a car and get it put onto the track come hell or high water. The stress and pressure that time imperative produces is enormous but necessity *is* the mother of invention. The world in general could definitely take a leaf out of F1's book in how it approaches its problems. That will only truly work when things like politics and the like are put to one side. Which they obviously never will be. In a million years.

Anyway, let's put Armageddon to one side now, shall we? I'd like our book to finish on a high.

The new regs are proof that Ross and his team at F1 HQ are responding to the demand to bring the sport element back into F1 and make it more entertaining. And the budget cap may entice new teams into the fray too. Whether these adaptations work or not is yet to be seen but I'd wager that some will and some won't. And what about more races? I know that's been mooted. If Bernie were still in charge we'd be up to about forty by now. We wouldn't be having support races. We'd be having F1 matinees! Having a few more races would certainly be challenging for teams but given the amount of people they now employ, why not? What was it Jean Todt said with regards to this? 'If you do not like zee heat, get out of zee kitchen.' He's a sympathetic soul. The thing is, F1 can no longer rely just on people who are zealots and workaholics.

**Johnny:** One of the big questions I have is how long Mercedes are going to stay in the sport. At the moment the Mercedes-AMG

Petronas Formula One Team is the most successful division in the whole of Mercedes-Benz. That is obviously one heck of an achievement and is testament to what the ethos that is required to win in F1 can achieve. It brings the best out in everybody. I've heard rumours to the contrary but I think they'll stay in the sport for as long as they remain competitive and hopefully that will be a very long time.

Right then, it's time to finish off. Where do you see F1 in ten years' time, Champ? I'll give you my predictions.

Bernie will have bought the sport back and will be preparing to sell it yet again. Eddie will have bought out Haas and will be selling carpets – sorry, rugs – from the back of the garage on race day. Lewis will have doubled Michael's tally of championships and will have retired to open a chain of F1-themed tea rooms in the south Dorset area. Christian Horner will have replaced Victoria Beckham in the Spice Girls. Ross Brawn will have taken up stand-up comedy, Jean Todt will have morphed into a garden gnome, and, after the sad death of Keith Richards, Brundle will have joined the Rolling Stones.

Or, in the real world: Mercedes will have left the sport, as will Renault. Red Bull will be dominant again, Ferrari will still be frustrated, and Charles Leclerc and Max will have won at least two World Championships each. Your turn.

**Damon:** Not sure if Brundle is Stones material but I could see him interviewing Mick on stage after: 'So, Mick, how did "Sympathy for the Devil" go for you? I thought it rocked!"

So here I go. Elon Musk will buy F1 and, instead of electric motors, we'll be using his rocket engines. Lewis Hamilton will own the rights to all the catering, making F1 the first ever exclusively plant-based-diet sport. Kimi Räikkönen will surprise us all and be elected FIA President and immediately give everyone a year off just to go and do whatever they want. Johnny Herbert will have gene therapy to make himself twenty-five again so he can have another career. Unfortunately, because his Super Licence expired twenty years ago, he has to race in F2 and start all over again. Hamilton will retire in 2030 having won fourteen world titles. Reverse grids will be standard format and drivers will get only one set of tyres to last a weekend to prove F1's green credentials.

Do you know what, I think we should give the last word in our book to big Bernie. Forget all the crass comments he makes just to get attention; love him or loathe him, he's the one who gave our sport the platform it deserved all those years ago, and had it not been given that, I'd probably still be delivering parcels around central London and you'd be testing hoverboards!

Whenever he was asked to define F1, the mighty Mr Ecclestone always used to come out with the same speech. 'It's the best,' he'd say. 'It's the best drivers, the best designers, the best engineers, the best mechanics, the best truck drivers, the best fans, the best show. It's the best, OK?' Whaddya say, Herbert?

**Johnny:** True dat.

# AFTERWORD

**Damon:** Well, Johnny. It started off as a brilliant idea, didn't it? You and I were supposed to sit down and discuss the forthcoming season and a few other subjects close to our hearts, and look what happened. After writing the book we got as far as Australia where, on the Thursday, we were told we couldn't come in. At first I thought it was personal, as in, we don't want the likes of you and Herbert around these parts anymore – which would have been understandable – but I was wrong. Two of the McLaren mechanics had tested positive for COVID-19 and that was it. It was goodbye Melbourne, hello lockdown. Four months later, here we are again!

**Johnny:** Don't you have a theory about why all this is happening?

**Damon:** I do, Johnny. You've heard of the Maya civilization, of course?

**Johnny:** Naturally.

**Damon:** Well, the Maya civilization had their own calendar, called the Mayan Calendar, which predicted that the world would change dramatically on 21 December 2012. Given that the calendar is thought to have been created before 500 BC, I reckon we can allow them a few years' grace either way, and, because it was so close, that's where I'm pledging my allegiance. I'm with the Mayans, Johnny! In fact, as of now I will only be using the Mayan Calendar.

**Johnny:** I have absolutely no idea what all that means, but thanks. But it's not just COVID though, is it? We've got global warming, Black Lives Matter, Bernie's baby. Life is totally different to how it was when we started writing this book at the end of 2019, which is why we've decided to write an extra chapter. It's mainly to apologise to our lovely readers for anything in the previous pages that is now incorrect, obsolete, or both. We had no idea it was coming, you see.

**Damon:** That's pretty much the entire book, then! And what do you mean we had no idea it was coming? The Mayans did.

**Johnny:** Read my lips: NO MORE MAYANS! If you look at the calendar on the official Formula One website it goes from testing in Barcelona from 26–28 February to the Austrian Grand Prix from 3–5 July. At first glance it looks like a mistake, but of course it isn't. I think a lot of people doubted the sport's ability to be able to stage races again so soon, but F1 thrives on solving problems and on the whole I think it's coped very well indeed.

**Damon:** So what was it like, Johnny? Take us through the Grand Prix you did in Hungary.

**Johnny:** Well, on the Saturday morning when we got off the bus we went straight to the Eurofins COVID testing point. Everyone who entered the circuit, regardless of who they were and what day it was, had to be tested first. I suppose you'd expect that, but the set-up they had was mightily impressive. The paddock itself was obviously a bit quieter as there were far fewer people, but you still had the same boys and girls doing the same jobs. You also saw more of the drivers than you normally do, which was nice.

**Damon:** And what about the lack of spectators?

**Johnny:** Do you know, the only time I really noticed that there weren't any spectators was during the build-up on the grid. Then, once the cars were fired up, it was back to normal.

**Damon:** Serious question, and I'm sure this will be on the lips of every reader who saw the Austrian Grand Prix: during the presentation ceremony, were you inside the little box that presented the trophies? For those of you who didn't see it, instead of using a human being to present the trophies, they used what looked like a box with a robot inside, but me and millions like me thought it was you. I did post a tweet saying that I suspected human interference, but I stopped 'short' of naming any names. Go on. You can tell us.

**Johnny:** I'm a rubbish liar, you know that. Yes, it was me. I, Robot!

**Damon:** By the end of Hungary everyone must have been exhausted.

**Johnny:** Yes, there were a lot of very tired faces in the paddock. I know we'd all had a break, but returning to the action with a triple-header was always going to be a challenge. Like everything, though, we rise to it. I think everybody was just relieved to be back.

**Damon:** Having these races served up to me on TV has been like a breath of fresh air. All that sensory and intellectual stimulation

F1 provides us with had disappeared almost overnight thanks to COVID, and it was only when the coverage of the Austrian Grand Prix began that I realized not just how much I'd missed the sport but how conditioned I'd become during the months of lockdown to only reading and hearing about COVID. But I'll tell you what else the restart has done: it's put all the predictions we made at the start of the season to the test, and I don't think we were too far wrong. The races themselves have been great and I especially enjoyed the wet qualifying at the Styrian Grand Prix. Isn't it funny how similar the backdrop was at the Styrian Grand Prix to the Austrian Grand Prix? I've no idea why. The two British boys, Norris and Russell, did very well in testing conditions, but Lewis's pole was just ridiculous. After Austria Valtteri Bottas must have fancied his chances of pushing on for a double and potentially taking hold of the championship, and then Lewis does that *and* he wins the race. At the end of the day though, Johnny, that's exactly what we'd expect from Lewis.

**Johnny:** The highlight of that weekend for me was Lando getting his first podium, and you're right, Damon, both he and George Russell did themselves proud during qualifying. One thing we didn't predict at the start of the season was Sebastian Vettel leaving Ferrari, which has obviously triggered a very interesting game of musical seats. Personally, I thought Daniel Ricciardo would have replaced Seb, and I was quite surprised when his name didn't feature. I think he'll do very well at McLaren. He'll suit them. Leclerc versus Sainz Jr, though. In my mind that's a very exciting prospect and it's good to see two younger drivers at Ferrari again.

**Damon:** Isn't your friend coming back into F1? The one who you said should retire, and eventually did.

**Johnny:** So I understand. He's only coming back to try to prove me wrong. I'm sure of it!

**Damon:** One thing we haven't touched on yet is the death of George Floyd, which has had almost as much of an impact on the world as COVID-19. Police brutality against black people in the United States has been well documented but has often gone unpunished, and unfortunately it's taken something as drastic as a man dying after a policeman kneeled on his neck for nearly eight minutes in broad daylight to provide the motivation for real change. Its impact on F1 has been less significant than COVID, but for Lewis it's been huge. His support of the Black Lives Matter movement and his work on securing a unified display of support from the drivers has been impressive.

**Johnny:** Absolutely. What really brought this home to me and put me on Lewis's side was when I read somewhere that he'd asked Toto Wolff whether the first thing he thought about on waking up in the morning was the colour of his skin, and of course Toto said no. As the only black driver in the sport it's obviously something that Lewis is reminded of all the time, which is why his persistence in trying to get every driver to take the knee is understandable. F1 is obviously a predominantly white sport and although I haven't spoken to Lewis about this I'm pretty sure that, in addition to spreading the word about Black Lives Matter and ending racism in general, he'll have one eye on pushing the FIA to promote diversity in the sport and become more inclusive.

The response to Black Lives Matter was pretty disjointed at first, and the scenes in Hungary at the End Racism protest, for example, were shambolic: some drivers wore End Racism T-shirts, some didn't, and some drivers weren't even there. But the whole thing was much more coordinated for the British Grand Prix, and the FIA gave more time for the kneeling protest before the national anthem.

**Damon:** The great thing is that once we got the season going it was pretty damn exciting. And I managed to make it to the British Grand Prix on 2 August and the 70th Anniversary Grand Prix just a week later. I can't believe that the sport we love so much is seventy years old, Johnny. It's even older than us! It was obviously a huge shame not having the crowds there, but Sky did commemorate it by getting the cast to wear 1950s-style clothing. You cut a bit of a dash in your natty threads and bow tie, while I managed to look more like that puppet meerkat from the Compare the Market adverts. Great result with Max and Red Bull outfoxing the Mercs. And all that stuff about Racing Point brake ducts. F1 is alive again!

Anyway, you and I have been banging on for what seems like seventy years with this book now. We're just a couple of old farts, really. A couple of old chancers rabbiting on about something we used to know something about. Why on earth people still listen to us I have no idea. In fact, dear reader, what on earth possessed you to buy this book?

**Johnny:** I think it's time for your lie-down, don't you? While we're on the subject of the future, just when we thought we'd heard the last of the mighty Bernie, he goes and extends his dynasty by one. Ace, I believe he's called. At last, a son and heir!

**Damon:** Over the next few years Bernie will pass on all his secrets about F1, burger vans and what it takes to make a few billion quid to his new son, and one day Ace Ecclestone will rule the world. We'll have to do another book, Johnny, just to see whether it happens. Actually, let me check my Mayan Calendar. It might make reference to it. Ah yes, here it is: 'In 2045, Alexander Charles

Ecclestone, otherwise known as Ace, will take possession of Planet Earth, having inherited it from his late father, Bernie, who bought the Earth back for a quid having sold it for a trillion pounds to an unnamed man without ever having owned it in the first place.'

**Johnny:** I wonder what odds you'd get on that.

**Damon:** Short ones.

# INDEX

DH indicates Damon Hill.
JH indicates Johnny Herbert.

# INDEX